PE

THE WEAVER'S SONGS

Vinay Dharwadker was born in Pune in 1954, and was educated at St. Stephen's College, Delhi University, and the University of Chicago. He is the author of a book of poems, *Sunday at the Lodi Gardens* (1994), and an editor of *The Oxford Anthology of Modern Indian Poetry* (1994), a co-editor of *The Collected Poems of A. K. Ramanujan* (1995), and the general editor of *The Collected Essays of A. K. Ramanujan* (1999). His other edited books include *Cosmopolitan Geographies: New Locations in Literature and Culture* (2001). He has published translations of modern Hindi, Marathi, Urdu and Punjabi poetry, as well as essays on literary theory, translation studies and Indian English literature. He teaches Indian languages and literatures at the University of Wisconsin-Madison, where he also serves as the Director of the Centre for South Asia.

Contents

TRANSLATOR'S NOTE

Kabir's poems have circulated in several languages across north India for the past five or six centuries, and he is probably the most frequently quoted poet in the modern Hindi world. He nevertheless remains an enigma—a shadowy presence behind the poetry, a voice, a simulacrum, a form of imagination constantly eluding our grasp. After nearly 200 years of scholarly research on his life and work, he appears to be a singer who has disappeared into his songs: he has ceased to be 'a person', and has become 'a whole climate of opinion' instead. In fact, in W. H. Auden's words memorializing W. B. Yeats in 1939, he is the type of poet whose death was 'kept from his poems', and who literally 'became his admirers' (Auden 1991, 275, 247).

These remote echoes from the twentieth century are significant because they are symptoms of the ways in which Kabir's poetry has stayed alive for more than half a millennium. Yeats himself first encountered a sample of it in Rabindranath Tagore's translations, which were published in *Songs of Kabir* in 1915 with an Introduction by Evelyn Underhill. The brief fable of the *haṃsā* in the twelfth song in that book must have resonated strongly with the Irish poet, for its symbolism of the soul as a swan or a bird on a journey beyond the human and natural realms seems to have influenced his conception of 'The Wild Swans at Coole' shortly afterwards. Tagore's translation was prosaic and speculative, but it conveyed enough of the idea—which the Kabir tradition had borrowed from older Indian and Persian traditions—to have an impact on Yeats.

Tell me, O Swan, your ancient tale.
From what land do you come, O Swan? to what shore will
you fly?
Where would you take your rest, O Swan, and what do you
seek?
Even this morning, O Swan, awake, arise, follow me!
There is a land where no doubt nor sorrow have rule: where
the terror of Death is no more.
There the woods of spring are a-bloom, and the fragrant
scent "He is I" is borne on the wind:
There the bee of the heart is deeply immersed, and desires no
other joy. (Tagore 1915, 55–56)

A more attentive rendering of the kind I offer in this volume reveals that the poem is lighter, more lyrical and suggestive, than the older version indicates:

Dear Swan,
talk of ancient things.
What country have you come from,
what shore will you alight on?
Where have you stopped and rested,
what goal have you set your heart on?
It's now the morning of consciousness,
let's leave together.
We won't be filled with grief and doubt in that place,
the fear of death won't strike us there.
Here the forests of desire are in bloom,
their fragrance assails us straight ahead.
A place that ensnares the beetles of the heart
can offer no hope of happiness.

Despite the opacity of Tagore's English, Kabir's song conveyed its mood to Yeats quite precisely, and induced him to create an analogous atmosphere when he wrote about the 'mysterious, beautiful' swans on the lake at Coole Park, Lady Gregory's estate in Galway, in 1916.

The resonances of the poetry associated with Kabir in modern times are not only poetic but also philosophical and conceptual. In the 1960s, Jacques Derrida, Roland Barthes and Julia Kristeva, among others in France, discovered that the words *texte* and 'text' contain the metaphor of 'textile', allowing us to view a text as a woven fabric, and hence as an instance of textuality; a group of texts as an interwoven continuum, and hence as an embodiment of intertextuality; and even the world as a continuous text, and hence as a vast fabrication or ideological construct (Makaryk 1993, 568–72, 639–42). But some three and a half centuries earlier, a canonical version of Kabir's poems had already conceived of God as a Master Weaver, and the universe as an interlacing of warp and weft on His divine loom. More presciently, the poems had imagined the human body itself as God's handiwork in the form of a fine-spun cotton sheet, in a world where reality is nothing but illusion.

It was an allegorical image of astonishing acuity. Medical science, for example, now tells us that when the fertilized human egg begins to divide and replicate in the womb, it first generates a flat sheet of cells, one cell thick, that rolls itself into a cylinder to form the 'tube' of the spine, around which the embryo then builds itself with layers of tissue. For the Kabir text fixed in the early seventeenth century, the human body is always already a *kosha*, an envelope, woven on the loom of procreation like a sheet of diaphanous muslin, to be wrapped around mind, consciousness and self. The penetrating quality of such conceptions has repeatedly renewed the poetic power of Kabir's verse, raising it to the level of a perpetually modern classic.

In the course of the twentieth century, Kabir has come to be construed as an 'individual author' in the modern sense of the term, and to occupy a position of primacy in the history of Indian literatures and religions. He is widely regarded as the first major poet in the Hindi language; as the earliest author of the bhakti movement in Hindi literature; and as the *ādi sant*, the first and predominant figure, in the *sant paraṃparā* of north India, a multifaceted tradition of philosophical, theological and social argument that began to dismantle the structures of classical Hinduism around the fifteenth century, and to replace them with a new architecture of ideas. Moreover, Kabir is a primary influence on the early Sikh Gurus, and hence plays an important role in the formation of Sikhism as a distinctive, antithetical religion.

At the same time and for similar reasons, Kabir has also come to occupy a position of prominence in world literature. As a fifteenth-century poet concerned with God, the experience of God, and the quest for an equivalent of salvation, he ranks among the foremost Asian and European mystics of the past millennium. As a social thinker, satirist and strong critic of older, established religions, he stands among the major reformers of the period who help define the multifarious transition from the late middle ages to early modernity around the globe (Dvivedi 2000, 170–75; Dass 1991, 1–21; Underhill 1915, 1–43).

My principal goal in *The Weaver's Songs* is to present readers in the twenty-first century with a fresh, compact yet representative selection of poems attributed to Kabir in reliable English translations, along with a commentary that would enable them to understand the poetry in its historical and cultural contexts. This goal, however, is complicated by the fact that the poems carrying Kabir's signature-line have reached us in an unusually varied and voluminous form. The complexity of the textual transmission implies that we cannot approach the poet as if he were an individual author, and that we cannot interpret his words, or the words ascribed to him, without working our way through a great deal of historical mediation. But if we comprehend the processes in Indian culture that have configured his poetry over the past five or six centuries, we can begin to appreciate the probable nature of his achievement as well as the structure of his imagination.

This book is divided into four main parts. The first consists of an Introduction entitled 'Kabir, His Poetry and His World', which discusses what we know of the poet's life and circumstances, the transmission of his poetry in the written, musical and oral modes since the century after his death, the issues surrounding the authorship of the poems ascribed to him, and the interpretation of the poetry itself. Since the process of selecting and translating the poems proves to be inseparable from the process of decoding their history and authorship, the Introduction also explains my strategies as editor, translator and critical commentator, and thus offers a comprehensive overview of the subject and method of this book.

The second part contains my translations of one hundred poems preserved in Kabir's name. The poems are distributed over five sections, with each section representing material from a particular source or set of sources, and the sequence of sections reflecting the interrelations of chronology, poetic form and mode of textual transmission. My choice of poems draws upon ten major sources and categories, and thus covers the broad range of materials found in the tradition as a whole. This is the first book, in fact, to offer a balanced representation of the multiple facets of Kabir's poetry in English translation.

My translations follow a fairly consistent pattern. For the convenience of readers in English, the translations carry titles (except in the case of the aphorisms), even though the original poems do not. In each rendering, one verse-paragraph in English represents one verse in the original, and therefore constitutes the primary unit of meaning in the process of translation. Since each verse in the original consists of one sentence or one set of interdependent sentences, and the verse-boundary always coincides with a syntactic boundary, my approach to translation differs directly from Walter Benjamin's, who takes 'words rather than sentences to be the primary element of the translator' (Benjamin 1969, 79).

At the end of each translation, I identify the text that I have rendered by citing its first verse or refrain (or both) as well as its source. In the case of my translations from the *Ādi Granth* and the Goindval Pothis, the first verse precedes the refrain in the original, and I specify the poem's position in the *Granth* by rāga, shabad number under rāga, and page number(s) according to the standard pagination. In the case of poems from the *Kabīr Granthāvalī*, the refrain comes before the first verse; in the instance of the *Bījak*, I cite only the first verse of a poem, because the source does not specify any refrains; and in the case of poems from the oral and musical traditions, I cite only the refrain. For all the sources other than the *Ādi Granth*, I identify particular editions of the sources (which are cited in full in the Bibliography at the end of the book), and furnish the necessary page numbers.

The third part of *The Weaver's Songs* contains my Notes to the poems. I have provided a separate note for each poem, in which I have listed all the available variants of the original as well as any previous English translations. In addition, each note offers critical comments on the poem itself, as well as explanations of my decisions as a translator, when necessary.

The fourth and final portion of the book consists of a Note on Transliteration, the Glossary and the Bibliography. The Glossary provides a comprehensive list of terms from Indian languages that I have used in the book, together with definitions and explanations. Readers will find it indispensable because I have used a large number of technical and non-technical Indian words and phrases in the main body of this volume without always pausing to explain them there. The Bibliography contains an alphabetical listing, by author (or by title, in the case of works without specified authors), of the primary and secondary material that I have cited or used in this book, together with annotations on some unusual items.

I have avoided scholarly footnotes or endnotes because the quantity and complexity of the material on Kabir can be quite overwhelming. Instead, I have used the author-date system of citation, mentioning an author's name and the year of publication, as well as the relevant page number(s) when necessary, either in the main body of my commentary or in parentheses. In the case of works without specified authors, I have mentioned only their titles and page numbers. Each parenthetical citation appears at the end of a sentence or a paragraph, with multiple citations separated by semicolons. All these items are keyed to the Bibliography at the end of the book.

Italics, diacritical marks, spelling and capitalization raise complicated issues in a book of this sort, and I have simplified them as much as possible. As terms for canons, 'Veda', 'Purāṇa' and 'Qur'ān' are not italicized, but the titles of particular Purāṇas, such as the *Brahmavaivarta Purāṇa*, are. Words from Sanskrit, Hindi and other languages that appear frequently in the book—such as 'bhakti', 'jāti' and 'shabad'—are not italicized, but words that appear infrequently are printed in italics. Modern personal names and the names of places and institutions, such as 'Parasanath Tivari', 'Banaras', 'Rajasthan' and 'Dadu Dayal Panth', do not carry diacritical marks. But other terms, most of which are common nouns, verbs and adjectives, as well as certain proper nouns and the titles of works in Indian and other languages, do contain diacritical marks for the sake of precision and clarity. The system of diacritical marks that I have adopted for the various languages used in this book is explained in the Note on Transliteration. I have also minimized the use of capitals at the beginning of non-English words or phrases, since capitalization is not a feature of the Nagari and Farsi scripts.

My material in this book draws on eleven distinct languages and speech-varieties: Sanskrit, Arabic, Farsi and modern Hindi and Urdu, as well as older forms of Avadhi, Bhojpuri, Braj Bhāshā, Rajasthani, Khadī Bolī and Punjabi. Since all of them, with the sole exception of Bhojpuri, are full-fledged literary languages embedded in distinct written and oral cultures, I have had to adopt three separate systems of transliteration: one for Sanskrit; one for Arabic, Farsi and Urdu together; and one for the other seven languages and speech-varieties as a group. This is especially necessary for the accurate reproduction of the styles of spelling in the older manuscript sources for Kabir. All the non-English words used in the book are listed alphabetically (in the order of the English alphabet) in the Glossary at the end, where I have provided the transliterated spelling in the headword, and have indicated alternative spellings in the accompanying annotation.

The epigraphs for the four sections of my Introduction are taken from Kedarnath Singh's long poem, 'Uttar Kabīr', which appeared in his book, *Uttar kabīr aur anya kavitāeṃ*, in 1995. Singh, a leading innovator of 'post-modernist' Hindi poetry since the 1960s, conceived of the poem in response to a minor incident during a journey that took him through Magahar, the town in north-eastern Uttar Pradesh where Kabir probably passed away. As his own epigraph to the poem explains:

> One morning in December 1989, while the train I was on happened to pass through the vicinity of Magahar, my gaze fell unexpectedly on a fairly large building, in front of which hung a sign bearing the name of Kabirdas. Upon asking about it I learnt that the building was a spinning mill established by the government to commemorate Kabir, but now virtually shut down—it was supposed to ensure that there would be a constant supply of yarn for the looms in that region full of weavers. Hearing about this, I wondered: How would Kabirdas have responded to this

> information—he who, just a short distance from that spot, has been at rest for centuries in his deep *samādhī* on the banks of the River Ami? (Singh 1995, 132)

The poem is cast as a dramatic monologue in Kabir's voice, and projects him as though he had come back to life in post-modern times. In the passages I have used for my epigraphs, the poet therefore speaks to us across the centuries, in terms that are at once ours and also unmistakably his own.

I first studied and translated Kabir in 1983–86 at the University of Chicago at the suggestion of A.K. Ramanujan. I presented some of my early work to audiences at the University of Chicago (1987) and Columbia University (1994). Six of these translations appeared in *Religions of India in Practice* (1995), edited by Donald S. Lopez, Jr.; my thanks to Princeton University Press for permission to use them here. I am also grateful to Namvar Singh for recommending me for this project. At Penguin India, my thanks go to Kamini Mahadevan for her unfailing tact, patience and enthusiasm; and to Kalpana Joshi and her colleagues for their extraordinary care with the editing, design and production. This book, too, is for Aparna Dharwadker, and for our children, Aneesha and Sachin.

INTRODUCTION

Kabir, His Poetry and His World

1. *The Life of a Weaver*

And now . . .
it's the same bank of the Ami
where I stand upright again
with Infinity wrapped
in a small, poor man's bundle
slung over my shoulder. . . .
Who has survived
who hasn't?
And even the one who has survived—
how much of him is left
at his own proper location
in his own proper time? . . .

Kedarnath Singh, 'Uttar Kabīr' (1995), pp. 133, 137

The historical figure we know as Kabir probably lived in the eastern half of north India in the fifteenth century. For the past 200 years or so, the Kabir Panth, one of the religious organizations associated with his name, has assigned him an extraordinary lifespan from 1398 to 1518. Ever since the British orientalist H. H. Wilson published his pioneering essays on the subject in English in 1828 and 1832, modern scholars have sought to find more plausible dates for Kabir.

In 1950, and then again in 1964, the distinguished Hindi literary historian Parashuram Chaturvedi sifted through several decades of debate and several bodies of evidence to conclude that the poet most probably lived between the late fourteenth and mid-fifteenth centuries (845–70). The American historian of religions David N. Lorenzen reopened the discussion in 1991, when he used Anantadas's *Kabīr Parachāī*, a text composed around 1625 and affiliated with the Ramananda Sampradaya, together with historical accounts of Raja Vir Singh, an early sixteenth-century ruler of Baghelkhand, to argue that Kabir may actually have flourished around the year 1500 (9–18). However, two detailed studies by Gurinder Singh Mann and one by Pashaura Singh, all dealing with the textual history of the *Ādi Granth* and published between 1996 and 2001, have demonstrated once more that the poet was a predecessor and not a contemporary of Guru Nanak (1469–1539), the founder of Sikhism. The information we now have about the formation of Sikh scripture and Kabir's place in it strongly supports the claim that he was born in or about 1398 and died around 1448, just before the mid-point of the fifteenth century.

The poetry preserved in Kabir's name in the older surviving manuscripts indicates that he spent the greater portion of his life in Banaras. Known by the ancient name of Kashi as well as the modern Sanskritised name of Varanasi, Banaras has long been identified as 'Shiva's city', one of the principal sacred sites on the Hindu map of the subcontinent. While most sources agree that the poet grew up, underwent an apprenticeship, and eventually practised an occupation in Banaras, some suggest that his birth and death may have occurred elsewhere. In all likelihood, Kabir spent a part of his life or passed his final days in the town of Magahar, which now lies in Basti district, approximately 15 miles west of Gorakhpur and 100 miles north of Banaras. A poem with his signature-line that appears as shabad 15 in Rāga Gauḏī in the *Ādi Granth* (as compiled in 1604) seems to confirm the story that Banaras and Magahar constituted the two 'ends' of his life:

Now tell me, Rāma,
what's my future trajectory?
    I've renounced Banaras:
    a huge mistake.
Like a fish out of water,
stranded on a bank,
    I'm left without the austerities
    of my previous births.
I've squandered my whole life
in Shiva's city:
    now that it's time to die,
    I've risen and come to Magahar. . . .
Kashi, Magahar: for a thoughtful man,
they're one and the same.
    My devotion's depleted:
    how will it land me on the other shore? . . .

The connection between Kabir and Magahar, however, is more than poetic. Since at least the late seventeenth century, residents of the town have claimed that the poet was either buried on its outskirts, or entered his *samādhī* there. One colonial account indicates that a local nawab named Bijli Khan built a mausoleum at that location on the banks of the river Ami in 1450, and that Fidai Khan, a nawab from outside the region, repaired it around 1567 (Keay 1931, 95–97). Whether these two men invested their resources in the monument specifically to commemorate the poet remains uncertain, but as recently as 1985 the Sunni Vaqf

Board of Lucknow possessed a deed dated 1698–99, which 'registers the gift of the village Kabirpura Karmua for the upkeep of the Muslim tomb of Shah Kabir' in Magahar (Lorenzen 1991, 17). The honorific title 'Shah' mentioned in the document suggests that the building may already have come to be regarded during Aurangzeb's reign as the *dargāh* of a sufi *pīr*. This is broadly consistent with the fact documented in Abdul Haq Dehlavi's *A<u>kh</u>bār al-A<u>kh</u>yār* (composed between 1590 and 1619) and Mohsin Fani's *Dabistān-i Mazāhib* (mid-seventeenth century), that Indian sufis in the Agra, Delhi and Kashmir regions were reading Kabir's poetry during the reigns of Jahangir and Shah Jahan. The tradition has continued throughout the colonial and post-independence periods, with a family of hereditary Muslim caretakers maintaining the mausoleum as a place of sufi worship and pilgrimage down to the present.

The position of Magahar in the poet's biography, however, is complicated by two disparate factors. On the one hand, descriptions and photographs published by the missionaries G. H. Wescott (1907) and F. E. Keay (1931) and the contemporary Hindi scholar Shukdev Singh (1981), among others, show that the old Muslim tomb in Magahar stands next to a Hindu-style temple, which supposedly memorializes the spot where he entered his *samādhī*, and is maintained by sādhus belonging to the Kabir Chaurā Maṭh of Banaras. On the other hand, as early as 1598, Abū'l Fazl, the author of the *Ā'īn-i Akbarī*, the official chronicle of Akbar's reign, recorded the existence of two other *samādhīs* for Kabir: one at Ratanpur, now a dozen miles from Bilaspur, in Chattisgarh, and another at Puri-Jagannath, in Orissa, both maintained by the Dharamdasi branch of the Kabir Panth from the seventeenth or eighteenth century onwards (Vaudeville 1974, 33–35).

Whether Kabir was born and died in Banaras, or in Magahar or elsewhere, the poetry attributed to him and the discourse that has accumulated around it consistently claim that he belonged to the community of weavers in the Banaras-Magahar region. Nita Kumar's ethnographic and historical work on Banaras in the 1980s has confirmed afresh that weavers have lived and worked in the city for the greater part of the past 1,000 years. Banaras has been famous for its silk and cotton weaving since early modern times, if not earlier, and remains a centre of international distinction for this craft, alongside such cities as Dhaka and Kanchipuram. Until the early twentieth century, Banarasi weavers produced their high-quality silk and cotton fabrics on handlooms that seem to have undergone little technological change over the previous seven or eight centuries. Even after the introduction of the jacquard machine and the Hattersley domestic loom around 1928, they have continued to practise their craft in ways that may go back to the beginning of the last millennium. Silk weaving, especially for saris, is still done on looms installed in *kāraḵhānās* or workshops in weaver's homes, and work-patterns in modern family businesses remain centred around the personalities of their master weavers, whose individual styles combine labour and leisure, technical skill and commercial acumen, and moodiness and imagination in different measures (Kumar 1989, 147–52).

One of the Kabir poems in the *Ādi Granth*—shabad 54

in Rāga Gauḏī, preserved since the first decade of the seventeenth century—captures the general atmosphere of a Banarasi weaver's workshop with great precision, even though its primary theme is more abstract and enigmatic:

The weaver thought,
Let me weave
    a body for my self—
but he couldn't have his wish,
and left his house
    in great frustration.

Nine yards, ten yards,
twenty-one yards—
    that completes one stretch of cloth.
Sixty threads in the warp,
nine panels interlocked,
    seventy-two extra threads
    added to the weft.

He counts its yardage, but can't,
he measures its weight, but can't—
    and yet it needs
    five pounds of sizing.
When he asks for the sizing
and doesn't find it ready at once,
    he kicks up a fuss in the house.

The weaver, master of his craft,
    master of his house,
sits through a daylong session at the loom,
but resigns in the end, despairing,
    Why has this moment come to pass?
He abandons the pots of sizing, the bobbins all wet,
    and walks off in a huff.

No thread emerges
    from the empty shuttle,
no shed stands ready
for picking and beating—
    the yarn in the heddles is tangled.
Kabir says, let go of the mess,
let that poor wish remain
    unfulfilled.

Weaving turns up as an allusion and a figure in a number of poems in the written, oral and musical traditions surrounding Kabir, and its recurrence reinforces his portrayal in commentaries as well as paintings as a skilled artisan, both literally and metaphorically (see, for instance, the seventeenth-century Mughal painting reproduced on the cover of Dass 1991).

During the early modern period in India (approximately, from 1498 to 1757) and the modern period as a whole (from about 1757 to the present), weavers have been a vital force in the economy of Banaras. Between the third quarter of the nineteenth century and the last quarter of the twentieth, for example, they have constituted as much as 25 per cent of the city's population at certain moments, and have supported a cottage-industry and trade employing as many as half a million workers at a time (Kumar 1989, 148–52).

Banaras, however, has been dominated by a Hindu majority for much of the past millennium, with a high proportion of its citizens belonging to the *dvija* or 'twice-born' caste-groups (brahmins, kshatriyas, and vaishyas), even though its community of weavers has usually been composed of a Muslim majority and a Hindu minority, at least in the modern period.

In contrast, Magahar has been a town populated predominantly by Muslim and Hindu weavers (besides Buddhists and *ādivāsīs* or 'aborigines') for several hundred years, with few upper-caste citizens until the post-independence period.

Moreover, since about the thirteenth century, a Muslim weaver in the Banaras-Magahar region has been known as a julāhā (a term of Farsi origin), whereas a Hindu weaver has been called a korī (a word of Sanskrit origin). Banarasi Hindus of the *dvija* caste-groups classify the Muslim julāhās as *mlechchhas* (outsiders, people of a foreign race or faith), and the Hindu korīs as shūdras ('servants'). As the Hindi scholar and writer Hazariprasad Dvivedi first noted in this context in 1941, the upper castes' classification of korīs as shūdras follows the paradigm of the *Brahmavaivarta Purāṇa*, which places nine types of artisans—gardeners, ironsmiths, sea-shell artisans, weavers, potters, bronze-workers, carpenters, artists and goldsmiths—in this category (Dvivedi 2000, 15–16).

The consequence of these factors is that the priestly, administrative and mercantile classes of Banarasi society have derided Magahar as a 'dirty' or 'polluted' town for centuries, and its inhabitants as 'low' and 'stupid', much as they have heaped contempt on the julāhās and korīs of their own city (Vaudeville 1974, 45; Kumar 1989, 153). The Kabir poems in the early manuscripts and the later sources respond several times to this provocation, especially in the aphoristic form of the sākhī, as in this instance from 1604 in the Sikh tradition:

Everybody, O Kabir,
    reduces my caste to a laughing stock:

but it devotes itself to the Creator,
    and I martyr myself to its cause.

The older demographic and cultural patterns in the Banaras-Magahar region are part of a wider geographical distribution and a longer historical cycle. Weavers have comprised almost two dozen distinct jātis or social groups in north India since the end of the classical period, and have inhabited towns and villages—usually in ghettos segregated by the upper castes—scattered over a crescent-shaped area stretching from Punjab to Bengal (Dvivedi 2000, 16–17).

In the Banaras-Magahar region itself, the Muslim julāhās have come to dominate the silk-weaving industry in recent decades, which has expanded to an unprecedented degree since the end of the nineteenth century. During this period, the julāhā silk-weavers of Banaras have accumulated capital, achieved upward mobility, and acquired a higher social status. As a part of this collective transformation resembling a class shift, they have adopted the community surname of Ansari, and have distanced themselves from the other julāhās, who, they claim, are socially inferior and do only 'coarse work' (Kumar 1989, 147–56; 1992, 97).

In the thirteenth and fourteenth centuries, as Muslim armies moved eastwards from Delhi in a concentrated phase of conquest and settlement across the Ganga-Jamuna Doab, all the way to the eastern wetlands of Bengal, shūdra jātis of weavers may have converted en masse to Islam. Hazariprasad Dvivedi used colonial records to speculate on the subject in the 1940s, and in the early 1990s the American historian Richard M. Eaton analysed the phenomenon quite comprehensively for the eastern half of north India between the thirteenth and sixteenth centuries, but the precise circumstances and mechanisms of such conversions remain unclear (Dvivedi 2000, 15–24; Eaton 2000, 113–34). Julāhās themselves seem to date their Islamicization to the thirteenth or fourteenth century, at least in some of their modern oral traditions. The 300 years preceding Mughal rule also appear to be the period when some jātis of weavers—such as the *jugis* of rural Bengal—began their association with Nath yoga, a system of thought and practice that projects itself outside the sphere of orthodox Hinduism as well as emergent saguṇī bhakti (Dvivedi 2000, 19–20).

Around the end of the fourteenth century, Kabir was probably born into a family of weavers in the Banaras-Magahar region, whose clan or community, originally korīs in the Hindu fold, may have converted to Islam and thus become julāhās a few decades earlier. If such was the case, it is likely that the poet grew up in a family or community that still retained pragmatic, quotidian connections with its earlier low-caste way of life.

It is also probable that the julāhā community endured disparagement at this time and in this environment for two divergent reasons: for being shūdras by origin, and for being *mlechchhas* by religious persuasion. These probabilities would explain the conflicting characteristics of Kabir as he appears in the poetry ascribed to him: his name is Muslim, but he seems to belong to a maligned or stigmatized community, without access to the social equality that Islam promises; he has the social identity of a Muslim, but he does not accept the basic tenets of Islam (such as the prophethood of Muhammad), and does not seem to know the faith with the familiarity of an insider; and his thought reveals an intimate understanding of the philosophical, theological and ritual aspects of Hinduism, but remains consistent with certain general features of sufism (without acceding to its distinctive institutions, such as the *silsilāh*).

The manuscripts from the sixteenth to the eighteenth centuries that preserve Kabir's poetry or comment on his life and work explicitly identify him as a weaver. On most occasions, they refer to him as a julāhā, but sometimes they also call him a korī, using the latter word as a generic signifier for someone in that occupation. In the *Ādi Granth*, this vacillation between a 'Muslim' designation and a 'Hindu' one is linked to the larger trope of God as a Master Weaver, where the Sikh Gurus (as editors) seem ideologically to prefer the term korī because it casts the Creator as a shūdra artisan—an idea that must have been virtually unthinkable for orthodox Hindus in seventeenth-century Banaras. As shabad 36 in Rāga Āsā says:

You haven't puzzled out
any of the Weaver's secrets:
    it took Him
a mere moment
to stretch out the whole universe
    on His loom.

While you were there,
listening
    to the Vedas and Purāṇas,
I was here,
spreading out
    the threads for my warp.

He fashioned His loom
    out of earth and sky:
He plied the sun and moon
simultaneously
    as His twin shuttles.

When He worked the pair
of treadles in the pit below
    in tandem,
I acknowledged Him
in my mind
    as a master weaver.
I found His signs,
the signs of a weaver,
    inside my house:
in a flash
I recognised Him
    as Rāma.
Kabir says, I've smashed
    my loom:
only the Weaver
can mesh
    thread with thread.

The edges of the poet's name, however, blur historically and conceptually into all the ambiguities of personal, social and religious identity. 'Kabīr' is a truncation of the Arabic *al-Kabīr*, which means 'the great [one]', and is one of the ninety-nine epithets of Allāh in the Qur'ān. For modern readers, Kabir has no other name, but the oldest surviving manuscripts in his case—the Goindval Pothis of the Sikhs, prepared in the Gurmukhi script around 1570–72, under the direction of the third Guru, Amardas—refer to him in their colophons and signature-lines in two different ways. For a total of forty-one times they identify him as Kabīru, Kabīr, Kabīrā, Kabīre, Kabaru, or Kabarī, but for a total of forty-eight times they designate him as Kamīr, Kamīru, Kamīrā, or Kīmīr (my counts are from Callewaert 2000).

While the latter series may represent only an accidental inconsistency in transcription, the frequency of its distribution over a set of fifty poems and their colophons, together with the semantics of the alternative name, may indicate something else. 'Kamīr' and its variants appear to be related to the common Hindi-Urdu words *kam*, *kamī*, and *kamīr*, all of which are derived from the Farsi term *kam*, which characterises its referent as low, deficient, less, mean, base, or despicable. The Kartarpur Pothi of 1604, a canonical manuscript of the earliest portion of the *Ādi Granth* prepared under the fifth Guru, Arjan, changes the poet's name almost uniformly to 'Kabīr' and its variants, allowing 'Kamīr' and 'Kamīru' to occur only three times between them in the entire text (Callewaert 1996).

Combined with the fact that the Fatehpur manuscript of 1582, inscribed in the Nagari script in northern Rajasthan, contains only 'Kabīr' and its variants, the Goindval and Kartarpur Pothis together suggest four intriguing possibilities: (*a*) that the scribe(s) of the Goindval Pothis made an innocent but persistent error in transcribing the poet's name with 'Kamīr' and its variants; (*b*) that Guru Amardas and the scribe(s) of the Goindval Pothis assembled the fifty Kabir poems from at least two distinct lines of transmission, one of which employed 'Kabīr' and its variants, while the other used 'Kamīr' and its variants, or both of which drew ambivalently on both paradigms; (*c*) that Guru Amardas and his scribe(s) experimented consciously with the 'Kamīr' paradigm as an alternative to 'Kabīr', or vice versa, for ideological reasons; and (*d*) that, conversely, more than three decades later, Guru Arjan and the scribes of the Kartarpur Pothi experimented deliberately with the 'Kabīr' paradigm as a homogenising alternative to 'Kamīr', but for different ideological reasons.

Two types of transmutation may have been at work here, because the poet's alternative names are opposed to each other on several levels at once. In the Muslim traditions, 'Kabīr' is Arabic and Qur'ānic, and therefore 'primary', whereas 'Kamīr' is Farsi and non-canonical, and hence 'secondary'. At the same time, 'Kabīr' represents something great and defines an attribute of God, whereas 'Kamīr' signifies something mean, base or deficient and refers to low origins in the human world. Furthermore, 'Kabīr' is imaginable as a personal name for a member of the *ashrāf*, the Muslim elite of the Sultanate period, consisting of wealthy, powerful and cultivated traders, religious officials, soldiers and administrators, mostly immigrants of Arabic, Iranian or Central Asian lineage (Eaton 2000, 97–102). However, 'Kabīr' is not convincing as a name for a julāhā who comes from a community universally mocked for its ethnic origins and its recent (and therefore 'shallow') conversion to Islam, as well as its illiteracy and uncouthness—whereas 'Kamīr' seems entirely plausible as a name for a person from precisely such a background.

The dance of linguistic, ethnic, economic and theological oppositions between the two names is so enticing that the early transmitters of Kabir's poetry in Punjab may well have relished the irony of substituting either 'Kamīr' with 'Kabīr' or 'Kabīr' with 'Kamīr', and thereby transmuting the poet's image at the stroke of a pen. In the first case, a preference for 'Kabīr' would raise a weaver from a socially inferior position to a rhetorically and even spiritually superior position, and thus change the status of his discourse—precisely the effect that has permeated the Kabir phenomenon for the past 500 years. In the second case, the choice of 'Kamīr' would almost iconically mark the poetry with its social origins, and thus underscore its revolutionary potential, but it would lack the indexical power of 'Kabīr' to surround the words with an aura of implied greatness. The remote possibility that Kabīr's name as we have it now may be a textual and ideological invention imposed on him several generations after his death reminds us that he himself seems destined to be nothing more than a shadow in the shadows of history.

Whether his real-life name was Kamir or Kabir, whether he was a Muslim julāhā or a Hindu korī, and whether or not he came from a family of weavers whose community had converted to Islam only in the thirteenth or fourteenth century, this poet seems most likely to have been a cotton weaver—rather than a silk weaver—in fifteenth-century Banaras. The poems in the manuscripts we have inherited do not mention silk, but together with later sources they allude a number of times to raw cotton, cotton yarn, bales of cotton cloth, coarse cotton sheets and finespun cotton fabric. One of the great poems in the tradition, *Jhīnī jhīnī bīnī chadariyā* (rendered here under the title 'Sheet')—which has been transmitted primarily in the oral and musical modes, and has been rated in the late twentieth century as the most popular of the Kabir songs—imagines God as a cotton weaver who weaves each human body on His loom as a sheet of sheer muslin, working thread by thread through the period of its gestation in a mother's womb:

He wove the sheet
    so fine, so fine,
He wove the sheet so fine.

What was the warp?
    What was the weft?
What was the thread
    with which He wove the sheet?

Iñgalā and Piñgalā,
    the warp, the weft,
Sushumnā the thread
    with which He wove the sheet.

He spins the eight-petalled lotus
    as his spinning-wheel,
with five elements
    and three great qualities

He weaves the sheet.

He weaves the sheet
    through ten months
in a mother's womb,
    beating in the weft,
testing and checking
    every strand,
He weaves the sheet.

Saints and humans
    wrap themselves in His sheet,
but the wrapping soils the sheet
    so fine, so fine.

His servant Kabir
    wraps himself in the sheet
with effort and care,
    he keeps it spotlessly clean,

this sheet, so fine, so fine.

If Kabir was a cotton weaver, in all likelihood he belonged to a class of artisans at the bottom of the economic scale. The poetry contains a range of references to his destitution and the life of poverty in general, focusing especially on his unrewarding labour at the handloom, his lack of steady income, his family's financial difficulties, and the arrogance and ostentatiousness of the rich. A poem such as shabad 11 in Rāga Soraṭhī in the *Ādi Granth* explores the effects of poverty on the human psyche—loss of self-worth, abjection, humiliation at having to beg for survival—but turns them around to achieve humility before God:

Mādhav, sweet lord,
how will I ever be
    in your blessèd company?
If you're a niggard,
I'll have to beg
    for your gracious gifts.

Don't starve your devotee:
take back this rosary of yours.
    I only ask for the dust
of the saints' feet:
I don't wish to be
    an object of someone's charity.

All I want is a couple of pounds
of ground wheat,
    a quarter pound of ghee,
some salt to go with it:
that'll suffice
    for survival twice a day.

All I need is a cot
with four legs,
  a pillow, a mattress.
I ask for a coarse sheet
to cover me:
  you'll have my adoration.

I haven't been covetous.
I've heaped ostentation
  on just one thing: your Name.
Kabir says, I've convinced
my heart to be content:
  for when the heart's content,

it comprehends Hari.

In Kabir's personal life, the social consequences of poverty would have been quite unambiguous: as an artisan in the urban underclass of fifteenth-century Banaras, he would have found it virtually impossible to acquire either literacy or formal education. From the poetry itself it is clear that no Hindu *shikshā*-guru (teacher) or *dīkshā*-guru (spiritual master) would have accepted either a shūdra or a *mlechchha* as a pupil under such circumstances, and no Muslim maulavī would have educated a julāhā without demanding a prohibitive fee. A number of poems portray Kabir as an illiterate man who reciprocally scorns paper and pen, books and orthodox learning, Veda and Qur'ān, paṇḍit and maulavī (Vaudeville 1974, 49–50).

Without literacy, formal education and spiritual initiation, Kabir would have found no entry into the world of high-caste and upper-class priests, theologians, scholars, poets, chroniclers and connoisseurs of the arts who controlled intellectual life in post-classical Banaras, within and outside the circles of royal patronage (for a later period, see Freitag 1992, 3–16; Lutgendorf 1992). This means that he probably composed his poems orally, recited or sang them mostly to illiterate and lower-class audiences, and had limited access, if any, to socio-economically privileged audiences interested in bhakti. His social position thus would have been unambiguously subaltern, and he would have had to overcome potentially insurmountable obstacles to receive any approbation as a poet, thinker or spiritual practitioner.

Given the *pratibhā* or brilliance of the surviving poems, and especially their intellectual breadth—which allows them to range freely over the domains of theology, philosophy, social thought, mythology, music and mysticism—Kabir's audiences since the late sixteenth century have persistently tried to claim that he was actually a brahmin by birth, or at least was initiated into legitimate spiritual practice by a brahmin *dīkshā*-guru.

One series of biographical accounts constructed after about 1600, for example, has suggested that he was the illegitimate child of a brahmin widow in Banaras, who abandoned him at birth, leaving him to be discovered by a childless julāhā couple named Niru and Nima, who then adopted him and raised him in a community of poor Muslim weavers. It has also asserted that Kabir was a precocious adolescent, and acquired a *dīkshā*-guru by tricking a high brahmin—the philosopher and theologian Ramananda—into accepting him as a disciple and initiating him into bhakti. The stories in this series acquired their influential forms in the *Kabīr Parachāī*, composed by Anantadas around 1625, and the *Bhaktirasabodhinī*, composed by Priyadas about 1712, both of whom were commentators of the Ramananda

Sampradaya, and tried to absorb Kabir, however implausibly, into a particularly conservative variety of saguna Vaishnava devotion.

A different series of birth-stories originated with the Kabir Panth at a later date, and attempted to take the poet completely out of his controversial social and human context. These narratives claimed that he was really 'born' in a blaze of light over a lake (Lahartārā Tālāb, not far from the Kabir Chaurā Maṭh in Banaras), and entered human society and history as a manifestation of the *Satguru*, God as the True Master (Keay 1931, 95; Lorenzen 1991, 23–27, 43–48).

Regardless of whether he was a legitimate or an illegitimate child, an offspring or merely a foundling, high caste or low caste by birth, Hindu or Muslim, or even a manifestation of God 'without attributes', the historical Kabir appears to have acquired a strong local or regional reputation as a poet, social critic and bhakta, perhaps in his own lifetime, but certainly in the decades after his death. The early reputation seems to have hinged on the audacity and persuasiveness of his views, touching upon issues that lay at the heart of Hindu and Muslim beliefs in north India during the fifteenth and sixteenth centuries, as we see in these poems that are among the earliest attributed to him.

If you love your followers, Rāma,
settle this quarrel, once and for all.

Is Brahmā greater, or where He came from?
Is the Veda greater, or its origin?

Is this mind greater, or what it believes in?
Is Rāma greater, or the one who knows Him?

Kabir says, I'm in despair. Which is greater?
    The pilgrim-station, or Hari's devoted slave?

Kabīr Granthāvalī, pada 27

Tell me, O paṇḍit,
    what place is pure—
where I can sit
    and eat my meal?

Mother was impure,
    father was impure—
the fruits they bore
    were also impure.
They arrived impure,
    they left impure—
unlucky folks,
    they died impure.

My tongue's impure,
    my words are impure,
my ears, my eyes,
    they're all impure—
you brahmins,
    you've stolen the fire,
but you can't burn off
    the impurity of the senses!

The fire, too, is impure,
    the water's impure—
so even the kitchen's
    nothing but impure.
The ladle's impure
    that serves a meal,
and they're impure
    who sit and eat their fill.

Cow-dung's impure,
the bathing-square's impure—
its very curbs
are nothing but impure.
Kabir says,
only they are pure
who've completely cleansed
their thinking.

Ādi Granth, Rāga Basanta Hiṇḍolā, shabad 7

Broadcast, O mullāh,
your merciful call to prayer—
you yourself are a mosque
with ten doors.

Make your mind your Mecca,
your body, the Ka'aba—
your Self itself
is the Supreme Master.

In the name of Allāh, sacrifice
your anger, error, impurity—
chew up your senses,
become a patient man.

The lord of the Hindus and Turks
is one and the same—
why become a mullāh,
why become a sheikh?

Kabir says, brother,
I've gone crazy—
quietly, quietly, like a thief,
my mind has slipped into the simple state.

Ādi Granth, Rāga Bhairava, shabad 4

The rhetorical boldness of such pieces, their uncompromising theological and social criticism, and their philosophical intricacy explain why Nabhadas, alone among the early Vaishṇava and Ramanandi commentators on Kabir, seems to have been both acute and unbiased when he chose to describe the poet in the following terms in verse 60 of his *Shrībhaktamāl*, composed around 1600:

Kabir didn't honour the world's conventions,
such as caste, the four stages of life, the six philosophical systems.
He sang of a faith that opposed bhakti
as a non-faith.
He showed that yoga, ritual sacrifice, fasting and charity were trivial and base
without the practice of devotional worship.
His ramainīs, shabdas, and sākhīs
are the truth about Hindus and Muslims.
His words didn't belong to a faction:
what he said was good for everybody.
The world's disposition is inflexible:
he didn't say things to please someone.
Kabir didn't honour the world's conventions,
such as caste, the four stages of life, the six philosophical systems.

A few stories in Kabir's poems as well as other sources circulated before the middle of the seventeenth century imply that the poet's audacity may have had repercussions in his lifetime. Two poems in the *Ādi Granth*, for example, establish a pair of persistent paradigms: in one, a powerful religious functionary attempts to punish the poet for his unorthodox criticism of doctrine and ritual; in the other, an authoritarian ruler tries to torture or kill him for his general defiance of authority (Dass 1991, 187–88, 238; Vaudeville 1974, 44–45; Lorenzen 1991, 23–42). If the persecution was a fact of Kabir's life but failed to silence him, it may have unintentionally enhanced his reputation as an independent thinker, and added to his aura of 'greatness' among his contemporaries. If, however, it succeeded in hurting or intimidating him, it may have provided the reason for his migration from Banaras to Magahar towards the end of his days.

After nearly two centuries of research on Kabir, we still cannot reconstruct the historical figure behind the name with much confidence. But if the composite portrait that emerges from all the circumstantial evidence is an index of historical fact, then we might conclude that this poet lived in and around Banaras from about 1398 to 1448; that he belonged to the community of Muslim julāhās in the region, either by birth or by adoption, and became a cotton weaver by occupation; that he was a poor artisan, a subaltern from the lowest socio-economic levels of fifteenth-century north Indian society, with no practical opportunity in his immediate environment for either education or spiritual initiation; that he nevertheless succeeded in composing and circulating poetry in the oral and musical modes, and in acquiring a reputation as a poet, critical thinker and religious practitioner; that he was perhaps persecuted for his outspoken and unorthodox views about religion and society, and was forced to flee from Banaras; and that he passed away in Magahar, in the vicinity of the monuments that constitute his Hindu-style *samādhī* and his Muslim-style *dargāh* today.

While this picture is meagre when compared to the

portraits that post-independence Hindi scholars have constructed, and is mostly a representation of his life and personality on the exterior, it may be sufficient to begin a systematic exploration of the poetry attributed to him (see especially Chaturvedi 1954, 1964; Tivari 1961; Gupta 1969; Sarnamsingh Sharma 1969).

2. *The Fabric of the Text*

A needle's lost
in the earth's heart
and the tailor has vanished
into that needlepoint. . . .
I want to descend
to the deep dark roots of that scream
I want to penetrate
every rock every head every thought
like the earth's original, isolated scream
so that I can reach through
to the last thread in the total fabric
which
no matter where you pull it from
which way you stretch it
always
falls short. . . .

Kedarnath Singh, 'Uttar Kabīr' (1995), pp. 136, 135

In the decades after Kabir's death around 1448, his reputation as well as his poetry appear to have spread across much of north India in three complementary and interdependent modes: by word of mouth, through the musical rendition of his verses, and in written versions of different sets of compositions attributed to him. The poetry is likely to have travelled with an assortment of people on the move: sādhus and yogis, pilgrims and merchants, scribes and poets, painters and musicians, and even soldiers and bureaucrats. In the first 200 years of its posthumous existence—from the end of the Sayyad dynasty in the Delhi Sultanate to the reign of Shah Jahan—it seems to have been disseminated along the period's principal routes of trade, migration and pilgrimage. It may have spread first from Banaras to Delhi and Punjab in the north, to the Braj area and Rajasthan in the west, and to Bihar, Bengal and Orissa in the east, along a branching east-west corridor. A little later, it may also have been dispersed from two distinct points of origin—the Banaras region and the Delhi-Punjab region—along separate north-south corridors towards Gujarat and Maharashtra.

The verbal and musical forms of Kabir's compositions almost certainly influenced the work of Guru Nanak, so the poet's reputation and his verse may have reached the Lahore area in Punjab, some 700 miles from Banaras, by the first quarter of the sixteenth century. A number of poems carrying Kabir's signature-line had definitely found their way to central Punjab and northern Rajasthan half a century later. Fifty of them were included in the Goindval Pothis between about 1570 and 1572; and a different set of fifteen was incorporated into a more conservative collection of bhakti poems, called *Pada suradāsajī kā*, prepared for the education of a Kachchhvāha prince of Fatehpur, near Sikar, in 1582 (Mann 1996, 2001; Bahura 1984).

Paper, ink and pen appear to have reached India quite late, arriving in the twelfth and thirteenth centuries in the north with Muslim soldiers, administrators and sufis migrating over land from Central and West Asia, and on the Malabar coast with Arab and Jewish traders plying the Arabian Sea. By the sixteenth century the practice of writing with pen and ink on paper had spread all over the subcontinent: near its end, the *Ādi Granth* celebrates the technological revolution of its times with a hymn in praise of paper, as well as a recipe for the preparation of ink. It is therefore conceivable that Kabir's poems were first written down towards the end of his lifetime, or in the years following his death, and that writing was involved in the transmission of his poetry from an early stage in its history.

The post-classical history of writing materials is significant in this case because poems claiming Kabir's authorship have been disseminated along three main lines of manuscript production since the second half of the sixteenth century. The oldest of these is the so-called *northern* line, maintained by the Sikh community at its institutional centres in Punjab. In retrospect, this line begins with the Goindval Pothis around 1570, reaches a normative form in the Kartarpur Pothi of 1604 (which constitutes the core of the *Ādi Granth*), and continues to produce new texts and reproduce earlier manuscripts until the tenth and final Guru, Gobind Singh, closes the canon in the 1680s. After Guru Gobind elevates the *Ādi Granth* to the status of the *Guru Granth Sāhib*, the 'living Guru', just before his death in 1708, this line focuses on manuscript reproduction until it enters print in 1864–65.

The history of the northern manuscript line coincides broadly with the birth and development of the Nanak Panth, or the religion we now call Sikhism, and the distinguishing features of its manuscripts emerge from the doctrines and practices of the community gathered around the ten Sikh

Gurus. It is also interbraided with the formation of the Gurmukhi script and of the basic domain of the Punjabi language and its early literature. The line is vital to the transmission of Kabir's poetry because the Sikh Gurus began to compile the principal texts of their faith in two main categories after the mid-sixteenth century: *bāṇī* or poems composed by the Gurus themselves, and *bāṇī* authored by others, among whom are poets called *bhagat*s or devotees, who do not belong to the *panth* but whose beliefs and utterances accord closely with, or serve as counterpoints to, those of the legitimate Gurus. In this division, which remains central to the *Ādi Granth* after 1604, Kabir is the foremost of the *bhagat*s represented in the canon: the Goindval Pothis already include fifty of his poems, and the final form of the scripture contains 228 poems and 243 aphorisms attributed to him (Dass 1991, 1–21).

The second main manuscript line for Kabir is the *western* one, which belongs geographically and culturally to the region of Rajasthan. It begins with the Fatehpur manuscript of 1582, prepared under royal patronage near the town of Sikar, and branches out in the seventeenth and eighteenth centuries into the institutions and practices of two emergent *saṃpradāya*s, the Dadu Dayal Panth (based in Naraina, with institutions also in the nearby city of Jaipur now) and the Niranjani Sampradaya (based mainly in western Rajasthan, with possible connections in Orissa). The former community is founded around the turn of the seventeenth century by Dadu Dayal (1544–1603), most likely a Muslim cotton-carder who identifies himself as a nirguṇa *upāsak* and organizes the *panth* in order to actively promote the worship of a God without attributes. The *panth* develops two main internal divisions over time, one consisting of sādhus without worldly connections who travel widely to promote their faith, and the other of householders who retain their worldly ties but nevertheless practise nirguṇī *upāsanā*; in addition, from the eighteenth century onwards, the Dadu Panthi sādhus subdivide themselves into five distinctive orders (Chaturvedi 1964, 488–539). Beginning with Dadu Dayal around 1600, the sādhus and other members of this *panth* cultivate a remarkable discipline of compiling, editing, copying and preserving large collections of texts in several languages and genres.

The Niranjani Sampradaya is probably founded earlier, by Swami Haridas (around 1455–1538) in Didwana, Rajasthan, with *maṇḍals* or branches emerging later in Nagaur, Bikaner and Jodhpur. Like the Dadu Panth, the Niranjani Sampradaya promotes the worship of a God without predicable qualities, but it specifically conceives of godhead not only as nirguṇa but also as *nirañjan*, absolutely pure and flawless, without any taint whatsoever. However, unlike the Dadu Panth, which defines itself as a strictly nirguṇa *saṃpradāya*, the Niranjani Sampradaya cultivates a 'catholic' stance, incorporating Nath yoga into its doctrines even while 'tolerating' saguṇī bhakti as well as idol worship and *varṇāśrama* dharma (Chaturvedi 1964, 337–56). In the eighteenth century, if not earlier, Niranjani sādhus consolidate a practice parallel to and interlocked with that of their Dadu Panthi counterparts, of compiling and preserving large anthologies of poetry and other types of texts in manuscript.

These two *panths* play a pivotal role in our context because Dadu Panthi manuscripts of the 1620–1824 period and Niranjani manuscripts surviving from the 1769–1804 period contain relatively large sets of poems attributed to Kabir

(Tivari 1961). The Dadu Panthi line is particularly complex, not only because it is prolific, but also because it includes compilations in specialized genres. One of these is the *pañchavāṇī*-style anthology which, as its name indicates, brings together 'five discourses', specifically the compositions of five *sant*s or holy men that the Panth celebrates: Dadu Dayal, Kabir, Namdev, Raidas and Hardas (in that order). The other genre is the *sarbañgī*-style anthology which, in accordance with its label, contains poems and other types of texts that exemplify 'all the parts' of the Panth's nirguṇa *mat* or doctrine of a God without qualities (see Callewaert 1978, 1991, 1993; Singhal 1990). As I shall show a little later, these two kinds of collections of disparate material employ rather different principles of selection and organization, and therefore orient themselves along different rhetorical axes.

The third and most recent line of manuscript production is the *eastern* one, centred around the Kabir Panth and its various *shākhā*s or branches in the eastern parts of north India. This line claims to be the oldest and most authentic one in relation to the poet, but its manuscripts do not attain an inspectable form until 1805, well after the Italian Capuchin monk, Marco della Tomba, stimulates European interest in Kabir with his writings and translations (prepared between 1758 and 1775), and shortly before British administrators and missionaries begin to collect, analyse and publish information on the poet (Vaudeville 1974, 5–6). Moreover, the Panth does not consolidate its competing recensions of a principal text, the *Bījak*, until much later, and then does so only in the medium of print, in early editions published between 1868 and 1937.

The Kabir Panth's numerous branches are scattered from Bihar and Orissa to Rajasthan and Gujarat, and they are usually identified by their *gaddīs* or institutional seats at specific locations. Among the major branches are the Phatuha *shākhā*, with its *gaddī* at Phatuha, near Patna, Bihar; the Bhagatahi branch, with a seat at Dhanauti, in Chhapra district, Bihar; the Chaurā branch, with its centre at the *maṭh* and temple in Banaras; and the Dharamdasi *shākhā*, with one important *gaddī* at Dhamakhera, near Bilaspur, Chattisgarh, and another at Puri-Jagnnath, Orissa, where it maintains a *samādhī* associated with Kabir—which Abū'l Fazl documented in 1598—and a second *samādhī* associated with its founder Dharamdas, a wealthy merchant who supposedly became a disciple of the poet (Wescott 1907, 105–06; Keay 1931, 97–103).

The Kabir Panth's manuscripts and printed books articulate four main versions of the *Bījak*, with the earliest manuscript compiled in Bihar in 1805. The Dharamdasi version of the *Bījak* is the first to enter print, being published by lithograph in 1868, accompanied by a commentary ascribed to Raja Vishwanath Singh of Baghelkhand, whose dynasty in the modern period is linked to the town of Rewa in north-eastern Madhya Pradesh. This version is connected to the Dharamdasis' contention that they have been patronized by Baghelkhand royalty since the time of Raja Vir Singh, who is mentioned in the *Babarnāmā* and who died about 1530, but the chronicles produced at his successors' court, though discussed sympathetically by David N. Lorenzen, do not provide conclusive proof to support the claim (Lorenzen 1991, 9–18). Of the other three, the Chaurā version is dated

1885 in manuscript and 1928 in print; the Phatuha version is dated 1893 in manuscript as well as print; and the Bhagatahi version (produced at the *shākhā*'s Mansar Maṭh in Bihar) is dated 1937 in book form.

Since 1868, the various versions of the *Bījak* have gone through nearly fifty editions and printings, spawning several major commentaries in Hindi (and even one in Sanskrit), leading up to the large Gangasharan Shastri edition (with a commentary) published in 1989. The theological positions of the competing *shākhās* of the Kabir Panth differ from each other, sometimes to a significant degree, but their aggregate output is the only one among the various manuscript lines to be devoted exclusively to Kabir, and to maintain that he is a 'manifestation' of the *Satguru* or primordial godhead (compare, for example, Hess and Singh 1983; Ajaib Singh 1984; Shastri 1989).

Whether we look for parallels in the period of the Renaissance in Europe (with which the historical Kabir was contemporaneous) or outside it, the textual history of this body of poetry is one of the most complex to be associated with a single author in world literature. At a minimum, it involves a constellation of about thirty indispensable source-texts in manuscript and print that evolve extraordinary relationships with each other between about 1570 and 1937. Table 1 offers an essential, schematic overview of the chronology and affiliations of these source-texts, alongside the principal modern editions that represent and supplement them. The large amount of information presented in this tabulation adds up to four major features of the Kabir corpus as a whole, which may be described and explained as in the pages following the table.

TABLE 1: Principal Manuscript and Print Sources of Kabir's Poetry, 1570–2000

Note: Items analysed and incorporated in Tivari 1961 are marked [T], whereas those used in Callewaert 2000 are marked [C].

No.	*Date(s)*	*Identification*	*Description*
	Manuscipts		
1.	1570–72	Goindval Pothis	Northern line; Sikh; preserved in Jalandhar and Pinjore, Punjab. Compiler: Guru Amardas. Gurmukhi script; 4 notebooks, 2 extant; Kabir: 50 padas. Analysed in Mann 1996, 2000. [C]
2.	1582	Fatehpur Ms.	Western line; Vaishṇava, royal patronage; ms. no. 49, reserved collection, Maharaja Sawai Man Singh II Museum, Jaipur. Nagari script; 163 folios; Kabir: 15 padas. Facsimile ed. in Bahura 1984; also analysed in Bryant 1984. [C]
3.	1604	Kartarpur Pothi (*Ādi Granth*)	Northern line; Sikh; preserved in Kartarpur, Punjab. Early core of *Ādi Granth/ Guru Granth Sāhib*; compiler: Guru Arjan; scribe: Bhai Gurdas. Gurmukhi script; 974 folios; Kabir: 228 padas, 243 shaloks (counts vary). [T][C]

contd . . .

No.	Date(s)	Identification	Description
4.	1614	*Pañchavāṇī* Ms. I	Western line; Dadu Panth; preserved in Sanjay Sharma Collection, Jaipur. Nagari script; Kabir: 370 padas. [C]
5.	1620	Rajjabadas, *Sarbaṅgī*	Western line; Dadu Panth; extant mss. dated 1714 (Banaras), 1744 (Naraina), 1760 (Jaipur), 1779 (Banaras). Multilingual work; compiler: Rajjabadas; contains 3,927 compositions in 12 genres by 137 authors. Nagari script; Kabir: 159 padas, 196 sākhīs, 1 *aril*. Complete text in Singhal 1990; also analysed in Callewaert 1978. [T][C]
6.	1627	Gopaladas, *Sarbaṅgī*	Western line; Dadu Panth. Compiler: Gopaladas; contains compositions by 182 authors. Nagari script; 364 folios; Kabir: 352 padas, 609 sākhīs. Text in Callewaert 1993. [C]
7.	1636	*Pañchavāṇī* Ms. II	Western line; Dadu Panth; ms. no. 12, Dadu Mahavidyalaya, Jaipur. Nagari script; Kabir: folios 140–91. [C]

contd . . .

No.	Date(s)	Identification	Description
8.	1658*a*	H. N. Sharma Ms. I	Western line; Dadu Panth; *bastā* no. 7, Harinarayan Sharma Collection, Jaipur. Nagari script; Kabir: 400 padas, 7 ramainīs, 800 sākhīs. [T]
9.	1658*b*	*Pañchavāṇī* Ms. III	Western line; Dadu Panth; ms. no. 34, City Palace, Jaipur; Callewaert's ms. 'V'. Nagari script; Kabir: 348 padas (folios 140–220, 488). [C]
10.	1660/ 1669	Jaipur Ms. I	Western line; Vaishṇava; ms. no. 3322, City Palace, Jaipur; Callewaert's ms. 'C'. Nagari script; Kabir: 185 padas (folios 7–35). [C]
11.	1675	*Pañchavāṇī* Ms. IV	Western line; Dadu Panth; ms. no. 875, Guru Nanak Dev University, Amritsar; Callewaert's ms. 'A'. Nagari script; Kabir: 393 padas (folios 165–236). [C]
12.	1681	Jaipur Ms. II	Western line; Vaishṇava; ms. no. 1853, City Palace, Jaipur; Callewaert's ms. 'J'. Nagari script; Kabir: 222 padas (folios 1–72). [C]

contd . . .

No.	Date(s)	Identification	Description
13.	1682–88	*Ādi Granth/ Dasam Granth*	Northern line; Sikh; edited by Guru Gobind Singh, with additions to and changes in 1604 text of Kartarpur Pothi/*Ādi Granth*; elevated to status of *Guru Granth Sahib* in 1708. Gurmukhi script; Kabir: 541 compositions (counts vary). [T][C]
14.	1684*a*	H. N. Sharma Ms. II	Western line; Vaishṇava; preserved in Harinarayan Sharma Collection, Jaipur. Nagari script; 330 folios. [T]
15.	1684*b*	Jaipur Ms. III	Western line; Vaishṇava; ms. no. 12, Vidyạ Bhushan Samgraha, Jaipur. Contains 60 different works by various authors. Nagari script; 330 folios; Kabir: folios 1–20, 213–62, 319. [C]
16.	1711	Dadu Ms. I	Western line; Dadu Panth; preserved at Dadu Mahavidyalaya, Jaipur; Tivari's ms. 'Dā 3'. Unusual contents; works in several genres by several authors; scribe: Jagannathadas, disciple of Lakshmidas; completed at Didwana, Rajasthan. Nagari script; 416 folios; Kabir: 343 padas. [T]

contd . . .

No.	Date(s)	Identification	Description
17.	1714	Sabha Ms. I	Western line; Dadu Panth; ms. no. 1409, Nagari Pracharini Sabha, Banaras; Tivari's sixth Sabha ms. Immense anthology in six parts, including a *Pañchavāṇī*, Rajjabadas's *Sarbaṅgī*, other works by Dadu Panthi authors, and works by Nath yogis. Nagari script; 791 folios; Kabir: 387 padas, 884 sākhīs, 7 ramainīs (folios 1–218). [T]
18.	1769	Niranjani Ms. I	Western line; Niranjani Panth; preserved at Dadu Mahavidyalaya, Jaipur; Tivari's second Niranjani ms. Scribe: Niranjani sādhu Mohanadas; completed at Sambhar, Rajasthan. Nagari script; 536 folios; Kabir: folios 409–518 [T]
19.	1770	Sabha Ms. II	Western line; Dadu Panth; preserved at Nagari Pracharini Sabha, Banaras; Tivari's eighth Sabha ms. Scribe: Ramadas, disciple of Ratanadas. Nagari script; 332 folios. [T]

contd . . .

No.	Date(s)	Identification	Description
20.	1773	Dadu Ms. II	Western line; Dadu Panth; preserved at Dadu Mahavidyalaya, Jaipur; Tivari's 'Dā 2' ms. Contains a *Pañchavāṇī*, Raghavadas's *Bhaktamāl*, Rajjabadas's *Sarbaṅgī*, and 11 other works. Nagari script; 695 folios. [T]
21.	1774	Dadu Ms. III	Western line; Dadu Panth; preserved at Dadu Mahavidyalaya, Jaipur; Tivari's 'Dā 1' ms. Scribe: Motiram, disciple of Vishnudas, in disciple-tradition of Baba Banavaridas; completed at Dadari, Rajasthan. Nagari script; 650 folios. [T]
22.	1790/ 1796	Jagannath, *Guṇagañjanāmā*	Western line; Dadu Panth. (*a*) 1790 ms. preserved at Nagari Pracharini Sabha, Banaras; scribe: Dayaram, son and disciple of Laladas; completed at the Dadu Panth centre in Naraina, Rajasthan. (*b*) 1796 ms. preserved at Dadu Mahavidyalaya, Jaipur; contains compositions in 9 genres and 2 languages by 65

contd . . .

No.	Date(s)	Identification	Description
			authors; divided into 179 thematic aṅgas. Nagari script; 400 folios; Kabir: 400 sākhīs. Text in Singhal 1990. [T] [C]
23.	1804	Niranjani Ms. II	Western line; Niranjani Panth; preserved at Dadu Mahavidyalaya, Jaipur; Tivari's first Niranjani ms. Nagari script; 669 folios; Kabir: 662 padas, 1,377 sākhīs, 13 ramainīs, 7 *rekhtā*s, 4 other works. [T]
24.	1805	Phatuha *Bījak* Ms.	Eastern line; Kabir Panth, Phatuha branch; preserved at Bihar Rashtrabhasha Parishad, Patna. Nagari script. Used as a source-text in Shukdev Singh 1972.
25.	1824	Sabha Ms. III	Western line; ms. no. 109, Nagari Pracharini Sabha, Banaras; commonly known as Sabha ms. 'Kha'; Tivari's second Sabha ms. Nagari script; 60 long folios; Kabir: 404 padas, 621 sākhīs, 8 ramainīs. Used as source-text in Shyamasundaradas 1928. [T]

contd . . .

No.	Date(s)	Identification	Description
Printed Books			
26.	1868	*Bījak* (Dharamdasi)	First version of *Bījak* in print, published in lithograph edition, with commentary by Raja Vikram Singh of Baghelkhand.
27.	1873	Kishandas, *Kabīr Padasaṃgraha*	First Niranjani print edition.
28.	1883	*Bījak* (Phatuha)	First print edition of Phatuha text.
29.	1900	*Kabīrasāhabkī Shabdāvalī*	Influential popular edition of the Kabir text, as constructed by the Radhasoami Satsang.
30.	1910–11	K. M. Sen, *Kabīr ke gīt*	Transcriptions of 100 Kabir songs sung by 'wandering yogis' in Bengal; in Hindi with Bengali translations, in 4 small volumes.
31.	1916	Upadhyaya, *Kabīr Vachanāvalī*	Popular edition, marked by an uncritical approach to texts and issues.
32.	1926	Vicharadas, *Bījak*	Influential edition of and commentary on the text, by a sādhu of the Kabir Panth.
33.	1928	Shyamasundaradas, *Granthāvalī*	First modern scholarly edition of Kabir's poetry, based on manuscripts at Nagari Pracharini Sabha, Banaras.

contd . . .

No.	Date(s)	Identification	Description
34.	1937	*Bījak* (Bhagatahi)	First print edition of Bhagatahi text.
35.	1941	H. P. Dvivedi, *Kabīr*	Critical exposition, with Hindi text of 100 Kabir padas as recorded in Sen 1910–11; and of 156 padas from other sources, such as *Shabdāvalī* (1900), Upadhyaya 1916, Vicharadas 1926, and Shyamasundaradas 1928.
36.	1961	P. N. Tivari, *Kabīr Granthāvalī*	Modern standard edition, based on all three manuscript-lines, with emphasis on western line; 200 Kabir padas, 21 ramainīs, 744 sākhīs, reconstructed from sources marked [T] above.
37.	1969	M. P. Gupta, *Kabīr Granthāvalī*	Scholarly edition with commentary, using material from all three manuscript-lines; polemical response to Tivari 1961.
38.	1972	Shukdev Singh, *Kabīr Bījak*	Scholarly edition of *Bījak*.
39.	1989	Shastri, *Bījak* (Chaurā)	Edition of Chaurā version, with new commentary.
40.	2000	Callewaert *Kabīr Vāṇī*	Variant texts of 593 Kabir padas from earliest mss., 1570–1681 period (marked with [C] above).

a. Geographical Dispersion

Table 1 shows that the early geographical dispersion of Kabir's poetry across much of north India proved to be irreversible. Occurring within the first century and a quarter of the poet's death, the dispersion must have meant that individual poems as well as clusters of poems began to inhabit new local and regional environments that were quite different from the environment in the Banaras-Magahar region in which they had originated.

Five hundred years ago, north India was already highly differentiated into regions by languages, speech-varieties, scripts and dominant cultural practices, among other variables. Once some or all of the poems composed by the historical Kabir had spread to such parts of the country as Punjab and Rajasthan, they could neither return to their place of origin nor sustain a living link to it. Thus, when the poems entered the written mode on a significant scale in the late sixteenth and early seventeenth centuries, they were already *regionalized*. The various Kabir manuscript-lines have retained that regionalizm ever since, and their geographical distribution cannot be retroactively undone.

b. Multiple Languages and Scripts

One of the primary differentiating factors among regions in India for the past one thousand years or so has been language, so the early and heterogeneous regionalization meant that Kabir's poetry was already *multilingual* when it acquired its earliest written forms in the Goindval Pothis, the Fatehpur manuscript, and the Kartarpur Pothi. By the end of the seventeenth century, its verbal texture had absorbed the grammar, syntax and semantics of half a dozen major languages and speech-varieties of north India: Bhojpuri, Avadhi, Braj Bhāshā, Rajasthani, Khaḏī Bolī and Punjabi (Chaturvedi 1954, 208–29). By this time, it had also acquired traces of several other languages, especially lexical items from Sanskrit, Arabic and Farsi, as well as a specialized vocabulary and stock phrases commonly used by religious practitioners across north India (a jargon usually called *sādhukkaḏī* or *sant bhāshā*). Moreover, from the first stages of its textual history, this body of verse appeared in different scripts in different locations, with the Gurmukhi, Nagari and Farsi scripts predominating in the sixteenth and seventeenth centuries, and the Kaithi, Gujarati and Bengali scripts, among others, adding to the complexity of the written transmission in subsequent times (Tivari 1961).

For the past 400 years, and increasingly so with each passing century, it has been impossible to strip away the effects of local speech-varieties and regional languages and scripts from the texture of the poems. Table 1 shows that, at the beginning of the twenty-first century, we cannot reduce the body of poetry to a homogeneous or monolingual text. In fact, we cannot even determine precisely which medium Kabir may have actually composed his verses—Bhojpuri or Avadhi—because all he seems to say about it is contained in the following aphorism, found in a very late text:

My speech is of the East:
    no one can understand its signs.
Whoever can understand my speech
    is truly a man of the East.

The irreversible multilingualism of the Kabir text has specific characteristics. The corpus in its entirety, viewed across manuscript-lines, appears in multiple scripts and contains a large number of languages. A particular poem may thus appear in variant forms in different manuscripts and manuscript-lines, with each such form articulated in a distinct language or speech-variety. In several instances, any one manuscript in a given line is composed quite consistently in a particular language or speech-variety belonging to the region in which it is produced.

This neat separation of linguistic mediums, however, is muddied by three kinds of cross-currents. First, a poem often retains a strong verbal base in one language, which may be the medium in which it was initially composed, but then undergoes a specific regional variation in which it seems to acquire the patina of a second language at the levels of lexicon and grammar. Many Kabir shabads in the *Ādi Granth*, for example, retain their overall Purabi or eastern (Avadhi) flavour, even though their verbal textures display a marked 'Punjabification', and they stand apart linguistically from many of the shabads of the Sikh Gurus, which are composed directly in Punjabi (Mann 2001, 5; Chaturvedi 1954, 208–29).

Second, some of the important manuscripts prepared between the sixteenth and eighteenth centuries—such as those of Rajjabadas's *Sarbañgī* (manuscripts from 1714–79, but composed around1620), and Jagannath's *Guṇagañjanāmā* (manuscripts from 1790–96, but composed earlier)—are explicitly multilingual, and therefore do not impose a regional or linguistic uniformity upon their materials. In such cases, Kabir's work may appear in different literary mediums within a single source, so that a Rajasthani version of one poem may turn up next to a Braj Bhāshā version of another (Singhal 1990).

Third, as Parasanath Tivari, Kabir's leading scholarly editor in the post-independence period, demonstrated persuasively in 1961, all the major manuscripts in the Gurmukhi and Nagari scripts contain linguistic 'errors' that derive from their mis-readings of intermediary manuscripts in the Farsi script. So even when a particular manuscript in a particular script constructs a linguistically homogeneous text for all its poems, it imports traces of other languages and scripts into its texture—an inescapable consequence of the very process of transmission in Kabir's case (Tivari 1961, pt. 1, 55–146). However, some poems that seem to have passed through more than one intermediary medium of transmission end up with verbal textures containing words and grammatical forms from a mixture of languages, which is often loosely called *sādhukkaḏī* or *sant bhāshā*; whereas some poems deliberately adopt the 'mixed medium' or generic conventions of *rekhtā* (Vaudeville 1974, 64).

Nevertheless, virtually all the poems in the early manuscripts are grammatically well-formed, which implies that their makers and transmitters have been in control of their various verbal mediums. If a particular variant of a poem mixes two or more registers, dialects or languages, its admixture is almost certain to be part of a deliberate authorial or editorial design. The additional fact that each of the six main tongues in the aggregate Kabir text—Bhojpuri, Avadhi, Braj Bhāshā, Rajasthani, Khaḏī Bolī, and Punjabi—functions as a self-consistent literary medium across the various manuscript-lines and modes of transmission suggests that Shyamasundaradas's influential description in 1928 of Kabir's language as a *panchamel khichchaḏī*, a crude 'mishmash of five elements', was seriously misguided and misleading (Shyamasundaradas 1959, 57–60; Vaudeville 1974, 63–69).

On the basis of a much closer and better-informed study of the received text, Parashuram Chaturvedi and Parasanath Tivari argued in the 1950s and 1960s that Kabir's poetry is a grammatically complete and skilfully constructed verbal artifact. But, like the American linguist Michael Shapiro in the 1990s, who demonstrated the grammatical intricacy and self-consistency at work in the Punjabi poetry of the *Ādi Granth*, Chaturvedi and Tivari were unable to reconceptualize the Kabir text as a fundamentally *multilingual* body of verse (Chaturvedi 1954, 208–29; Tivari 1961, pt. 1, 214–60; Shapiro 1995). In fact, we now need to go further and argue that the translation of Kabir's poems into multiple scripts and literary mediums at an early stage became one of their primary poetic features for subsequent transmitters. That is, the multilingualism of the Kabir corpus may have begun in (or even before) the sixteenth century as an unavoidable historical and cultural accident, but by the end of the main phase of manuscript production around 1824, it had become an integral part of the tradition's design. But how exactly the mixture of *bhāshās* and *bolīs* we find in the Kabir poems relates to *rekhtā*—both as a historical state of the Hindi-Urdu linguistic spectrum and as a specific poetic medium, style or form—and to hybridity—as a general principle of language, textuality, culture and identity—remains to be explored (Faruqi 2001; Ahmad 1993).

c. Modes of Transmission

Besides regionalization and multilingualism, the important manuscripts in the various lines listed in Table 1 display an active interdependence among the oral, musical and written modes of transmission in the constitution of the poetry. As Pashaura Singh observes of the *Ādi Granth*, 'variations in the early manuscripts . . . [are] examples of regional or dialectal forms used in the oral transmission of a singing tradition' (2000, 123).

This reciprocity, however, takes specific forms in certain combinations. All three main manuscript-lines build upon the mutually constitutive roles of the oral and written modes of transmission in determining verbal texture. We therefore find that the written text of the poetry accommodates patterns apparently belonging to prior oral composition and transmission, and various orally transmitted versions of the poetry reveal a dependence on written forms recorded earlier in time (Tivari 1961, pt. 1, 53–54).

However, the eastern textual line suppresses the musical dimension of the poems, and extends the mode of handwriting into the medium of print in the final decades of the nineteenth century, before its manuscripts achieve full closure or disclosure. In contrast, the northern and western lines of transmission highlight the musical aspect of Kabir's poetry from their respective beginnings in the late sixteenth century. But they do so in divergent ways, using different principles of textual organization, while at the same time allowing the written, musical and oral versions of a poem to modify each other to an extent comparable across the two lines. Thus, between about 1570 and 1824, the important manuscript sources of Kabir become the sites at which the oral and musical modes merge with the written mode in varying proportions, blurring the boundaries between form and meaning, repetition and variation, and canonicity and improvisation.

The complementary roles of orality, music and writing, however, are more than an aspect of transmission: these modes are actually also modes of representation, and therefore are closely connected to the text's organization and meaning. The Kabir manuscript-lines diverge from each other not only because they canonize different sets of poems, but also because they employ rather different principles of arrangement that have theological as well as hermeneutical consequences.

The *Ādi Granth*, for instance, which represents the paradigmatic form of the northern line, uses an emboxed structure to accommodate about 3,000 poems composed by six Sikh Gurus, some fifteen of their companions within the faith, and another fifteen *bhagats* or model devotees outside the faith. The main body of the *Granth* is divided into thirty-one sections, each of which is defined by the classical Hindustani or regional (male) rāga or (female) rāginī to which all its poems are musically set. In Gurinder Singh Mann's words, the section for any particular rāga

> begins with hymns of four stanzas (*chaupadas*) and goes on to include hymns of eight stanzas (*ashtpadis*), four stanzas of six verses each (*chhants*), and other longer compositions containing a sequence of couplets and stanzas (*vars*). These smaller units within each [section] open with hymns by Guru Nanak and include the compositions of his successors and those of the Sikh bards and the Bhagats. The hymns of the Bhagats are treated as distinct units but follow the same principle of organization based on the number of stanzas. (2001, 5)

Sikh commentators disagree on the interpretation of the text's musical dimension, and the Gurus themselves warn explicitly against essentializing the musical settings; as Mann goes on to note,

> Guru Ramdas puts this strongly. He claims that God is beyond *rags* . . . , and that liberation [mukti] can be attained only by serving God, leaving *rags* and other sounds along the way . . . In the Sikh belief system, a *rag* is simply an effective carrier of the message, which is the element of primary significance in devotional singing. There is absolutely no provision to deify *rags*. (88)

Nevertheless, the structure that contains the 228 Kabir shabads in the *Granth* and distributes them among nineteen rāgas and rāginīs, has a straightforward theological significance. In the Sikh conception, God—*Akāl Purakh*—has no attributes and may be imagined only as *Ik Oṃkār*, the articulation and resonance of the 'One and Only' primordial sound represented by the syllable OṂ. One of the ways of approaching this unmanifest sound is through the patterning of human sounds (also called shabads) that is vocal music. In subsuming its text under musical settings, the multilayered *Granth* thus accords the meaningful discourse of its poems a mystical dimension—the power to connect directly to God, imagined as the purest and most primordial of sounds, through the pure sound of music that opens up a path out of the taintedness of everyday reality. As Pashaura Singh indicates, this perspective emerges first in Guru Nanak's works, which stress 'the mode of devotional singing as the only efficacious means of liberation' (129).

In contrast, the western or Rajasthani line emphasizes two other sets of principles of organization. The *pañchavāṇī*-style manuscripts not only arrange their poems by author (Dadu Dayal, Kabir, Namdev, Raidas and Hardas), but within the section for each author, by rāga and rāginī. This manuscript genre is primarily author-centred and only secondarily music-centred, and its textual function appears to be to allow a reader to experience the 'phenomenological interiority' of each *sant*'s particular version of bhakti or nirguṇī *upāsanā*. Such an experience is vital because each of the five authors canonized in a *pañchavāṇī*-style manuscript achieved mukti from *saṃsār* on the Dadu Panthi scale of values, and therefore is a model to be emulated.

In further contrast, the *sarbaṅgī*-style manuscripts arrange their poems in an emboxed structure different from that of the *Ādi Granth*, with the outermost frame defined by theme, the next one by genre or verse-form, the third one by rāga or rāginī and the innermost one by author. Rajjabadas's *Sarbaṅgī*, completed around 1620, for example, contains 144 thematic sections, each of which brings together poems and other texts in one or more of several genres (pada, sākhī, *shloka*, *kavitta*, *chaupāī*, *bait*, *aril*, etc.). The padas in each section are arranged by musical setting, with one or more author's padas included under any one rāga or rāginī. The text is written in the Nagari script but it is deliberately multilingual, with the *bait*s in Farsi, the *shloka*s in Sanskrit, and the poems in the other genres in Rajasthani or in varieties of Hindi overlaid with Rajasthani. The text as a whole contains 3,927 separate compositions, including 890 padas, 2,691 sākhīs, 173 *shloka*s, and 173 *bait*s, which are attributed to a total of 137 named poets (with a few pieces left unattributed).

The *sarbaṅgī* genre is thus heavily text-centred, with theme and form (or genre) predominating over musical setting and individual author (Singhal 1990). In the *pañchavāṇī* model, the poets' personalities and spiritual accomplishments mediate between the reader and God, whereas in the *sarbangī* model the themes themselves give the poems their mystical dimension.

The eastern line of texts, represented most authoritatively by the *Bījak*, rejects both the music-centred order of the *Ādi Granth*, and the theme-centred arrangements of the *sarbangī* manuscripts in the western line. Excluding all *sant*s other than Kabir, it builds up a single-authored text (which renders it author-centred, but differently from the western *pañchavāṇī* tradition), in which the shabdas, for example, are arranged quasi-alphabetically according to the *akshar*s or letters with which they begin. So poems that begin with words beginning with *sa*, for instance, are clustered together, but the clusters for different letters are themselves not ordered in the standard alphabetical sequence of the Nagari script (see the text in Shukdev Singh 1972). Instead, the letters identifying the clusters of shabdas are scrambled into an esoteric pattern, which readers of the *Bījak* can decode only if they have been initiated into the Kabir Panth. Thus, the principle of ordering the poems according to their starting *akshar*s in the eastern textual line, like the divergent principles used in the northern and western manuscripts, is a 'mystical' principle connecting text, reader, poet and God.

We can therefore say that in the northern line the musical mode 'contains' poetic forms, authors and verbal meanings within itself, in that order; in the western line, authors and themes, as defined in the written mode, serve as alternative master categories that contain musical settings, poetic forms and verbal meanings, in that order; whereas in the eastern line alphabetical letters—in their oral and written aspects together—determine the sequence of forms and meanings, in that order, without any reference to the musical mode. The combinations and hierarchies of the three modes of representation and transmission provide the principles of textual organization in the three main manuscript-lines, and all three principles flesh out, as it were, the 'mysticism' of Kabir's poetry.

d. Textual Mediation

The multiplicity of regions, modes, languages, scripts and manuscripts involved in the first spread of the Kabir text exposed its poetry to mediation by a variety of individuals, groups and institutions at an early date. In fact, all the sources of this poetry that we have inherited since the late sixteenth century are populated entirely by intermediaries: we have no independent access to the historical poet or his work, and we therefore cannot strip away the layers of mediation to uncover an original author or an original text.

Furthermore, most of the mediating structures that have transmitted Kabir's supposed words to us are predisposed towards something else. The *Ādi Granth*, for example, is concerned with defining the *pakkī bāṇī* or the 'solid and permanent discourse' of faith in the Nanak Panth, the original form of Sikhism; whereas Rajjabadas's multilingual *Sarbañgī* is designed to underwrite the beliefs and practices of the Dadu Dayal Panth (Mann 2001, 111; Pashaura Singh 2000, 18; Singhal 1990). Even in the case of the Phatuha, Bhagatahi, Chaurā and Dharamdasi branches of the Kabir Panth—which claim to have originated in Kabir's lifetime with some of his companions and disciples—the intentions, interests, ideologies and practices of a number of individuals and groups intervene distractingly between the historical author and the words that represent him.

Over a period of half a millennium or more, such mediations have imposed two other irreversible trajectories upon the manuscripts: (*a*) continuous textual *enlargement*, and (*b*) internal discursive *variation*. The steady expansion of the Kabir corpus over time is graphically illustrated in the chronological framework of Table 1 above, as also in the concrete particulars of the sources listed there. When Guru Arjan closed the Kartarpur Pothi in 1604, for example, he assigned a set of 228 lyric poems and 243 aphorisms to Kabir; when Rajjabadas completed his *Sarbañgī* around 1620, he ascribed a set of 156 lyric poems and 181 aphorisms to Kabir that overlapped only in part with the selection in the Sikh canon (Mann 2001; Callewaert 2000; Dass 1991; Singhal 1990). While preparing his comprehensive modern edition of the *Kabīr Granthāvalī* in the 1950s—almost three and a half centuries after the Kartarpur Pothi—Parasanath Tivari found that the seventeen manuscript and print sources he had classified as the most legitimate for his purposes yielded 1,713 lyric poems and 4,395 aphorisms, for a total of 6,108 distinctive compositions ascribable to Kabir (Tivari 1961, pt. 1, [a]-[c]).

Since the early seventeenth century, the expansion of the Kabir text has occurred roughly in proportion to the increase in the number of mediating institutions or organized communities, and to the crests or peaks in their activities. The quantity of discourse ascribed to Kabir increased by incremental amounts over and above the Sikh collections of the 1570–1604 period when the Dadu Panth and the

Ramananda Sampradaya became active in the seventeenth century, rose further when the Niranjani Panth took a lead in the process of dissemination in the eighteenth century, and climbed dramatically in the nineteenth and twentieth centuries when the Kabir Panth, with its four main branches, as well as the new Radhasoami Satsang added their modern resources to the process. In general, the greatest quantitative augmentation of the discourse associated with Kabir has taken place in the era of dissemination in print and other mass-media, which have enabled the production, reproduction and circulation of texts, music and performance on a scale impossible to achieve before the nineteenth century.

The precise nature of the internal variation induced by the pervasive mediation of the text becomes perceptible when we look closely at the distribution of individual poems across manuscripts, groups of manuscripts and manuscript-lines. The basic pattern is best discerned by comparing Parasanath Tivari's methodologically groundbreaking edition of the *Kabīr Granthāvalī* (1961) and the technologically-aided alternative prepared by Winand M. Callewaert et al., *The Millennium Kabīr Vāṇī* (2000).

Tivari used seventeen manuscript and print sources of the 1604–1937 period as his primary texts, which are marked with a [T] in Table 1 above. These sources together yielded 1,573 padas, 134 ramainīs, and 4,395 sākhīs in all. When he did a statistical count of which of these poems appeared in an invariant form in how many sources, he found the numbers displayed in Table 2 (Tivari 1961, pt. 1, [b]-[c]).

Almost four decades later, the Dutch philologist Winand M. Callewaert and his collaborators, Swapna Sharma and

Dieter Taillieu, used ten manuscript sources dating between 1570 and 1681 to gather versions of all the padas attributed to Kabir that were in circulation in north India within 250 years of the poet's death (by my dating). They discovered that the ten earliest manuscripts still available in the 1990s, which I have marked with a [C] in Table 1 above, all belonged to the northern and western traditions, and contained a total of 593 padas among them, with the distributional patterns for 590 of them shown in Table 3 (Callewaert 2000, 75–80).

TABLE 2: Distribution of Kabir poems among textual sources used in Parasanath Tivari's *Kabīr Granthāvalī* (1961)

No. of Sources with Poems in Common	*No. of Padas Found In Invariant Form*	*No. of Ramainīs Found in Invariant Form*	*No. of Sākhīs Found in Invariant Form*
9	0	0	1
8	0	0	16
7	0	0	69
6	1	0	259
5	17	0	344
4	68	1	436
3	155	20	1,010
2	339	28	836
1	999	85	1,424
Total in 17 sources	1,579 PADAS	134 RAMAINĪS	4,395 SĀKHĪS

In Tivari's case, we find that out of 1,579 padas distributed among seventeen distinct sources of the 1604–1937 period, only one pada was common in *invariant* form to six sources, seventeen padas were common to five sources, and sixty-eight padas were common to four sources. Of the great majority of the padas, as many as 999 appeared in one source each, and 339 appeared in two sources each, while a total of only 241 padas appeared in three or more sources each. Similar statistics turn up for the ramainīs and sākhīs, so the inescapable conclusion is that, since no pada is common to seven or more of the seventeen sources, the manuscripts

TABLE 3: Distribution of Kabir Padas among textual sources used in Winand M. Callewaert et al., *Millennium Kabīr Vāṇī* (2000)

No. of Manuscripts with Padas in Common	*No. of Padas in Variant forms counted in these Manuscripts*
10	0
9	2
8	12
7	46
6	90
5	95
4	93
3	67
2	58
1	127
TOTAL NO. OF PADAS IN 10 EARLIEST MANUSCRIPTS	590

and books in Tivari's selection diverge widely from each other in this type of accounting.

In the case of Callewaert et al., we find that of the 590 padas they counted in *variant* forms in the ten earliest Kabir sources (belonging to the 1570–1681 period), no pada was common to all ten manuscripts, two padas were common to nine manuscripts, twelve were common to eight manuscripts, and only forty-six were common to seven manuscripts. As many as 127 padas appeared in only one source each, and fifty-eight appeared in only two sources each, so that a total of 185 padas appeared in no more than two sources, and only 150 appeared in six to nine manuscripts each. Again, we have to conclude that the earliest manuscripts do not intersect with each other on a significant scale in this type of quantitative analysis, which is more liberal than Tivari's because it focuses on the padas in all their variant forms.

The logical inferences to draw from these statistics are quite startling. No single poem attributed to Kabir appears in all the written and printed source-texts, or in all the early manuscripts—or even in all the manuscript-lines—that we have, whether we are as inclusive with our source-texts as Tivari was or as exclusive as Callewaert was. Different sets of poems, containing up to a few dozen poems each, turn up in common among manuscripts belonging to particular manuscript-lines, or among interrelated written and printed sources.

The great majority of poems carrying Kabir's signature-line are pieces that appear in common only in very small groups of interlinked sources, or remain isolated in individual sources. Thus, even a tiny core of poems that may be 'universal' to the Kabir tradition does not seem to exist. At best, we have two or three competing cores of poems recorded at early stages of the text's history, each consisting of roughly forty to seventy poems, spread over different groupings of manuscripts, with partial overlaps among some of them, and no intersection connecting all of them. This probably happens, as Callewaert suspected, because *the different surviving manuscript-lines actually obtained their material from different sources* in the fifteenth and sixteenth centuries. From this we have to infer that, in all likelihood, more than one mode of representation—drawing on more than one origin—transmitted Kabir's poetry along more than one path from Banaras to Punjab and Rajasthan in the decades after his death (Callewaert 2000, 23–26). It is historically impossible to go back to the period between 1448 and 1570 and to somehow reconstruct a unitary origin and a unified body of words from which all subsequent versions emerged. In this specific sense, the composition and distribution of Kabir's poetry are now radically indeterminate.

3. The Thread of Authorship

How strange
to become a mere name
rubbed and whittled away
on the lips of one's own town
in the course of time
to be sifted through the sieve of one's own language
and so to become
a tale in people's memories
How scary
to become a metaphor. . . .

Kedarnath Singh, 'Uttar Kabīr' (1995), p. 140

If there is no thread of poems to interweave the manuscript-lines, and no historical individual to texture the whole with a coherent design, how are we to make sense of the Kabir phenomenon? During the nineteenth and twentieth centuries, scholars ranging from H. H. Wilson, G. H. Wescott, F. E. Keay and Hazariprasad Dvivedi to Parasanath Tivaṛi, Mataprasad Gupta, Charlotte Vaudeville and Winand M. Callewaert noted that the received text cannot be the work of a single person in the fifteenth century, and that its size and internal variation make it impossible to interpret cohesively. But they continued to expect the text to function as if it were a closed and self-consistent structure in a homogeneous linguistic medium (and edited it accordingly), and to refer to its author as if he were an autonomous individual with a determinate personality, working with well-defined intentions in specific historical circumstances (for example, see Keay 1931, 62–63; Chaturvedi 1954, 54–56; Vaudeville 1974, 49).

The difficulty with such an approach is that we have a text before us that refuses to behave like a fixed and coherent body of discourse. The poetry is evidently dispersed over an extensive and culturally varied area, and is irrecoverably regionalized; its multiple modes of representation and transmission entangle it in fundamental questions of poetic order and meaning; it surfaces in history in a plurality of scripts, languages and manuscripts; it is thoroughly mediated by an assortment of groups and institutions; and it consequently expands and diversifies internally over the centuries. In fact, because it is disjointed, multimodal, multilingual and functionally open, it is antithetical to the kind of text that scholars trained in the Western, post-

Enlightenment discipline of philology would like it to be.

The challenge is to 'crack the code' that is 'Kabir', and the best solution may be to construe the received text as the work of a *community of authors*. If we accept the empirical fact that the poetry attributed to this poet has been open to intercession for half a millennium, the concept of collective authorship implies that a large number of potential mediators have had the opportunity to compose, rewrite, revise and edit particular poems and groups of poems on his behalf. This means that, during the five and a half centuries since the historical author's death, 'Kabir' has ceased to be a proper noun, and has turned into a common poetic pseudonym, a discursively constituted mask or an interchangeable public persona. More specifically, 'Kabir' has become a zone of intersubjectivity, a common consciousness upon which individuals from assorted times, places, backgrounds and languages converge for an array of disparate purposes.

The notion that Kabir, as we know him, is actually a community of poets and a bundle of poetic effects is remarkably consonant with a number of Indian and Western conceptions of authorship and textuality that diverge from their correlates in philology. The Kabir tradition itself, for example, tells us that 'There are as many Kabirs as there are leaves in a tree', and that 'The discourse of Kabir is infinite'. Colonial and post-colonial philologists have routinely discounted the ironic simile in the first claim, and the theological subtext in the second (that Kabir was a manifestation of God), because both statements in their separate ways undermine the ideology of an author as a unique, self-determining human individual. But the figure of the leaves in a tree tantalizes us with the possibility that the poet may be only a model or a type, that authorship in this case may be an aggregate affair, and that the text may be open to endless proliferation.

The Sikh tradition offers an instance in which community authorship is not only acknowledged but also procedurally canonized. The six Gurus who contribute shabads and other compositions to the *Ādi Granth* all do so under the shared signature of 'Nanak', and therefore collaborate in speaking in a 'collective' voice. Only the *Granth*'s editorial colophons, placed on the margins of the *bāṇī* itself, meticulously differentiate the Gurus from each other as the historical authors of specific compositions. The paradigm of collaboration in Sikh scripture directly affects Kabir because, in one famous instance (shabad 12 in Rāga Bhairava), Guru Arjan composes a poem with Kabir's signature-line and records the fact that he is doing so (Dass 1991, 2, 234; Pashaura Singh 2000, 284–86). In the larger corpus outside the *Granth*, mediators participate similarly as Kabir's surrogate authors, co-authors, editors or translators, but without signing their own names, or without the benefit of a 'byline'.

Moreover, such enactments of collective authorship in the middle period of Indian history (roughly 1200 to 1750) are part of a two-layered principle in the bhakti movement. According to this principle, when an individual becomes a bhakta, he (more rarely, she) attaches himself to a guru, and at the same time joins the broader community of devotees or 'company of saints'. When he begins to produce discourse devoted to God as one of his primary (karmic) means of attaining mukti, the community of bhaktas around him serves not only as an audience, but also as a reservoir of textual energy and a pool of potential collaborators. Whenever the bhakta speaks as a poet, he also always speaks for the community as a whole, and the community also always speaks for him. Thus, as A. K. Ramanujan has noted,

> The Vīraśaiva saints, for instance, . . . are often thought of as a family, as a society. . . . They are thought of as one, plural yet singular: the saint as a fourth person singular, if you wish, a virtual presence outside the normal three-person grammar of daily systems. . . . The saints form a cult, develop a culture of their own, speak a common dialect or raise one to poetry. . . . They, with their followers, form a new society, a second society within the larger one. Thus together, they constitute . . . a community seeking *communitas*. (Dharwadker 1999b, 282–83.)

This form of fellowship has at least two parallels in the traditions centred around Europe. In the terms of the psychoanalytical account of writing developed by the Czech theorist Julia Kristeva, for example, the bhakta's 'company of saints' defines both the domain of intersubjectivity and the domain of intertextuality that underwrite and 'authorize' his discourse. In much older terms, the bhakti ideal of community and communication accords just as closely with the concept of *paraṃparā* in Sanskritic India as with the concept of 'tradition' in Latinate Europe.

Both *paraṃparā* and tradition comprise a process and a structure designed to transmit the constitutive elements of a culture—such as ideas, values, texts, practices or laws—from generation to generation. In a literary culture, the very mention of *paraṃparā* or tradition invokes an ideal of collaboration, for as the blind Argentinian writer Jorge Luis Borges pointed out around the mid-twentieth century, a tradition may be metonymically thought of as 'a single poem polished by generations of men' (Borges 1981). Even with its shades of neo-Platonism and Berkeleyan idealism, Borges's trope captures the condition of the Kabir corpus with empirical exactness: each of the 200 padas and twenty-one ramainīs selected from seventeen sources in Tivari's *Kabīr Granthāvalī* (1961), and each of the 593 padas gathered from the earliest manuscripts in Callewaert's *The Millennium Kabīr Vāṇī* (2000), is evidently a piece of poetry polished by several generations of men.

The most vivid example of collaborative textual refinement may be the pair of poems that I have entitled 'Allāh-Rāma' and 'Allāh-and-Rāma' in this book. The first of these is one of the earliest recorded poems with Kabir's signature-line, pada 8 in the Goindval Pothis of 1570–72:

Allāh-Rāma,
I live by Your Name:
show me Your mercy,
my Lord.

If Allāh resides
inside a mosque,
then whose is the rest of the land?
Hindus claim His Name
inhabits an idol:
but God can't be found
in either place.

The southern country
is Hari's home,
the west is Allāh's camping ground.
Search your heart,
your heart of hearts:
that's His abode,
that's His camp.

The brahmin fasts
once a fortnight,
the qāzī fasts for Ramadān.
Each devotes
eleven months to himself,
then looks for rewards
    in a month of fasts.

Why go off to Orissa
for ritual immersions?
Why bow your head in a mosque?
You're a crook at heart,
you pretend to pray:
why go all the way
    on a hajj to the Ka'aba?

These men and women,
the whole lot of them,
are nothing but Your forms.
I'm a child
of Rāma-and-Allāh,
    everyone's my guru-and-*pīr*.

Kabir says, listen,
O men and women:
seek shelter with the One and Only.
Repeat His singular Name,
you creatures: for only then
will you be able
    to cross life's ocean.

This pada invented the topos of 'I am the child of one God'—one of the origins of Kabir's fame as an original proponent of religious unity, tolerance and secularism. The poem still speaks to us with a fresh voice, but its texture contains conceptual and aesthetic flaws: the last two verses fail to wrap up the argument conclusively, and the final verse falters rhetorically. In the three and a half centuries after it was first written down, however, the invisible craftsmen of the Kabir tradition chipped away at it until it acquired the poetic precision it needed. The polished version turned up in 1910–11, when Kshitimohan Sen recorded songs sung by 'wandering yogis' in the Bengal countryside:

If Khudā inhabits the mosque,
then whose play-field is the rest of the world?

If Rāma lives in the idol at the pilgrim-station,
then who controls the chaos outside?

The east is Hari's domicile, they say,
the west is Allāh's dwelling-place.

Look into your heart, your very heart:
that's where Karīm-and-Rāma reside.

All the women and men ever born
are nothing but Your embodied forms:

Kabir's a child of Allāh-and-Rāma,
They're his Guru-and-Pīr.

The central ideas and images of the old version are still in place, but the structure is now controlled and symmetrical, the argument is clear and complete, and the wording has achieved the maximum brevity. In a text of collaborative authorship, each poem is explicitly a palimpsest, to be recomposed until all its particular poetic possibilities have been exhausted. If ideological instrumentality were not an issue, one might even say that the hundreds of variations that make up the great bulk of the Kabir corpus are collective experiments in the aesthetics of palimpsestic textuality.

In order to make sense of the Kabir phenomenon using conceptions of authorship and textual production as collective enterprises, it is necessary to briefly reconsider the dynamics of literary culture in the middle period of Indian history. Bhakti literature often represents the formation of its texts and textual communities as a benign—even beatific—process, but this is inevitably an idealized projection (Ramanujan 1973, 61–65). In historical actuality, freshly composed texts enter a world of discourse that is always already populated by other texts, and often trigger a virulent process of praise and blame, acceptance and rejection. Especially when this happens in a period, place or circumstance that is not governed by the concept of a text as its author's 'property', verbal artifacts can become objects of aggressive contention and competition. In north Indian culture after the end of the classical period (around 1200), intermediaries of several sorts—individuals, groups, institutions—usually compete fiercely with each other for control over new texts in the public arena.

Under such circumstances, mediators seek to dominate texts for the sake of one or more of three main objectives. One is the goal of *canonization*, in which a group or an institution attempts to establish a particular body of discourse as the 'law' or norm for a particular community (see, for example, Pashaura Singh 2000, 25). Even when a community produces a text that it wishes to canonize for itself, the process can be disruptive and violent, pitting internal factions against each other and fracturing the community centrifugally, or pitting the community as a whole against other communities and thus embattling it centripetally.

The gradual development and canonization of the *Ādi*

Granth between the time of Guru Nanak (died 1539) and that of Guru Gobind Singh (died 1708) had both types of effects concurrently. In one direction, the process split the legitimate Gurus and their followers from a succession of competitors and dissenting groups within the emergent Sikh community; in the opposite direction, the process exposed the Sikhs to protracted conflict with the Mughals, resulting in the execution of Guru Arjan in 1606, during Jahangir's reign, and of Guru Teg Bahadur in 1675, during Aurangzeb's reign (Mann 2001, 25; Dass 1991, 6, 24–25).

A second goal for which intermediaries often compete over texts is *appropriation*, the process of arrogating something to oneself as one's exclusive property. In post-classical and early modern India, a text frequently becomes an object of appropriation by various agents after its author's death because it is, or is perceived to be, a potential instrument of power or wealth. Religion has been big business on the subcontinent for more than the past millennium, and the political economy of faith has rested as much on the exercise of power over people's hearts and minds for political ends, as on the use of such power to generate wealth for individuals, institutions, communities and classes. As I shall show later in this section, Kabir's poetry became an object of appropriation early in its history, and continues to be a major site of contention in the political economy of subcontinental religions down to the present.

A third objective for which mediators battle over texts in middle-period India is *ideological containment*. The dynamics of an existing order of canons, discourses and texts depends not only on the ability of groups and institutions to appropriate new texts that enter the public domain, but also to prevent them from doing any damage. Intermediaries press for specific modes of containment—which typically include suppression, mitigation and diversion—when they find a particular body of discourse threatening a desirable status quo. While some communities have sought to canonize Kabir's poetry in one institutional form or another since the early seventeenth century, others have tried to contain its revolutionary potential.

The consolidation of the bhakti movement after about 1400, especially in north India, often involves the contentious processes of canonization, appropriation and containment simultaneously, which affect the formation of its textual traditions as well as its grass-roots communities. The competition among embattled discourses and texts is particularly intense in the broad division between nirguṇa *mat* and saguṇī bhakti, with the fault line emerging between the conception of God as completely devoid of predicable attributes, and the conception of God (and gods) as endowed with definite, usually anthropomorphically predicated, qualities. In the contest for words and meanings, hearts and minds, power and wealth, mediating agents usually resort to half a dozen distinct but overlapping strategies which may be conceptualized as follows:

1. the *erasure* of a text, or its expulsion from the sphere of publicity, so that it either ceases to exist or retreats underground;
2. the *re-inscription* of a text, or the process of editing, revising or rewriting it, so that its message is significantly modified;
3. the *composition* of a new text or a portion of a text, to supplement or even substitute for the text under

contestation, so that the latter is altered to a significant extent;

4. the *criticism* of a text in a separate commentary, making it an object of praise or blame, and thus raising or lowering its value on the imaginary stock exchange of a community's opinion (Frye 1957, 18);
5. the *allegorization* of a text in a separate commentary, inducing the original to say something it does not state explicitly, while leaving its actual content and expression intact (Kermode 1983, 40); and
6. the *mythologization* of a text's author, using the mode of either hagiography or commentary, usually in order to elevate him in relation to an audience, so that he seems larger than life, or vice versa.

Intermediaries use these strategies, individually and in combination, as much for canonizing texts as for appropriating and containing them. Some of these methods are more extreme or invasive than others, but all of them enable mediators to gain control of a text's material form, its meaning, its actual circulation in the public arena, and its reception in the world. In the Kabir case, the shape and substance of the corpus as we have received it indicate that the 'community of authors' who eventually became his ventriloquists and ghostwriters subjected his original poetry to all these methods of transmission and transformation.

Using this framework, we can now say that the poetry composed by the historical Kamir or Kabir probably became public property in the oral and musical modes, and perhaps also in writing, before 1448. After his death, it turned into an object of canonization, appropriation and containment for a number of mediating groups, which re-inscribed and allegorized it in different ways and to different degrees for different ends, and which also mythologized the poet and criticized the poetry in different styles. All three of the major manuscript-lines that have survived down to the twenty-first century chose to elevate Kabir's life and personality, and to canonize his work. The northern line, however, most probably edited his text and composed new poems on his behalf in order to emphasize his rejection of both Hinduism and Islam in their orthodox forms (a primary theme for Guru Nanak); to elaborate upon his mysticism, in its 'sober' as well as 'intoxicated' aspects; and to deepen his domesticity—a central value in Sikh social thought (Pashaura Singh 2000, 285–86; Mann 2001, 111–12, 115).

In contradistinction, the western line of manuscripts seems to have re-inscribed and augmented his verse in order to foreground his lyrical and emotional devotion to God, and possibly to underplay his social radicalism, particularly his harsher attacks on Hindu and Muslim ritual and social practice—a concern especially for the Dadu Panth, which has attracted both Hindu and Muslim followers (Chaturvedi 1964). The eastern textual tradition, in contrast to the first two lines, appears to have modified Kabir's message and added new material to it in order to portray him chiefly as an ascetic and a philosopher, and also to sharpen his satire and invective, not only against paṇḍits and mullāhs, but also against all types of saguṇa bhaktas (whether Vaishṇava or Shaiva) because the Kabir Panth stresses asceticism and operates mainly in the embattled heartlands of saguṇī bhakti in the Vaishṇava and Shaiva modes.

The contentiousness of the community of authors who

appropriated Kabir, however, is clearest among the mediators outside the three main manuscript-lines after the sixteenth century, and within the eastern textual tradition after the eighteenth. Starting around 1600, the Ramananda Sampradaya developed some hagiographical works and commentaries, such as Anantadas's *Kabīr Parachāī* (about 1625) and Priyadas's *Bhaktirasabodhinī* (about 1712), chiefly as instruments of containment, using them to mythologize Kabir in such a way as to expunge or mitigate his nirguṇa radicalism. Between the seventeenth and nineteenth centuries, the Niranjani Panth—working on the borders of the main Rajasthani tradition—contained Kabir by re-inscribing his poetry within a 'catholic' framework combining elements of nirguṇī *upāsanā* and saguṇī bhakti (Chaturvedi 1964).

In the early twentieth century, the Dharamdasi branch of the Kabir Panth published works such as the *Anurāg Sāgar*, which systematically mitigated and diverted the poet's message to a surprising degree, even while appearing to maintain his canonical status (Ajaib Singh 1984). This move was part of a larger fraternal competition within the Kabir Panth that started around 1865, in which the Dharamdasi, Chaurā, Phatuha and Bhagatahi *shākhā*s aggressively appropriated and re-defined Kabir, producing a succession of editions of the *Bījak* and other works that catered astutely to the colonial and post-colonial marketplace (Dwyer 1981, 273–79).

Around the same time, the Radhasoami Satsang, a new religious community founded in 1861 by Shiv Dayal, a Hindu banker of Agra, appropriated Kabir's text for its canon, but re-inscribed and allegorized it quite heavily, expanded and modernized its text with new compositions, and achieved great commercial success with a publishing enterprise, the Belvedere Press (Tivari 1961, pt. 1, 113–15). Over the past four centuries, the Ramanandis, the Niranjanis, the Dharamdasis, the Kabir Panthis (more generally) and the Radhasoamis have overtly deflected the Kabir text from its trajectory in the older manuscript traditions, and have turned it into an object of appropriation in the broader political economy of Indian religions.

To push back the speculative and stereotypical picture of Kabir as a poor, unlettered cotton weaver of fifteenth-century Banaras, and to re-imagine him, for a moment, as a large, composite, and shifting band of interlocutors is to achieve a different kind of clarity. We can now begin to understand why the text we have received is so multifaceted and intractable, why it contains divergent themes, what makes it a site of appropriation and containment, and why it cannot be the correlate of a benign process of community formation. We can also start to account for the textual differences separating the Sikh *Ādi Granth*, the Dadu Panthi and Niranjani *Granthāvalī*, and the Kabir Panthi *Bījak*, the extensive changes on the fringes of the corpus over a period of 400 years, and the possible absence of a common core of poetry across the main manuscript-lines.

In other words, a theory of collective authorship makes it evident that, as half a millennium unfolds, groups of ghostwriters appropriate various segments of the older text and create new sectors of discourse, pushing the body of Kabir's verse deeper and deeper into the waters of worldly business and politics.

4. *The Design of the Poetry*

I look
not from the secure shelter of Rāma
but through that big hole
right in the middle of Time
That's the vantage point from which I see
a narrow black shiny strip of tarmac
zooming out
as if it were crossing Infinity. . . .
But this thing called mukti—
if you look at it
from another angle
as rocks look at their own inarticulate heat
or as trees look at it
then what is it what is it. . . .

Kedarnath Singh, 'Uttar Kabīr' (1995), pp. 136, 141

Given these considerations, I have kept two aspects of the Kabir phenomenon foremost in mind while selecting the poems that comprise the central portion of this book: that the poetry we have inherited is the work of a community of authors, and that the chorus of voices ventriloquizing for the poet is not always innocuous. But I have also allowed the poems to speak for themselves, across this distance in time, place and language, without overwhelming them with circumstantial inferences. So one of my principal objectives has been to pick poems that represent as many facets of the Kabir tradition as possible, including its regional distribution, its multiple modes and manuscript-lines, its mediating institutions, its protean evolution from the sixteenth century to the twentieth, and its important poetic forms, genres and styles. At the same time, I have tried to choose pieces that represent its best poetry as well as its most resonant social, philosophical and theological arguments. The variety of materials that I have sought to include in these pages is tabulated by category in Table 4 at the end of the Introduction.

In keeping with the assortment of criteria involved, I have divided the central portion of this volume into five sections. Section I, 'Sixty Threads in the Warp', contains seventeen poems from the northern line of texts, drawing twelve shabads from the *Ādi Granth* of 1604, and five padas from the Goindval Pothis of 1570–72. Section II, 'I've Painted My Body Red', brings together fifteen poems from the western manuscript-lines, twelve of which are in the pada form and three in the ramainī form, representing both Dadu Panthi and Niranjani sources, and *pañchavāṇī* as well as *sarbaṅgī* collections.

Section III, 'The Ganga Drains the Ocean', focuses on seven poems from the eastern textual line, one of which is a ramainī and the rest of which are shabdas from the Kabir Chaurā version of the *Bījak*. Section IV, 'Neither Line Nor Form', complements the first three parts by bringing together a substantial selection of forty-six aphorisms from all three traditions, with ten shaloks from the *Ādi Granth*, ten sākhīs from the *Kabīr Granthāvalī*, and twenty-six sākhīs from the *Bījak* (with several aphorisms in common among these sources).

Finally, Section V, 'This Sheet, So Fine, So Fine', complements the first four parts of the selection by offering fifteen songs transcribed from various north Indian oral sources and classical and regional musical performances in the twentieth century, some of which overlap with poems recorded much earlier in writing. In aggregate, the poems in these pages consist of fifty shabads, padas, or shabdas, four ramainīs, and forty-six shaloks or sākhīs, for a total of one hundred separate compositions transmitted in one material medium or another between about 1570 and 1995, a period of four and a quarter centuries.

As I remarked earlier, the arrangement of poems has theological and hermeneutical consequences for the main textual traditions surrounding Kabir. My second objective therefore has been to present my selection of poems and my translations more or less in the order in which they appear in particular sources, and to present the sources themselves in their broad historical progression. The poems in section I appear in the musical order of the *Ādi Granth*, with the early padas from the Goindval Pothis subsumed under the sequence of rāgas and rāginīs created by Guru Arjan in 1604.

The poems in section II follow the thematic and formal order of the *Kabīr Granthāvalī*, modelled on the *sarbañgī*-style arrangement invented by Rajjabadas around 1620, with the padas preceding the ramainīs and the musical settings accorded an ancillary status. The poems in section III are placed in the esoteric order of *akshar*s or letters of the original in the *Bījak*, with the ramainīs now preceding the shabdas or padas, and the musical dimension suppressed altogether. In section IV, the shaloks from the *Ādi Granth* come before the sets of sākhīs from the *Kabīr Granthāvalī* and the *Bījak*, in the overall chronological sequence of these three sources, while the aphorisms from each source retain the order in which they occur in the original, with some overlap among the sets.

Finally, again, in section V, songs transcribed from Hindustani classical performances are followed by songs transcribed from regional folk traditions, which, in turn, are followed by lyrics recorded from non-canonical oral sources. This is the first book in English to represent the full range of major Kabir sources, and its selection and arrangement give the reader an unusually panoramic yet detailed view of the original.

So far as the translations themselves are concerned, my approach has been shaped by a variety of considerations. In the common terminology of sufism, the poets of the Kabir text are mostly 'sober' mystics, philosophers, theologians and social critics. As a community of verbal craftsmen, their overarching rhetorical, poetic and thematic concerns seem to be 'to speak the truth, the whole truth, and nothing but the truth' about 'the God beyond God', and about all the consequences that follow from an uncompromising commitment to the worship of this godhead without qualities (Shyamasundaradas 1930, 55). Whatever their conflicting worldly engagements might be, these poets collectively construct the Kabir text as an embodiment of truth in language, and hence tie all aspects of their poetry to the process of inventing, discovering, recovering and uncovering 'the truth'. Moreover, they are relentlessly rigorous logicians of 'salvation'.

Given the predominance of this theological and epistemological position in the main branches of the original, it is essential for a translator of Kabir to devise an approach that can accommodate such a conception of poetry, logic and truth. I have tried to meet this standard by rendering each poem into English as literally and accurately as possible with respect to its meaning and its argument. At the same time, I have tried to translate each piece as poetically as possible with regard to its texture, structure, genre, voice and disposition.

My strategy as a translator has therefore turned out to be surprisingly similar to Vladimir Nabokov's in his English rendition of Alexander Pushkin's classic nineteenth-century Russian verse-novel, *Eugene Onegin*, where Nabokov sought to render 'the whole text, and nothing but the text', in a crafty play on the oath of honesty that a witness takes before testifying in a modern court of law. I have employed a wide range of technical devices to accomplish this goal in the medium of contemporary English free verse, from alliteration, assonance, consonance, embedded rhyme and occasional end-rhyme to extended similes and synecdoches, metonymic metaphors, paradoxes and parallelisms. But the technicalities are only means to other ends, for in the end, as A. K. Ramanujan once put it, 'Only a poem can translate a poem' (1999, 231).

A selection prepared, arranged and represented along these lines reveals that the major sources of the Kabir tradition actually display a remarkable thematic and imaginative consistency at their core, disproving the philological claim—based on statistical counts, without attention to the content of the poetry—that the manuscript-lines are fundamentally disconnected from each other. This shared structure of ideas, images, arguments and dispositions also furnishes the basis for an answer to the larger question that has been hovering over my entire discussion: What exactly did the historical

Kabir accomplish in his lifetime that had the power to trigger an enormous process of textual colonization and to keep the conflict going for more than half a millennium?

The one hundred poems represented in this book, and especially the fifty padas and four ramainīs among them, suggest that Kabir succeeded in inventing a discourse with a remarkable combination of simplicity and complexity, which the poets of his community have never really relinquished. On one plane, the 'invention' of this discourse does not generate anything new, because virtually all its elements and their combinations were already in existence before Kabir's time. On another plane, however, it creates something fresh, because it alters, ever so slightly, whatever it takes from the past, and leaves nothing unchanged.

At the heart of 'Kabir's' way of thinking and speaking is the conviction that God is absolutely without attributes or qualities. Nirguṇa God, as I have already suggested, is closest in conception to 'the God beyond God' or the 'absolute godhead' that mystics in other religions also invoke (Ghose 1995). Because God is truly without attributes, we, in our ordinary states of consciousness, cannot imagine or know Him or It, and we cannot predicate what He or It 'is' in propositions, statements or narratives constructed in human language. The Kabir poets therefore frequently claim that God is inconceivable and unknowable, and that His or Its story is ineffable. They also offer us two other conceptions of their nirguṇa God: He or It is *nirañkār*, completely formless, and also *nirañjan*, absolutely pure and flawless, without any taint whatsoever. Furthermore, in any one of these conceptions, the Kabir poets project God as being indivisible into attributes, and hence appear to adopt a principle very close to the Qur'ānic principle of God's 'unity'.

All three characterizations of God deliberately use negative terms—nirguṇa, *nirañkār*, and *nirañjan*—and are part of the 'negative dialectics' that recurs in the Kabir poems, significantly echoing the dialectics of *neti*, *neti* ('not this . . . not that . . .') launched in a related philosophical and theological context in the *Bṛhadāraṇyaka Upaniṣad* around 800 B. C. (Olivelle 1996, 68.) Poetically, the Kabir poets also put this negative dialectics in motion on a much larger scale in the early northern and western manuscripts: they use as many concrete names of God as possible from the Hindu, Muslim, bhakti and sufi traditions, but undercut all of them by changing constantly from one to another, with the implication that even as we name God, He or It proves to be unnameable (see Table 1 in Dwyer 1981, 98–99). At the same time, they frequently return to a single name, 'Nirguṇa Rāma', which encapsulates the negative dialectics in a miniature paradox: even though 'Rāma' is God with specific qualities (a human incarnation of Vishnu), once we attach the epithet 'nirguṇa' to His Name, He insistently becomes His own unimaginable opposite.

The God beyond God is unmoving and immovable, the Kabir poets tell us, but He is the *Sirjanhār*, the Creator of the universe. In contrast to Him, His Creation or the created universe and all its contents are saguṇa (possess attributes), have *rūp* or *ākār* (have form or shape, are formed), and are *añjan* (are tainted, flawed, contaminated). As one of the padas in Gopaladas's *Sarbañgī* of 1627, taken from the Niranjani tradition and rendered musically by Kumar Gandharva in the 1980s, says:

Rāma
the Flawless One
is different:
the chaos scattered all around us
is tainted.
Creation's contaminated,
the syllable OṂ
is sullied:
impurity has created
this unholy spread.
Brahmā,
Shankara, Indra
are smirched:
Govind with his *gopīs*
is soiled.
Speech and sound
are foul,
the Vedas are stained:
impurity has perpetrated
so many forms.
Learning, reading, recitation,
the ancient books
are all corrupt:
knowledge, cheapened, mouthed for free,
is dirty.
The leaf in the oblation is rank,
the god in his shrine
is unclean:
infection serves
the infected.
Impurity dances,
impurity sings:

pollution displays
an infinite number
of guises.

The how and what, the when and where
of contamination:
it vanquishes
charity, goodness, austerity,
devotion.

Kabir says,
only one in a million
awakens to this:
but when he does,
he gives up what's tainted
and joins the incorruptible.

The created universe in its entirety is illusory or unreal precisely because it is constituted by attributes, forms and flaws that seem real to human subjects (who experience and engage with them through their sensory capacities, motor-capacities, minds and egos), but in fact are unreal because they are other than God, who alone is real. For the poets of the Kabir tradition—in a position that resembles the classical theology and metaphysics of Advaita Vedānta—all of Creation is therefore Māyā, the totality of illusion, in contradistinction from God, who remains the sum of all that is real.

Māyā, whom they personify (misogynistically) as Woman, has the power to delude human subjects into believing that its constituents—the flawed, formed and qualified contents of the universe—are real, and that there is no reality beyond them. Under the power of Māyā, the poets claim, the created universe as a whole appears to be an immense, chaotic sprawl of things; it is disorderly, topsy-turvy and irrational in its very structure. Māyā dominates Creation, and she even absorbs into herself all the gods who possess attributes, and who thereby become agents of illusion. As a famous pada in the western manuscript-line puts it:

We know
what Māyā is—
a great robber and thief,
a con-woman
in cahoots with con-men.

She wanders all over the world,
carrying her noose
strung with three strands—
she sits rocking in every place,
using her sweet tongue.

In Keshava's house
she masquerades as Kamalā,
in Shiva's mansion
she's Bhavānī. . . .

Or, as a shabda in the *Bījak* claims:

My good men,
what comes and goes,
bustling about the world,
    is Māyā. . . .

For those who worship the Master,
the ten avatars
are a masterful illusion.
    Kabir says, listen,
    O saintly men—
what springs to life
and expends itself
    is utterly different from Him.

The God beyond all gods is absolutely different from Māyā and stands apart from His Creation, but He ultimately exercises complete control over them.

The Kabir poets then argue that the human world exists within and is a small part of the created universe; is therefore made up of forms, attributes and impurities; and hence lies entirely within the domain of Māyā. Human beings, like other entities in Creation, are flawed, and tend to be driven by vanity, pride, greed, hatred, envy and violence (among other factors), as well as by pretensions and delusions. They are distracted from the truth of God's reality by the falsehoods or illusions of Māyā, and therefore take the 'wrong path' that keeps them trapped within the realm of tainted attributes and forms. One of the early shabads in the *Ādi Granth* presents a memorable illustration of this facet of human nature:

Brother, why do you strut about,
so full of yourself?
    How come you've forgotten
those ten months
when you were suspended
upside down
    inside the womb?

When the body's cremated,
it turns to ashes;
    when it's buried,
it's eaten by armies of worms.
The body's a jar of unbaked clay
containing water—
    that's its greatest claim to fame.

As a honeybee
accumulates its honey,

so a man accumulates his wealth.
But when he's dead, the others say,
Take him away, take him away!
Why have we let this corpse
lie here so long?
His wife accompanies his bier
from the inner rooms to the threshold;
beyond that, his friends bear him away.
The folks in his family
go as far as the cremation ground.
Beyond that,
the swan's all alone.
Kabir says, listen, O creatures,
those who fall into
the well of death
ensnare themselves
in make-believe Māyā,
like parrots who delude themselves
and fall into a bird-catcher's trap.

Their egotism, greed and pretentiousness, among other qualities, lead human beings to perpetrate acts of deception upon themselves and each other, which adds a profusion of man-made illusions to the illusions that already populate the domain of Māyā. In the eyes of the misanthropic Kabir poets, human beings are especially responsible for inflicting fake religions, false values, social and economic injustices and acts of violence upon the world. As a consequence, individuals, groups, institutions and society as a whole need to be changed, here and now.

In a changed world, human beings would clearly understand why the realm of Māyā—the whole of

Creation—is flawed, impure and unreal, what the 'true nature' of the God without attributes is, how they can undo the effects of Māyā and attach themselves to God, and how they might act more ethically while living in the human and natural worlds. In this context, one of the ideals of ethical life upheld by the poets of the Kabir tradition strongly resembles a Buddhist 'middle path' or a Stoical 'golden mean', as in the following song from the oral tradition:

I'm neither pious nor impious—
  I'm neither an ascetic nor a hedonist.

I don't dictate and I don't listen—
  I'm neither a master nor a servant.

I'm neither a captive nor a free man—
  I'm neither involved nor indifferent.

I haven't been estranged from anyone—
  and I'm no one's close companion.

I'm not going to a place called hell—
  and I'm not going to heaven.

I'm the agent of all my actions—
  yet I'm different from my deeds.

A few in a million can grasp this notion—
  they sit with poise, ensconced in immortality.

Such is the creed of Kabir—
  some things it builds, some it destroys.

For the poets of the Kabir tradition, each individual has to achieve liberation from Māyā for himself (or, as we would say today, herself). Adopting a position that resonates with the *Ṛg-veda* and the major Upaniṣads, they argue that a human being is born into this world with a physical body, and an *ātmā* or 'true self', which is a 'piece' of the godhead, housed within it. But in a variation that resembles the late-classical position of *viśiṣṭādvaita*, they suggest that the true self within a human being has the same 'attributeless nature' as God, yet stands in a relation to its body that is analogous to—though far more limited than—God's relation to Creation. They often refer to this *ātmā* as a *haṃsa* (a term borrowed from the Upaniṣads and Nath yoga), which corresponds to the swan that represents the soul in Indo-European mythology (and in the work of such modern poets as W. B. Yeats).

The *ātmā* or *haṃsa* is trapped within its body and within the domain of Māyā, and its goal in this lifetime must be to free itself from those bonds and be reunited with the God beyond God, from which it has been fragmented since the beginning of Creation. The true self is trapped in its body not only by the mechanics and effects of Māyā, but also—contrary to David N. Lorenzen's suggestion on this point—by the karma of the individual whose identity it defines (1995b, 18). Karma, or action in the world, always has 'fruits' or consequences, and these consequences generate residues (*anuśayas*) in their agent that bind him to further action. The chain of actions, fruits of action and causal karmic aggregates (*prārabdha*, *sañcita*, and *āgamin* or *kriyamāṇa*, according to the eighth-century philosopher, Shankarācharya), spans not only the period of a lifetime, but also the duration beyond the individual's bodily death.

The balance of *puṇya* (merit) and *pāpa* (demerit), of good and bad moral dispositions, that a human being acquires through good and evil actions in one lifetime activates the rebirth of his or her *ātmā* in another body for another lifetime, which, in turn, leads to another (re)death and another (re)birth, potentially in an unbreakable cycle spanning the entire period of existence of the created universe. To break the cycle with the relentless logic of karma itself—as in karmic theory from the early Upaniṣads to Advaita Vedānta—an individual must perform so many good deeds in successive lifetimes that his or her stock of merit comes to far outweigh the accumulated stock of demerit (Herman 1976; Potter 1980). Or, because goodness and evil are so subtle, and evil (unlike goodness) is so easy to perpetrate, an individual may seek God's intercession. If an individual devotes himself or herself totally to God, He may intervene on his or her behalf in this lifetime, and end the cycle of rebirths.

To obtain God's intercession, however, an individual must first establish access to Him. As the Kabir poets acknowledge, in the post-classical Indian world, an individual may try to establish access to God in one or more of several potential ways. He may patronize a Vedic priest and perform *yajñas* or ritual sacrifices; he may follow the precepts of Paurāṇic Hinduism and worship at a temple and undertake pilgrimages; he may pray five times a day at a mosque, under the direction of an officiating mullāh, and follow a full calendar of Muslim fasts, feasts, mortifications and sacrifices; he may read the Vedas, the Purāṇas or the Qur'ān for himself, or grasp their injunctions through the readings, recitations and commentaries of priests; or he may find a sufi *pīr*, a Nath yogi, a Tantric master or a Shaiva ascetic, and learn to sing ecstatic songs, perform *āsans*, intoxicate himself with secret liquors or chant mantras.

But the problem, the Kabir poets tell us, is that none of these supposed means actually establishes access to God. The Vedas and the Purāṇas are useless; the Qur'āns and Katebs are useless; the paṇḍits and their mantras are useless; the mullāhs and their prayer-calls are useless; the temples and the mosques are useless; the ritual sacrifices and the lengthy pilgrimages are useless; the yogis with their split ears and bodily contortions are useless; the starving *saṃnyāsī*s in forests are useless; the Shaiva *jaṅgama*s with their smeared ashes are useless; the sufi *pīr*s with their *silsilāh*s are useless; the dance of Krishṇa and the *gopī*s is useless; the story of Dasharath and Rāma is useless; the rules of purity and pollution, endogamy and incommensality, are useless; the secret codes of mantras and *tantra*s and *yantra*s are useless. All these means are useless for establishing a connection with God because they belong to the domain of man-made illusions, to the realm of Māyā, to the tainted and flawed universe of attributes and forms, and hence to a web of lies, deceptions and errors. Bhakti alone provides access to God, but even that contains false bhakti: there are fake devotees, such as saguṇa bhaktas, and there are make-believe forms of devotion, such as saguṇī bhakti. So the only path through all of this is that of 'true bhakti', which is utter and uncompromising devotion, based on nirguṇa *mat*, to the God beyond God.

But how does nirguṇī bhakti ensure access to God and His intercession? It does so, the Kabir poets say, by teaching the individual how to independently find the formless, flawless God within himself, in the form of the true self, the *ātmā* or *haṃsa* within. Unlike all other gods, this God is very easy to find—all it takes is a moment's search. To locate and recognize Him, an individual must look within himself, 'roaming' in his own mind; he must concentrate on God by remembering and repeating His Name without interruption; and he must let God's 'light' flood him and dispel the 'darkness'. In this process, the individual must accept God Himself as the One and Only True Master, the greatest of all Gurus, and let God show him the way to Himself.

To make himself worthy of God's 'teaching', he must develop an absolute and total love of God, and attach himself to His 'fellowship', the only 'true company'. When God receives that pure and complete devotion, He grants His devotee His complete grace: this is at once God's *saulabhya*, 'ease of access', in the conceptual vocabulary of bhakti, as well as His immediate 'presence', in the terms of sufism. Thus, one of the voices of Kabir in the *Ādi Granth* says, virtually in a sufi's language:

Light came to light. Darkness disappeared.
  Roaming in my mind, I found the gem called Rāma.

It destroyed my fear of life and death.
  He revealed His colours naturally, easily.

Where there's bliss, sorrow's far away.
  The heart contains the jewel of the love of God.

Whatever happens is all Your doing.
  Those who realize this commingle with the truth.

Kabir says, my wrongs abate: my heart's immersed
  in the One who's the Life of the Universe.

Once an individual has established contact with the God beyond God through *tyāg* (renunciation of the body and the senses, of Māyā), *upāsanā* (continuous, disciplined devotion), *vichār* (meditation), *jap* and *nām sumiran* (repetition and remembrance of His Name), and *dhyān* (unbroken concentration), his objective should be to attain mukti or 'final release' from karma and *saṃsār* and from existence in the created universe by merging permanently with Him.

To reach this end, he needs to enter *sahaj samādhī*, the easy, natural, and even spontaneous and simple state of 'union' with God (*sahaj* being a concept borrowed from Tantric Buddhism and Vaishṇavism), which occurs when he concentrates his entire being on the true self within him, and becomes identical with that, and only that, self (Chaturvedi 1954; Vaudeville 1974; Dvivedi 2000). Since the true self is a fragment of godhead, achieving complete and irreversible identity with it *is* the process of uniting with God.

The ineffable tale
    of that final simple state:

it's utterly different.

It can't be weighed on a scale,
    can't be whittled down.
It doesn't feel heavy
    and doesn't feel light.

It has no rain, no sea,
    no sun or shade.
It doesn't contain
    creation or destruction.

No life, no death exist in it,
    no grief, no joy.
Both solitude and blissful union
    are absent from it.

It has no up or down,
    no high or low.
It doesn't contain
    either night or day.

There's no water, no air,
    no fire that flares again and again.
The True Master permeates
    everything there.

Thus, the whole process of finding access to God, establishing and maintaining contact, and cementing that contact until what 'one' 'is' becomes indistinguishable from Him is a fully *interiorized* process. In this process, an individual must 'break the circuit of the senses' and 'extinguish' all sensory experience: there is no need for contact or engagement with anything in the external world, all of which is the antithesis of both the true self within and the God beyond God who is beyond the created universe outside.

As this abbreviated account indicates, the poets of the Kabir tradition are rigorous logicians of 'salvation'. But their perspective is not merely theological or academic: they are also unflinching social and psychological realists for whom metaphysics leads squarely into moral philosophy, ethics, social criticism and politics. The argument about mukti thus seems to be focused on a single goal, but it has several far-reaching outcomes in the domain of 'practical reason'. First, if God and human self are related as described above, for the nirguṇa bhakta, there can be no philosophically valid basis for either Hindu religious practice or Hindu social organization. From a nirguṇa standpoint, Vedic ritual, Paurāṇic temple worship, the caste system, the asymmetrical codes of commensality, the rules of endogamy, and even the authority of *śruti* and *smṛti* must be 'false'. As a late sākhī from the *Bījak* puts it:

The One who knows me is the One I know:
    I refuse to do

what the world or the Vedas
    tell me to do.

Second, if the individual *ātmā* is substantially identical to ultimate nirguṇa reality and is ontologically distinct from it but can achieve 'union' with it under specific conditions (of 'conditionlessness'), for the nirguṇa bhakta the structure of orthodox religious practice in Islam—mosque, mullāh, ritual prayer, fasting, hajj—must also be 'false'.

Third, if the whole logic of *sahaj samādhī* is that the self-God relationship requires no mediation, all the mediating agents, texts and locations of organized religion—priest, mantra, Qur'ān, temple, mosque, pilgrim-station—are necessarily 'false'. Moreover, even human gurus are unnecessary (as the Dadu Panth acknowledges), for God Himself is the *Satguru*, the One and Only True Teacher, a complete community of One. In the eyes of the nirguṇa bhakta, all human institutions that seek to mediate between him and God must then be 'false', including such organizations as the Kabir Panth and its branches, which attempt to mythologize and ritualize Kabir in contradiction of their own professed doctrine.

Fourth, the extended logic of *ātmā*, mukti, *sahaj samādhī* and nirguṇa God implies that the fundamental dynamics of absolute reality is non-violent. So violence then belongs to the realm of Māyā, and any religious or social practice that involves violent means or ends is false and tainted. As Hazariprasad Dvivedi, Linda Hess and Shukdev Singh, among others, have pointed out, in the nirguṇa bhakta's perspective, both Hindu and Muslim sacrificial rituals are violent, and paṇḍās as well as mullāhs are 'skilful butchers', so organized religion belongs to the web of corruption and impurity (see, for example, Dvivedi 2000, 242, pada 151; Hess and Singh1983, 46, shabda 11). An individual is accountable to God for every one of his or her acts of violence, and every form of oppression is wrong, because it is underwritten by violence. As an early shalok from the *Ādi Granth* frames it:

When you use force, you commit a crime,
  and God will make you answer for it.
When His scribe pulls out the written account of your deeds,
  for a blow to the mouth you'll get a blow to the mouth.

Finally, since Hinduism and Islam (and all other institutionalized religions) belong to the realm of Māyā, the nirguṇa bhakta must reject them as 'false' in their totality. This is the 'secularism' of the community of Kabir poets—but it is paradoxically a 'theological secularism'. In the modern period, we have come to view secularism as historically and conceptually possessing four basic orientations: (*a*) a *non-religious* disposition, in which secularists attempt to construct social principles and to deal with civil and civic matters by stepping outside the domain of religion altogether; (*b*) an *a-religious* orientation, in which secularists adopt an attitude of indifference to religion, and develop pragmatic strategies that ignore the division between the religious and the non-religious; (*c*) an *anti-religious* orientation, in which secularists explicitly oppose religion and seek to dismantle its institutions and structures; and (*d*) a *post-religious* disposition, in which secularists treat religion as a phenomenon of and in the past, and hence only of historical interest.

Between the sixteenth and eighteenth centuries, however,

the Kabir poets invented an astonishing fifth alternative. In this dissident conception of the secular, institutionalized religions—with their wealth, power, mediating structures and violent practices—determine what constitutes 'religion' and what is legitimately 'religious' in the human world. But the human world belongs wholly to the domain of Māyā, so these institutions and their definitions of dharma or 'religion' cannot reach beyond the limits of Māyā to the God without attributes. Nirguṇa God stands *outside* the immense scaffolding of organized human religions and what they define as 'religious' doctrine and practice, and since the 'secular' is that which lies outside the scope of the 'religious', *God as such is entirely secular.*

The consequence of this conception is that the process of attaining mukti—of liberating the individual *ātmā* from its imprisonment in karma and *saṃsār*, by enabling its union with absolute nirguṇa reality—is also a secular process. It is precisely such a secularism that makes both God and mukti completely accessible to anyone and everyone, regardless of caste, class, birth, gender, upbringing, status or rank, and that becomes indistinguishable from the deeply subversive egalitarianism and cosmopolitanism of the Kabir community.

It took the poets of the Kabir tradition some 250 years—from the death of the poet around the mid-fifteenth century to the end of the seventeenth century—to flesh out this self-consistent logic in almost 600 poems, crafted with the most minimal means. If the fifty poems that carry Kabir's bipolar signature in the Goindval Pothis of 1570–72 and the fifteen poems copied into the Fatehpur manuscript of 1582 are the earliest pieces in the tradition, and therefore the most likely to resemble his original compositions, the historical poet had already invented such a structure in a miniature or incipient form in his lifetime.

If those poems are any indication, Kamir or Kabir was at once a philosopher and a musician, a theologian and a social critic, a fearless speaker and a gentle bhakta—and his words had the *mādhurya*, the natural sweetness, of a poet. When that weaver departed from his house, he left his unfinished weaving on his loom, with fables, allegories, sermons, satires, aphorisms, riddles and songs stretched out as a warp 'in progress'. In the centuries since his departure, his collaborators have made the journey to his workshop and sat at his frame, shedding and picking, beating in the weft thread by thread, finishing the great design that he began.

TABLE 4: Categories of Materials Used for Selection of Poems
Modes of Transmission, Geographical Regions, Manuscript Lines, Musical Traditions, Institutions, and Particular Texts

Oral Mode	*Musical Mode*	*Written Mode*		
		Northern Ms.-Line	*Western Ms.-Line*	*Eastern Ms.-Line*
1. **Bihar-Bengal region** (K. M. Sen)	3. **Northern tradition** a. Goindval Pothis b. *Ādi Granth*	7. **Sikh institutions** a. Goindval Pothis b. *Ādi Granth*	8. **Dadu Panth** a. *Pañchavāṇī mss.* b. *Sarbaṅgī mss.*	10. **Kabir Panth** (*Bījak*)
2. **Banaras region** (H. P. Dvivedi)	4. **Western tradition** a. Dadu Panthi mss. b. Niranjani mss.		9. **Niranjani Panth** (Niranjani mss.)	
	5. **Folk traditions** (K. M. Sen, H. P. Dwivedi)			
	6. **Modern mass-media** (recordings in Hindustani classical style)			

POEMS

‘Sixty Threads in the Warp’

Poems from the Northern Texts

The Final State

The ineffable tale
    of that final simple state:

it's utterly different.

It can't be weighed on a scale,
    can't be whittled down.
It doesn't feel heavy
    and doesn't feel light.

It has no rain, no sea,
    no sun or shade.
It doesn't contain
    creation or destruction.

No life, no death exist in it,
    no grief, no joy.
Both solitude and blissful union
    are absent from it.

It has no up or down,
    no high or low.
It doesn't contain
    either night or day.

There's no water, no air,
    no fire that flares again and again.
The True Master permeates
    everything there.

The Eternal One remains
    unmoving, imperceptible, unknowable.
You can attain Him
    with the Guru's grace.

Kabir says, sacrifice yourself
    to the Guru,
and remain ensconced
    in the true community.

Refrain: *sahaja kī akatha kathā hai nirārī*
Verse 1: *taha pāvasa sindhu dhūpa nahi chhahīā*
Ādi Granth, Rāga Gau<u>d</u>ī, shabad 48

Body and Self

The weaver thought,
Let me weave
a body for my self—
but he couldn't have his wish,
and left his house
in great frustration.

Nine yards, ten yards,
twenty-one yards—
that completes one stretch of cloth.
Sixty threads in the warp,
nine panels interlocked,
seventy-two extra threads
added to the weft.

He counts its yardage, but can't,
he measures its weight, but can't—
and yet it needs
five pounds of sizing.
When he asks for the sizing
and doesn't find it ready at once,
he kicks up a fuss in the house.

The weaver, master of his craft,
master of his house,
sits through a daylong session at the loom,
but resigns in the end, despairing,
Why has this moment come to pass?
He abandons the pots of sizing, the bobbins all wet,
and walks off in a huff.

No thread emerges
    from the empty shuttle,
no shed stands ready
for picking and beating—
    the yarn in the heddles is tangled.
Kabir says, let go of the mess,
let that poor wish remain

    unfulfilled.

Refrain: *gaī bunāvana māho*
Verse 1: *gaja nava gaja dasa gaja ikīsa*
Ādi Granth, Rāga Gauḏī, shabad 54

Slander

Slander! Slander!
 People deride me—
folks truly love
 to smear and tarnish.
Slander's my father,
 slander's my mother.

If your name has been blackened,
 you'll go to Vaikuṇṭha—
the true Name's meaning
 will set itself in your mind.

There's so much calumny,
 my heart's purified—
my vilifier
 scrubs my clothes clean.

Whoever maligns me
 is my friend—
my heart goes out
 to every detractor.

The one who stops decrying me
 is my real critic—
such a denouncer
 vexes my life.

Defamation's
 my dearly belovèd—
revilement puts me
 in its debt.

Everybody
slings mud at Kabir—
my denigrator drowns,
I land on the other shore.

Refrain: *nindau nindau mo kau logu nindau*
Ādi Granth, Rāga Gauḍī, shabad 71

Birth and Light

What house can we call
    a house without fear?
People succumb and pray
to fear everywhere—
    so live fearlessly!

The birth of light,
the light of birth—
    they bear fruits and pearls
    made of glass.

On the riverbank
at the pilgrim-station,
the mind doesn't find
    true belief—
it remains entangled
in ritual's rights and wrongs.

The measure of evil
and the measure of good—
    the two are alike.
The touchstone you need
is in your house—
    give up your quest
    for other qualities.

O Kabir,
don't shed light
on the Name devoid of all qualities—
  let people know
  that object of knowledge
  exactly as it is.

Refrain: *kavanu su gharu jo nirabhau kahīai*
Verse 1: *joti kī jāti jāti kī jotī*
Ādi Granth, Rāga Gauḏī, shabad 9

The Senses

I've extinguished the flame:
there's no more smoke from the lamp.
Only the moon's left:
there's nothing else.

I've dried out the wick:
I haven't replenished the oil.
I've stopped beating the drum:
I've put the dancer to sleep.

I've broken the strings:
I've silenced the rebeck.
I've neglected my work
and ruined my routine.

Once I knew what I had to do,
I gave up singing:
my sermons, my satires,
my aphorisms, my tales.

Kabir says, those who break
the circuit of the senses
aren't very far
from the supreme station,

their destination.

Refrain: *bujhi gaī agani na nigasio dhūṃā*
Verse 1: *bātī sūkī telu nikhūṭā*
Ādi Granth, Rāga Āsā, shabad 11

The Master Weaver

You haven't puzzled out
any of the Weaver's secrets:
    it took Him
a mere moment
to stretch out the whole universe
    on His loom.

While you were there,
listening
    to the Vedas and Purāṇas,
I was here,
spreading out
    the threads for my warp.

He fashioned His loom
    out of earth and sky:
He plied the sun and moon
simultaneously
    as His twin shuttles.

When He worked the pair
of treadles in the pit below
    in tandem,
I acknowledged Him
in my mind
    as a master weaver.

I found His signs,
the signs of a weaver,
    inside my house:

in a flash
I recognized Him
    as Rāma.

Kabir says, I've smashed
    my loom:
only the Weaver
can mesh
    thread with thread.

Refrain: *korī ko kāhū maramu na jānāṃ*
Ādi Granth, Rāga Āsā, shabad 36

Trap

Brother, why do you strut about,
so full of yourself?
    How come you've forgotten
those ten months
when you were suspended
upside down
    inside the womb?

When the body's cremated,
it turns to ashes;
    when it's buried,
it's eaten by armies of worms.
The body's a jar of unbaked clay
containing water—
    that's its greatest claim to fame.

As a honeybee
accumulates its honey,
    so a man accumulates his wealth.
But when he's dead, the others say,
Take him away, take him away!
Why have we let this corpse
    lie here so long?

His wife accompanies his bier
from the inner rooms to the threshold;
    beyond that, his friends bear him away.
The folks in his family
go as far as the cremation ground.

Beyond that,
    the swan's all alone.

Kabir says, listen, O creatures,
those who fall into
    the well of death
ensnare themselves
in make-believe Māyā,
like parrots who delude themselves
    and fall into a bird-catcher's trap.

Refrain: *kāhe bhaīā phiratau phūliā phūliā*
Verse 1: *jaba jarai taba hoi bhasama tanu*
Ādi Granth, Rāga Soraṭhī, shabad 2

Poverty

Mādhav, sweet lord,
how will I ever be
    in Your blessèd company?
If You're a niggard,
I'll have to beg
    for Your gracious gifts.

Don't starve Your devotee:
take back this rosary of Yours.
    I only ask for the dust
of the saints' feet:
I don't wish to be
    an object of someone's charity.

All I want is a couple of pounds
of ground wheat,
    a quarter pound of ghee,
some salt to go with it:
that'll suffice
    for survival twice a day.

All I need is a cot
with four legs,
    a pillow, a mattress.
I ask for a coarse sheet
to cover me:
    You'll have my adoration.

I haven't been covetous.
I've heaped ostentation
    on just one thing: Your Name.
Kabir says, I've convinced
my heart to be content:
    for when the heart's content,

it comprehends Hari.

Refrain: *mādho kaisī banai tuma saṃge*
Verse 1: *bhūkhe bhagati na kījai*
Ādi Granth, Rāga Soraṭhī, shabad 11

Fable

The night's gone:
  don't let the day go by, too.
The bumblebees have left:
  the cranes have arrived, alighted.

The soul, a young girl,
  trembles, thinking:
I don't know
  what my husband's going to do.

Water won't keep
  in a jar of unbaked clay.
The swan has flown away:
  the body wilts.

Kabir says:
  My arms ache
from scaring off the crows.
  This tale has reached its end.

Refrain: *raini gaī matu dinu bhī jāi*
Verse 1: *thara thara kaṃpai bālā jīu*
Goindval Pothis, Rāga Sūhī, pada 3

Departure

Hari has sent His summons—
COME INSTANTLY.

Your time to act is up—
you have to submit a written account of your deeds.
Death's brutal messengers are here
to take you away.
What have you earned?
What have you spent and lost?
Come quickly, now—
the Dīvān has sent for you.

You beg and plead:
I still have a few things
left to do in the village.
Let me wrap them up—
give me a few hours—just tonight.
I'll cover your expenses.
We'll stop at a rest-house for our morning prayers,
when we're on our way tomorrow.

They're the fortunate ones,
all the folks who've kept
the company of good men,
and hence are imbued with Hari's colour—
they share in the Lord's substance.
They've found perennial happiness,
in this world, in that one—
they've won the priceless object.

In wakefulness and sleep, brother,
    you've squandered your life.
You've stacked up wealth and material things—
    all of which are someone else's.
Kabir says, those who're oblivious
    have lost track of their Master—
they're buried, they're stuck,
    they're one with the dust.

Refrain: *hari phuramānu daragahi kā āiā*
Verse 1: *amulu sirāno lekhā denā*
Goindval Pothis, Rāga Sūhī, pada 4

Ant

Beware of the world,
    brothers,
    be alert—
you're being robbed
    while wide awake.
Beware of the Vedas,
    brothers,
    be vigilant—
Death will carry you away
while the guard
    looks on.

The neem tree
becomes the mango tree,
    the mango tree becomes
    the neem,
the banana plant
spreads into a bush—
    the fruit on the coconut palm
ripens into a berry
right under your noses,
    you dumb and foolish
    rustics!

Hari becomes sugar
    and scatters Himself
    in the sand.
No elephant can sift
the crystals from the grains.

Kabir says, renounce
all family, caste, and clan.
Turn into an ant,
instead—
pick the sugar from the sand
and eat.

Refrain: *duniā husīāra bedāra jāgata musīata hau re bhāī*
Ādi Granth, Rāga Rāmakalī, shabad 12

Mosque with Ten Doors

Broadcast, O mullāh,
your merciful call to prayer—
    you yourself are a mosque
with ten doors.

Make your mind your Mecca,
your body, the Ka'aba—
    your Self itself
is the Supreme Master.

In the name of Allāh, sacrifice
your anger, error, impurity—
    chew up your senses,
become a patient man.

The lord of the Hindus and Turks
is one and the same—
    why become a mullāh,
why become a sheikh?

Kabir says, brother,
I've gone crazy—
    quietly, quietly, like a thief,
my mind has slipped into the simple state.

Refrain: *kahu re mulāṃ bāñga nivāja*
Verse 1: *manu kari makā kibalā kari dehī*
Ādi Granth, Rāga Bhairava, shabad 4

The Way

A wife gives birth to her husband.
An infant keeps his father
amused with games,
and suckles him without breasts.

Look, folks, look at the state
of this decadent age!
A son marries
his own mother.

A man who has no legs
leaps through the air.
A man who has no mouth
roars with laughter.

A man lies asleep
in the absence of sleep.
Milk churns in a can
in the absence of a churning-stick.

A cow delivers milk
with missing udders.
A long journey traverses
a missing road.

Kabir says in explanation:
    In a world of disasters,
you can't find your way
    without the True Master.

Refrain: *joi khasamu hai jāiā*
Verse 1: *dekhahu lokā kali kā bhāu*
Goindval Pothis, Rāga Basanta, pada 21

Purity

Tell me, O paṇḍit,
what place is pure—
where I can sit
and eat my meal?

Mother was impure,
father was impure—
the fruits they bore
were also impure.
They arrived impure,
they left impure—
unlucky folks,
they died impure.

My tongue's impure,
my words are impure,
my ears, my eyes,
they're all impure—
you brahmins,
you've stolen the fire,
but you can't burn off
the impurity of the senses!

The fire, too, is impure,
the water's impure—
so even the kitchen's
nothing but impure.
The ladle's impure
that serves a meal,

and they're impure
    who sit and eat their fill.

Cowdung's impure,
    the bathing-square's impure—
its very curbs
    are nothing but impure.
Kabir says,
    only they are pure
who've completely cleansed
    their thinking.

Refrain: *kahu paṇḍita sūchā kavanu ṭhāu*
Verse 1: *mātā jūṭhī pitā bhī jūṭhā*
Ādi Granth, Rāga Basanta Hiṇḍolā, shabad 7

Greed

This is the house you're in,
this is where you search
and eat what you find—
    don't go visiting
    someone else's house.

Your gait is like
the ambling gait of a cow—
you have a tail,
    its tuft of hair
    has a slick sheen.

You pick at the flour
left behind in the grinding mill,
you lick the stone clean—
    where are you sneaking off with that rag
    meant to wipe the mortar?

Your gaze is fixed
on the cooking pot.
Don't stare—
    you'll get the short end
    of a stick or club on your back.

Kabir says,
you're very well fed.
Don't devour any more—
  someone might brain you
  with a brick or stone.

Refrain: *isa ghara mahi hai su tū ḍhūṇḍhi khāhi*
Verse 1: *suraha kī jaisī terī chāla*
Ādi Granth, Rāga Basanta, shabad 1

The Jewel

Light came to light. Darkness disappeared.
  Roaming in my mind, I found the gem called Rāma.

It destroyed my fear of life and death.
  He revealed His colours naturally, easily.

Where there's bliss, sorrow's far away.
  The heart contains the jewel of the love of God.

Whatever happens is all Your doing.
  Those who realize this commingle with the truth.

Kabir says, my wrongs abate: my heart's immersed
  in the One who's the Life of the Universe.

Refrain: *paragaṭī joti miṭiā andhiārā*
Verse 1: *marana jīvaṇa kī sañkā nāsī*
Goindval Pothis, Rāga Prabhātī, pada 7

Allāh-Rāma

Allāh-Rāma,
I live by Your Name:
show me Your mercy,
my Lord.

If Allāh resides
inside a mosque,
then whose is the rest of the land?
Hindus claim His Name
inhabits an idol:
but God can't be found
in either place.

The southern country
is Hari's home,
the west is Allāh's camping ground.
Search your heart,
your heart of hearts:
that's His abode,
that's His camp.

The brahmin fasts
once a fortnight,
the qāzī fasts for Ramadān.
Each devotes
eleven months to himself,
then looks for rewards
in a month of fasts.

Why go off to Orissa
for ritual immersions?
Why bow your head in a mosque?
You're a crook at heart,
you pretend to pray:
why go all the way
on a hajj to the Ka'aba?

These men and women,
the whole lot of them,
are nothing but Your forms.
I'm a child
of Rāma-and-Allāh,
everyone's my guru-and-*pīr*.

Kabir says, listen,
O men and women:
seek shelter with the One and Only.
Repeat His singular Name,
you creatures: for only then
will you be able
to cross life's ocean.

Refrain: *ālahā rāma jīvāṃ terī nāī*
Verse 1: *alahu eku masīti vastu hai*
Goindval Pothis, Rāga Prabhātī, pada

'I've Painted My Body Red'

Poems from the Western Texts

Wedding

O bridesmaids,
sing wedding-songs:
King Rāma, my bridegroom,
has come to my house.

I've painted my body red,
I'll paint my mind all red:
the five great elements
are in the bridegroom's party.

Lord Rāma, my guest,
has arrived:
I'm young again,
I'm drunk and giddy with youth!

I'll set up the wedding canopy
in my body's lake,
and Brahmā himself
will chant the Vedas.

I'll walk around the fire
with Lord Rāma:
my blessèd, blessèd
fortune!

Three hundred and thirty million gods
and eighty-eight thousand sages
are here to attend
the ceremony.

Kabir says,
I'm off to my wedding:
I'm marrying
the Imperishable One.

Refrain: *dulahinīṃ gāvahu mañgalachāra*
Kabīr Granthāvalī, añga 2, pada 5; Rāga Gauḏī

Fever

Without Rāma,
my body's fever won't go down:
  the fire burns in water,
in water it flares.

You're an ocean,
I'm a fish inside You:
  I live in water
but water I crave.

You're a cage,
I'm the parrot inside You:
  what can Death, that pouncing cat,
do to me?

You're the True Master.
I'm Your disciple: a newborn child.
  Kabir says, we'll meet
when time has run its course.

Refrain: *rāṃma binu tana kī tapani na jāi*
Kabīr Granthāvalī, añga 2, pada 9; Rāga Gauḏī

The Provider

Kabir has quit
stretching and weaving,
he has written Rāma's name
all over his body,

Kabir's mother
sobs and weeps.
How, O Lord,
will these kids survive?

Whenever the loaded shuttle
flies through the warp,
the thread of Rāma's love
snaps.

Kabir says,
listen, dear mother,
the Lord of the Three Worlds
is our provider.

Refrain: *tananāṃ bunanāṃ tajyau kabīra*
Kabīr Granthāvalī, aṅga 2, pada 12; Rāga Gauḍī

Debate

If you love your followers, Rāma,
  settle this quarrel, once and for all.

Is Brahmā greater, or where He came from?
  Is the Veda greater, or its origin?

Is this mind greater, or what it believes in?
  Is Rāma greater, or the one who knows Him?

Kabir says, I'm in despair. Which is greater?
  The pilgrim-station, or Hari's devoted slave?

Refrain: *jhagarā eka niberahu rāṃma*
Kabīr Granthāvalī, aṅga 4, pada 27; Rāga Gauḏī

Mother and Son

Hari, you're the Mother
and I'm your son.
    Why don't you forgive me
    my faults?

Whenever a son
commits a wrong,
    his mother doesn't
    take it to heart.

Even when he grabs her by the hair
and hits her,
    she doesn't retract
    her love for him.

Kabir says, I have only
this one poor brain:
    if the child's in pain,
    the mother's in pain.

Refrain: *hari jananī maiṃ bālaka terā*
Kabīr Granthāvalī, aṅga 5, pada 37; Rāga Gauḍī

Banaras and Magahar

Now tell me, Rāma,
what's my future trajectory?
  I've renounced Banaras:
  a huge mistake.

Like a fish out of water,
stranded on a bank,
  I'm left without the austerities
  of my previous births.

I've squandered my whole life
in Shiva's city:
  now that it's time to die,
  I've risen and come to Magahar.

For so many years
I practised my penances in Kashi:
  now that I'm dying,
  I'm a resident of Magahar.

Kashi, Magahar: for a thoughtful man,
they're one and the same.
  My devotion's depleted:
  how will it land me on the other shore?

I say: Everybody recognizes
Ganesha and Shiva,
  but Kabir, though dead,
  absorbs himself in Lord Rāma.

Refrain: *aba kahu rāṃma kavana gati morī*
Kabīr Granthāvalī, añga 4, pada 46; Rāga Gau<u>d</u>ī

Let Me See You

How can I get
  to see You now?
Why should my heart be pacified
  if You don't let me have
a vision of You?

Am I a bad servant?
  Or are You merely
oblivious of me?
  Between the two of us, Lord,
whose fault is it?

You're said to be
  master and king
of all three worlds—
  You're the one who fulfils
all the heart's desires.

Kabir says,
  Hari, reveal Yourself.
Either tell me
  to come to You—
or bring Yourself to me.

Refrain: *ajahūṃ milai kaisai darasana torā*
Kabīr Granthāvalī, aṅga 4, pada 47; Rāga Bhairava

Storm

My good brothers,
 knowledge swept through
like a hurricane.
 It completely blew away
the reed-curtain
 of confusion and error,
it didn't let Māyā
 stay tied down.

It toppled the twin poles
 of vacillation,
it broke the beam
 of everyday love.
It tossed down
 the thatch of craving
from the top of the roof,
 it shattered the pot
of foolishness.

The rain that fell
 in the wake of the storm
soaked Your men to the skin.
 Kabir says, when I saw
the sun come out,
 my mind was filled with radiance.

Refrain: *santau bhāī āī gyānna ki āndhī re*
Kabīr Granthāvalī, añga 5, pada 52; Rāga Gauḏī

The Love of King Rāma

Dear heart,
don't do a thing
if you haven't worshipped
King Rāma.

People hear the words
of the Vedas and the Purāṇas
and begin to nurse their hopes
for the fruits of action.

All these enlightened people
are absorbed in the moment,
but they blame
the learned priests
for their disappointments.

The ascetic withdraws
into the forest
to master his senses,
and feeds on roots and stems.

So do all those shamans,
singers, scholars and saints
whose lives are written down
on plaque and parchment—
but it doesn't make
a jot of difference.

This one is thin and penniless,
he wraps his loins
in a loincloth—
but the love of God
that Nārad had
hasn't touched his heart or mind.

That one sits
singing holy songs
with great self-satisfaction—
but what God has he seen
or recognized?

Time and death
hack away at the world,
yet everyone describes himself
as a true seer within.

Kabir says
the only man
who serves a single master
is the one who knows
the love of Rāma.

Refrain: *mana re saryau na ekau kājā*
Kabīr Granthāvalī, añga 8, pada 86; Rāga Soraṭhī

Doer and Deed

O saints,
the doer is different
from his deeds.

He doesn't come and go,
he doesn't die,
he isn't born—
think this over
with a cool mind.

Just as sky and earth
are two,
so do Creator and Creation
stand apart.

Just as a cause
is held back
from its consequence,
so is my lord and lover
from me.

Who was the real wife
of the man named Dasharath,
father of Rāma?
And where did Dasharath's father,
Rāma's grandfather,
come from?

Rādhā and Rukmiṇī
were Krishṇa's queens,
and Krishṇa was the master
and husband of both,
but he also savoured the love
of sixteen thousand lovers—
who was the one
who did all that?

Vāsudev was Krishṇa's father,
and Devakī his mother,
but Krishṇa appeared
in the good Nanda's home.

Kabir says,
the doer isn't the one
who has gone and sold himself
as a slave
to his deeds.

Refrain: *sādhau karatā karama taiṃ nyārā*
Kabīr Granthāvalī, añga 12, pada 158; Rāga Āsāvarī

Māyā

We know
what Māyā is—
a great robber and thief,
a con-woman
in cahoots with con-men.

She wanders all over the world,
carrying her noose
strung with three strands—
she sits rocking in every place,
using her sweet tongue.

In Keshav's house
she masquerades as Kamalā,
in Shiva's mansion
she's Bhavānī.

She has settled down
as an idol at the priest's,
she has become
the holy water
at the pilgrim's destination.

She has planted herself
in the ascetic's hut
as an ascetic woman,
in the king's palace
she sits on the throne
as a queen.

In some homes
she's diamond and pearl,
in some she has become
a worthless cowrie-shell.

She has moved in
with the common devotee
and become a devotee herself,
she lives with the Muslim man
as his Muslim woman.

Kabir says, listen,
O holy men—
this is the whole
ineffable tale.

Refrain: *māyā mahā ṭhagini haṃma jānnīṃ*
Kabīr Granthāvalī, añga 13, pada 163; Rāga Bihāga

Meditation

Recollect Him, first, in your mind:
  no one else compares with Him.

Nobody can measure His full extent:
  He knows no beginning and no end.

Impossible to tell if He has a form or not:
  His lightness or heaviness can't be weighed.

Neither hunger nor thirst, neither sun nor shade:
  He exists in everything without sorrow, without
    happiness.

He's Brahman: unmanifest, unlimited.
  He permeates everything as absolute knowledge.

I've contemplated Him at length:
  there's no one else like Rāma.

Verse 1: *pahile mana maiṃ sumirau soī*
Kabīr Granthāvalī, ramainī 2; *bārahapadī* ramainī

Sapling and Seed

When learned priests
forget their stuff,
they read the good old Vedas—
without their books,
they don't have a clue
to the secret of things.

When they see
someone's suffering
they pounce on it
with words like karma,
they apply their theories
of the four *āshramas*.

They've taught the four ages
the *gāyatrī* mantra—
go ask them
whom it has set free.

Whenever they touch someone
they bathe
to purify themselves—
tell them who's really
the inferior one.

They take great pride
in their many good qualities,
but so much vanity
doesn't make them any good.

Only the One
who's the Destroyer of Pride
can deal with their arrogance.

Give up the thought
of being proud of your birth,
look for the text
of nirvana.

You'll find
the eternal bodiless
resting place
only when the sapling
has spoilt the seed.

Verse 1: *paṇḍita bhūle paḏhi guni bedā*
Kabīr Granthāvalī, ramainī 7; *ashṭapadī* ramainī

Moth

Joy is brief.
Sorrow and grief are endless.
The mind's an elephant,
mad, amnesiac.

Air and flame burn as one,
just as when the moth, its eye enchanted by light,
flies straight into the lamp,
and wing and fire flare together.

Who hasn't found
restful peace in a moment of pleasure?
So you brush aside the truth,
and chase the lies you hold so dear.

At the end of your days
you feel the temptation, you covet joy,
even though old age and death
are close at hand.

The world's embroiled in illusion, error:
this is the process always in motion.
Man attains a human birth:
why does he waste and destroy it?

Verse 1: *alapai sukha dukha āhi anantā*
Kabīr Granthāvalī, ramainī 15; *baḏī ashṭapadī* ramainī

Deadly Business

I try to give up Māyā,
 but I can't give her up.
Again and again
 she wraps herself
around me.

Honour is Māyā,
 pride is Māyā.
Where there's no Māyā,
 there's knowledge
of the ultimate reality.

Māyā is pleasure,
 Māyā is the chain
that shackles living things.
 Because of Māyā we renounce
the very breath of life.

Prayer-beads are Māyā,
 austerities are Māyā,
yoga, too, is Māyā.
 Māyā ties up
everybody.

Earth and water are Māyā,
 sky is Māyā.
Māyā spreads
 and surrounds us
on all four sides.

Māyā is mother,
  Māyā is father,
father and mother are Māyā.
  And, in the final count,
Māyā is wife and child.

Māyā carries on
  her deadly business
by killing.
  Kabir says, in this sport,
Rāma is my sole support.

Refrain: *māyā tajūṃ tajī nahi jāī*
Pañchavāṇī Manuscript IV (1675), pada 72; Rāga Gauḏī

'The Ganga Drains the Ocean'

Poems from the Eastern Texts

Warrior

The warrior does
the warrior's duty.

His stock of good deeds,
like money lent to others,
truly increases
by one-fourth.

He kills the living
to preserve the living—
he gives up his life,
yet stays alive
and watches all this happen.

The true warrior's the one
who goes down fighting
to keep his promise
to protect his clan.

He kills the five
enemy-senses
because he knows
the one true Self within.

The hermit who has learnt
this lesson from his master
overthrows his mind
right then and there.

Drunk on the senses,
his mind falls fighting
the moment he wounds his target.

Only the mind,
that self-crowned king,
dies in the battle—
and not the Self,
which never perishes.

Love is a void without Rāma,
it goes about
lost in itself.

Verse 1: *kshatrī kare kshatriyā dharmā*
Bījak, ramainī 83

Rāma's Essence

O saints, don't sleep while you're awake.
Time can't devour you,
the four ages can't destroy you,
old age can't ruin your bodies.

The Ganga, in reverse, drains the ocean,
and swallows up the moon and the sun.
A sick man finds the strength to strike down the nine planets.
Reflections in water emit an uncanny radiance.

The man without legs runs in all ten directions.
The man without eyes watches the whole world.
The rabbit, in reverse, feasts upon the lion.
Who can comprehend these wonders?

A jar that's upside down doesn't sink in water.
When upright, it fills with water and sinks.
No matter how inconsistent the actions of a man,
the Guru's grace still gets him across life's ocean.

The man who dwells in a cave envisions the whole world,
but he can't explain a thing outside the cave.
The arrow, in reverse, strikes the archer himself.
Only those who're fearless can comprehend this.

A man who's known as a singer never sings,
while a man who's a mute sings constantly.
A viewer watches the player on stage with a musical
instrument
only to increase his pleasure in the unheard sound.

For the one who sifts through the telling and talking,
    the whole adds up to an ineffable tale.
The earth, in reverse, rises and pierces the sky.
    These are the old masters' sayings.

A man quaffs the drink of immortality without a cup.
    A river brims with water but contains its flood.
Kabir says, anyone who tastes the essence of Rāma
    becomes immortal, and lives for ages and ages.

Refrain: *santo jāgata nīnda na kījai*
Bījak, shabda 2

The Simple State

Listen,
you saints—
I see that the world
is crazy.

When I tell the truth,
people run
to beat me up—
when I tell lies,
they believe me.

I've seen
the pious ones,
the ritual-mongers—
they bathe at dawn.

They kill the true Self
and worship rocks—
they know nothing.

I've seen
many masters and teachers—
they read their Book,
their Qur'ān.

They teach many students
their business tricks—
that's all they know.

They sit at home
in pretentious poses—
their minds are full
of vanity.

They begin to worship
brass and stone—
they're so proud
of their pilgrimages,
they forget the real thing.

They wear caps and beads,
they paint their brows
with the cosmetics
of holiness.

They forget the true words
and the songs of witness
the moment they've sung them—
they haven't heard
the news of the Self.

The Hindu says
Rāma's dear to him,
the Muslim says it's Rahīm.

They go to war
and kill each other—
no one knows
the secret of things.

They do their rounds
from door to door,
selling their magical formulas—
they're vain
about their reputations.

All the students
will drown with their teachers—
at the last moment
they'll repent.

Kabir says,
listen,
you saintly men,
forget all this vanity.

I've said it so many times
but nobody listens—
you must merge into
the simple state
simply.

Refrain: *santo dekhata jaga baurānā*
Bījak, shabda 4

The Ten Avatars

My good men,
what comes and goes,
bustling about the world,
    is Māyā.

The One who's the True Guardian
doesn't inflict
    death on anyone—
He doesn't come and go,
He has never moved
    from place to place.
Why would He change into
a Fish or a Tortoise?
    He didn't slay Shaṅkhāsura.

He's kind, compassionate—
He doesn't inflict
    cruelty on anyone.
Tell me, whom has He ever killed?
    He's a maker—
He never went by the name of Varāha,
He didn't lift up the weight of the earth.
    These aren't the Lord's actions—
    the world lies about them.

The one who burst out of a pillar—
    everybody believes in him.
He's Narasiṃha, the Man-Lion,
who tore into Hiraṇyakashipu's chest
with his claws—
    but he isn't the Creator.

The Lord didn't assume
the fifty-two forms
that tormented King Bali
in the netherworld—
    the one who did that
    was Māyā.
The whole world bustles about
indiscriminately—
    Māyā has deluded the world.

The True Master
wasn't Parashurāma,
He didn't slaughter the kshatriyas—
    that was a trick
    that Māyā played.
He doesn't recognize
separation and devotion—
    His creatures have invented
    these fictions.

The Guardian of the universe
wasn't the one
who marrie Sītā,
He didn't build the bridge across the sea
with rocks and stones.
    That was merely
the master of Raghu's clan,
who's commemorated for such deeds—
    anyone who memorializes him
    as though he were the Lord
    is a blind man.

The Creator wasn't the cowherd
who consorted with those cowgirls—
He didn't go to Gokul,
He didn't murder Kaṃsa.
The Master's gracious to everyone—
He hasn't been
the winner or the loser
in any war.

The Creator isn't the one
who's called the Buddha,
He didn't destroy the *asuras*.
Those who're ignorant
are deluded about the world—
Māyā has deluded the world.

The Creator isn't the one
who'll become Kalkī,
He won't be the future killer
of Kaligrahi.
Māyā's the o e
who has created this confusion—
she has impeded
the true renouncer,
the faithful wife.

For those who worship the Master,
the ten avatars
are a masterful illusion.
    Kabir says, listen,
    O saintly men—
what springs to life
and expends itself
    is utterly different from Him.

Refrain: *santo āvai jāya so māyā*
Bījak, shabda 8

Parting

Dear Swan,
where will you go
when you've left the lake?

You who picked up pearls
with your beak
in the middle of the lake,
I've helped you find
so many moments,
so many shades
of pleasure and play.

Now the lake is dry,
the lotus leaves have given up
their waterdrops,
the lotuses have lost
their freshness.

Kabir says,
after parting this time,
when will we meet again?

Refrain: *haṃsā pyāre saravara taji kahaṃ jāya*
Bījak, shabda 33

A City Ablaze

O Lord,
it's a conflagration!
It's raging without fuel—
one can't find a man
who has the power to put it out.
I know it has spread from You—
it's burning down
the whole world!

The seed of this fire
sprouts in water—
it douses the water
as it blazes.
It consumes nine women,
not just one—
no one knows
the true solution.

The city burns—
its guard sleeps contentedly.
He says,
My home's safe—
the town may burn,
but my things are unharmed.
O Rāma,
your colour blazes, shimmers.

A hunchback clings
around one's neck—
he worships the instruments
of the intellect.
A whole lifetime's
wasted in thinking—
this body remains
unsatisfied.

No one's more dim-witted
than a pretender,
a man who deceives
intentionally.
Kabir says,
in Rāma's eyes
everything's a Woman—
I can't do otherwise.

Refrain: *narahari lāgi dhauṃ bikāra*
Bījak, shabda 58

Holiness and Hell

An illusion of this sort
is a great misunderstanding.
What's the difference between
Veda and Qur'ān, holiness and hell,
male and female?

You've turned this body—
this pot of clay—
into a means to an end.
You've falsely confused
echo with sound,
effect with cause,
progeny with seed.
When the pot disintegrates—
when the body dies—
what's it called?
You moron!
You've lost sight
of the true search, the true end.

We're all one skin, one bone,
one shit, one piss,
one blood, one intestine.
All of Creation's composed
from a single point of origin—
then who's a brahmin,
who's a shūdra?

Brahmā is impulse, energy—
  Shankara is darkness, inertia—
  Hari is truth and light.
Kabir says,
  remain submerged
  in the Rāma without such qualities—
    no one's a Hindu,
    no one's a Turk.

Refrain: *aiso bharama bigurachani bhārī*
Bījak, shabda 75

'Neither Line Nor Form'

A Selection of Aphorisms

Shaloks from the Ādi Granth

1

Everybody, O Kabir,
makes my caste a laughing stock:

but it devotes itself to the Creator,
and I martyr myself to its cause.

kabīra merī jāti kau; shalok 2

2

The world's a pit of soot:
the blind fall right into it.

I sacrifice myself for those
who're stuck in there, yet succeed in climbing out.

kabīra jagu kājala kī koṭharī; shalok 26

3

Don't be vain, Kabir:
you're just a wrapping of skin on bone.

Even those who ride on horses, under parasols,
are buried quickly in the mud.

kabīra garabu na kījīai; shalok 37

4

Brother, the entrance to salvation is miniscule:
one-tenth the size of a mustard seed.

The mind remains a lumbering elephant:
how will it ever make it through that door?

kabīra mukati duārā sañkurā; shalok 58

5

Kabir's family sank to the bottom
the day his son Kamāl was born:

he gave up Hari's rosary and crassly brought
material wealth into the house.

būḍā baṃsu kabīra kā; shalok 115

6

Kabir, a fire raging on every side
consumed the house built of wood:

paṇḍit after paṇḍit perished in the blaze,
while every idiot got away.

kabīra koṭhī kāṭha kī; shalok 172

7

I went on a hajj to the Ka'aba,
but on the way I ran into God.

Picking a fight with me, He said:
Who told you to go there?

kabīra haja kābe hau jāi thā; shalok 197

8

When you use force, you commit a crime,
  and God will make you answer for it.

When His scribe pulls out the written account of your deeds,
  for a blow to the mouth you'll get a blow to the mouth.

kabīra joru kīā so julumu hai; shalok 200

9

Kabir, sow such a seed
  that its tree will flourish perennially:

cool shade, abundant fruit,
  foliage full of birds at play.

kabīra aisā bīju boi; shalok 229

10

Listen, dear girl: Does my Belovèd live in my Self,
  or does my Self live in my Belovèd?

I don't know: What's my Self, what's my Belovèd?
  What's inside my body? My Belovèd or my Self?

sunu sakhī pīa mahi jīu basai; shalok 236

Sākhīs from the Kabīr Granthāvalī

11

Nothing in me is mine:
  whatever's mine is Yours.

What's Yours I give to You:
what's there that's mine?

merā mujha maiṃ kichhu nahīṃ; aña 6, sākhī 2

12

Even if you were to transform
the seven oceans into ink,

the world's trees into pens, the whole earth into paper,
you couldn't write down the list of God's excellences.

sāta samunda kī masi karauṃ; aña 8, sākhī 2

13

When I was, Hari wasn't:
now that Hari is, I'm not.

All the darkness was erased
the moment I saw the Lamp.

jaba maiṃ thā taba hari nahīṃ; aña 9, sākhī 1

14

O Kabir, I'm worse than everyone else,
everyone's a better person than me:

anyone who comprehends this
is a dear friend of mine.

kabīra sabha te haṃma bure; aña 15, sākhī 32

15

My speech is of the East:
  no one can understand its signs.

Whoever can understand my speech
  is truly a man of the East.

bolī hamarī pūrabī; aṅga 18, sākhī 11

***Sākhīs from the* Bījak**

16

There's a mirror in your heart,
  but you can't endure the sight

of your face in it: you can bear to look
  only when you've ceased to doubt.

hṛdayā bhītara ārasī; sākhī 29

17

The path the paṇḍits have taken
  is also the one to which the common folk have flocked.

The steep slope of Rāma:
  that's the one Kabir is scaling.

jehi māraga gaye paṇḍitā; sākhī 31

18

The heartless man hasn't seen that country
  but talks and talks about it:

he lives on a diet of salt, but makes his living
selling camphor to others.

bina dekhe vaha desa kī; sākhī 34

19

What can the sandalwood tree do,
now that the snake has twined itself around it?

The poison has spread to all its limbs:
how will it absorb the elixir of life?

chandana sarapa lapeṭiyā; sākhī 38

20

The man with a truthful heart is best:
there's no happiness without the truth,

no matter how many millions of times
one tries to find it by other means.

sabha te sāñchā hai bhalā; sākhī 64

21

Judge your actions with your own mind:
make only honest transactions.

Falsehood is harmful at the very source:
so go acquire the diamond of truth.

sāñchā saudā kījiye; sākhī 65

22

Everybody understands
  the single drop merging into the ocean.

One in a million comprehends
  the ocean merging into a single drop.

būnda jo parā samudra meṃ; sākhī 69

23

Don't travel in the company of a man
  whose tongue never stops wagging,

whose heart isn't truthful: he'll be the death of you
  before you reach your journey's end.

jāke jibhyā banda nahīṃ; sākhī 83

24

As the entertainer with his monkey,
  so the living man with his mind:

he makes it perform its dancing tricks,
  then puts it on display, perched on his arm.

bājīgara kā bāndarā; sākhī 95

25

Mind and Māyā are one,
  Māyā fuses with the mind.

The three worlds are plunged into delusions.
  To whom can I explain this?

mana māyā to eka hai; sākhī 105

26

It's hard to be born a human:
you won't be born another time.

The ripe fruit that falls to the ground
doesn't grow back on the branch.

mānukha janama duralabha hai; sākhī 115

27

My eyes brim with tears
as I watch the mill grind:

when the twin stones turn in the mortar,
no one passes through intact.

chakkī chalatī dekhike; sākhī 129

28

The martyrdom of ritual sacrifice
for the milk that gives us ghee:

the life of the four Vedas boiled down
to half a verse by Kabir.

balihārī vahi dūdha kī; sākhī 131

29

The great are gone in their greatness,
every hair bristling with vanity.

Ignorant of the True Master,
the four castes alike are untouchable.

ba<u>d</u>e gaye ba<u>d</u>āpane; sākhī 139

30

Bone burns like wood,
hair burns like grass.

Kabir burns in Rāma's essence
like cotton burning in a house.

hāḏa jarai jasa lākaḏī; sākhī 174

31

Knowledge ahead, knowledge behind,
knowledge to the left and right.

The knowledge that knows what knowledge is:
that's the knowledge that's mine.

phahama āge phahama pāchhe; sākhī 188

32

The one who stays within the limits assigned to him is a man.
The one who roams beyond those limits is a saint.

To reject both limits and their absence:
that's a thought with immeasurable depths.

hada chale so mānavā; sākhī 189

33

The One who knows me is the One I know:
I refuse to do

what the world or the Vedas
tell me to do.

jo mohi jānai tāhi maiṃ jānauṃ; sākhī 200 (*chaupāī*)

34

Good company engenders happiness,
bad company breeds sorrow.

Kabir says, head for the place where you're sure
to find the true community.

saṃgati se sukha ūpaje; sākhī 208

35

As you stick to it at the beginning,
so stick it out to the end:

cowrie by cowrie, compile your capital
in lakhs and crores.

jaisī lāgī vora kī; sākhī 209

36

The One is one with the All,
the All is one with the One.

Kabir is one
with the knowledge without duality.

eka samānā sakala meṃ; sākhī 272

37

Accomplish one thing and you accomplish all.
Seek to do all and you lose the one vital thing.

When you water the root of a plant,
  it flowers and bears fruit to satisfaction.

eka sādhe saba sadhiyā; sākhī 273

38

Speech is priceless when it comes
  from someone who knows how to speak:

weigh it in your heart's balance
  before it leaves your mouth.

bolī to anamola hai; sākhī 276

39

When a man who's sleeping and dreaming
  opens his eyes and looks, awake,

he sees the living man engaged in a looting spree,
  without any give-and-take.

sapane soyā mānavā; sākhī 291

40

Sweet words are a balm,
  but harsh speech is an arrow:

it enters through the ear, hearing's vestibule,
  and pierces the body from head to toe.

madhura vachana aukhadī; sākhī 301

41

I've travelled at home and abroad,
  I've tramped the lanes of village after village:

and yet I haven't met a man of discrimination
  who can tell things for what they are.

desa bidese hauṃ phirā; sākhī 316

42

As soon as they speak, you recognize
  the ploys of saint and thief:

the workings of the inner self
  surface through the channel of the mouth.

bolata hī pahichāniye; sākhī 330

43

A ready-made man:
  a brainless thing, a featherweight.

What to do with him? He's a bright red flower,
  but devoid of fragrance.

banā banāyā mānavā; sākhī 333

44

The one who sits is a grocer.
  The one who stands is a milkman.

The one who stays awake is a nightwatch.
Death grabs and devours them all.

baiṭhā rahe so bāniyā; sākhī 338

45

He: neither line nor form.
Body: absent. Ground: groundless.

Behold the bodiless man, standing in the middle of
the circle of the sky.

rekha rūpa vaha hai nahīṃ; sākhī 347

46

The poem of witness is the eye of knowledge:
to understand it, gaze into your heart and mind.

Without the song of testimony,
the quarrels of this world don't end.

sākhī aṃkhī gyāṃna kī; sākhī 353

‘This Sheet, So Fine, So Fine’

A Selection of Songs

Sheet

He wove the sheet
so fine, so fine,
He wove the sheet so fine.

What was the warp?
What was the weft?
What was the thread
with which He wove the sheet?

Iñgalā and Piñgalā,
the warp, the weft,
Sushumnā the thread
with which He wove the sheet.

He spins the eight-petalled lotus
as his spinning-wheel,
with five elements
and three great qualities

He weaves the sheet.

He weaves the sheet
through ten months
in a mother's womb,
beating in the weft,

testing and checking
every strand,
He weaves the sheet.

Saints and humans
    wrap themselves in His sheet,
but the wrapping soils the sheet
    so fine, so fine.

His servant Kabir
    wraps himself in the sheet
with effort and care,
    he keeps it spotlessly clean,

this sheet, so fine, so fine.

Refrain: *jhīnī jhīnī bīnī chadariyā*
Kabīr Vachanāvalī, bhajan 223

The Flawless One

Rāma, pure Rāma,
the Flawless One,
is different:
the chaos scattered all around us
is tainted.

Creation's contaminated,
the syllable OṂ
is sullied:
impurity has created
this unholy spread.

Brahmā,
Shankara, Indra
are smirched:
Govind with his *gopīs*
is soiled.

Speech and sound
are foul,
the Vedas are stained:
impurity has perpetrated
so many forms.

Learning, reading, recitation,
the ancient books
are all corrupt:
knowledge, cheapened, mouthed for free,
is dirty.

The leaf in the oblation is rank,
the god in his shrine
is unclean:
infection serves
the infected.

Impurity dances,
impurity sings:
pollution displays
an infinite number
of guises.

The how and what, the when and where
of contamination:
it vanquishes
charity, goodness, austerity,
devotion.

Kabir says,
only one in a million
awakens to this:
but when he does,
he gives up what's tainted

and joins the incorruptible.

Refrain: *rāṃma niranjana nyārā re*
Gopaladas, *Sarbañgī* (1627), añga 45, pada 2; Rāga Bhairava

Breath

Why look for Me anywhere else, my friend,
when I'm here, in your possession?

Not in temples, not in mosques—
not in the Ka'aba, not on Kailash.

Not in rites, not in rituals—
not in yoga or renunciation.

Look for Me and you'll find Me quickly—
all it takes is a moment's search.

Kabir says, listen, O brothers—
He's the very Breath of our breaths.

Refrain: *mokoṃ kahāṃ dhūḏhe bande*
'Kabīr-vāṇī', pada 1

The Bhakta's Caste

O saintly men,

don't ask the man
devoted to the God without qualities
what his caste is.

The brahmin's good,
the warrior's good,
the trader's caste is good.

The thirty-six clans, they're all good—
it's your question, then,
that's crooked.

The barber's good,
the washerman's good,
the carpenter's caste is good.

Raidas, the saint, was good,
Supach, the seer, was good—
though they were scavengers.

Both Hindus and Turks
have demeaned themselves—
they can fathom nothing.

Refrain: *santana jāta na pūcho nirguniyāṃ*
'Kabīr-vāṇī', pada 2

Garden

Don't go to the gardens outside, don't go:
your body itself contains a bower in bloom.

There you can sit on a thousand-petalled lotus,
and gaze upon the ultimate infinite form.

Verse 1: *bāgoṃ nā jā re nā jā*
'Kabīr-vāṇī', pada 4

The Mystery of Māyā

O yogi,
the world of Māyā
    is hard to renounce.

When I renounced my home,
    I was trapped in my clothes;
when I renounced my clothes,
    I was stuck with my mendicant's rounds.

When I renounced desire,
    anger wouldn't leave me;
when I renounced anger,
    I was stuck with greed.

When I renounced greed,
    my ego wouldn't leave me—
my self-regard, my boastfulness,
    my attachment to appearances.

When my mind was finally detached,
    I renounced the world of Māyā:
my concentration, my ancient memory
    then fused with my words.

Kabir says, listen,
    my good brothers—
one in a million
    has solved this mystery.

Refrain: *avadhū, māyā tajī na āī*
'Kabīr-vāṇī', pada 5

Swan

Dear Swan,
    talk of ancient things.

What country have you come from,
    what shore will you alight on?
Where have you stopped and rested,
    what goal have you set your heart o

It's now the morning of consciousness,
    let's leave together.
We won't be filled with grief and doubt in that place,
    the fear of death won't strike us there.

Here the forests of desire are in bloom,
    their fragrance assails us straight ahead.
A place that ensnares the beetles of the heart
    can offer no hope of happiness.

Refrain: *haṃsā karo purātana bāta*
'Kabīr-vāṇī', pada 12

Fish

The fish in the water
is racked by thirst:
I hear about it
    and burst out laughing.

What you're looking for
is right at home:
and yet you roam from forest to forest,
    full of gloom.

Without self-knowledge
the world's all make-believe:
what's Mathura,
    what's Kashi?

Verse 1: *pānī bicha mīna piyāsī*
'Kabīr-vāṇī', pada 43

The Ineffable

What's visible isn't real—
what's real is ineffable.

What can't be seen can't be known—
what hasn't been said can't be believed.

The man who knows uses words and signs—
an ignoramus gapes in astonishment.

Some concentrate on a god without a form—
some on a god who has an outward shap

The man of knowledge understands—
the Creator's different from both of thes

The Creator's love remains invisible—
His syllables don't fall on human ears.

Kabir says, the man who comprehends
both love and renunciation—

he doesn't read the text of death,
the text of the world's extermination.

Verse 1: *jo dīsai so to hai nāhīṃ*
'Kabīr-vāṇī', pada 49

Apostasy

I don't know
what sort of Master
  you have.

Is He deaf
that the mullāh must screech
  from the mosque?

Surely He can hear
even the anklets that tinkle
  on an ant's feet!

You count your beads,
you smear your brow with marks,
  you grow long matted locks.

But deep inside yourself
you carry the vicious dagger
  of apostasy—

this isn't the way
  to attain the Master!

Verse 1: *nā jānai terā sāhaba kaisā hai*
'Kabīr-vāṇī', pada 67

Allāh-and-Rāma

If Khudā inhabits the mosque,
then whose play-field is the rest of the world?

If Rāma lives in the idol at the pilgrim-station,
then who controls the chaos outside?

The east is Hari's domicile, they say,
the west is Allāh's dwelling-place.

Look into your heart, your very heart:
that's where Karīm-and-Rāma reside.

All the women and men ever born
are nothing but Your embodied forms:

Kabir's a child of Allāh-and-Rāma,
They're his Guru-and-Pīr.

Verse 1: *jo khodāya masajīda basatu hai*
'Kabīr-vāṇī', pada 69

Neither This Nor That

I'm neither pious nor impious—
    I'm neither an ascetic nor a hedonist.

I don't dictate and I don't listen—
    I'm neither a master nor a servant.

I'm neither a captive nor a free man—
    I'm neither involved nor indifferent.

I haven't been estranged from anyone—
    and I'm no one's close companion.

I'm not going to a place called hell—
    and I'm not going to heaven.

I'm the agent of all my actions—
    yet I'm different from my deeds.

A few in a million can grasp this notion—
    they sit with poise, ensconced in immortality.

Such is the creed of Kabir—
    some things it builds, some it destroys.

Verse 1: *nāhīṃ dharmī nāhīṃ adharmī*
'Kabīr-vāṇī', pada 79

Rain

Rainclouds gather and darken
in the sky, O sādhu,
the rainclouds gather
and darken.

This string of clouds
has risen in the east:
the rain comes down,
rim-jhim, rim-jhim.

Secure the dams around your farms,
each to his own:
the water's overflowing
with force.

Put the bulls
of Love and Detachment to work:
plough, plough
the field of nirvana.

The man who comes home,
harvest and husking done,
he's the happy farmer
with real skill

With equal servings
on their plates,
both sage and scholar
eat their fill.

Verse 1: *gaganaghaṭā gaharānī sādho*
'Kabīr-vāṇī', pada 87

Creation

O ascetic—
    the ways of this Creation
are something else.

It changes a pauper
    into a king—
it turns an emperor
    into a beggar.

It stops the clove tree
    from bearing cloves—
it keeps the sandalwood flower
    from blooming.

It casts the fish into the forest
    as a beast of prey—
it leaves the lion
    swimming in the sea.

It transforms the castor plant
    into the sandalwood tree—
it spills the sandal's fragrance
    in every direction.

It squeezes the three worlds
    into a shard of the Cosmic Egg—
it grants a blind man
    the vision to witness this farce.

It gives a cripple the power
to leap over Mount Meru—
it lets him meander across
all three worlds.

It makes a mute shed light
on the science of knowledge—
it lets an endless stream of words
gush from his mouth.

It bundles up and dumps the sky
into the netherworld—
it raises Shesha, the serpent,
to rule over heaven.

Kabir says,
Rāma's the King—
whatever He does
is beautiful.

Refrain: *avadhū, kudarati kī gati nyārī*
'Kabīr-vāṇī', pada 112

Don't Stay

Don't stay—
 the land's a wilderness.

This world's a paltry paper packet—
 a spot of rain
 will wash it away.

This world's a garden of thorns—
 snarled and snared,
 we'll perish in pain.

This world's all tree and tinder—
 kindled, it will roast us
 like sacrificial victims.

Kabir says, listen, my good men,
 the True Master's name
 is our lasting abode—

 our station, our destination.

Refrain: *rahanā nahiṃ desa birānā hai*
'Kabīr-vāṇī', pada 130

NOTES TO THE POEMS

I. 'Sixty Threads in the Warp': Poems from the Northern Texts

1. The Final State

TEXT: *Ādi Granth*, Rāga Gauḏī, shabad 48; reproduced in Callewaert 1996, 1:333 and 2000, 609, pada 530. VARIANTS: None. TRANSLATIONS: Dass 1991, 77. Lines 1–7 in my version represent the refrain; each subsequent quatrain represents one verse in the original.

This poem describes the indescribable: the attainment of mukti. Mukti is the final liberation of the individual *ātmā* (which I render as 'the Self' or 'the true self') from the bondage of karma and *saṃsār*, of action and its effects and of the cycle of birth, death and rebirth. The poem equates the attainment of mukti with the attainment of the *sahaj sthiti*. The word *sahaj* describes something easy, natural, spontaneous, casual or simple; a *sthiti* is a condition or state; throughout this book, I have translated the whole phrase as 'the simple state'. (See the poem of that title below.) It is a 'final' state of the 'liberated' true self, and it has no predicable qualities. Most often, a human individual attains mukti at the moment of death, at the end of a particular lifetime in the world; but here 'Kabir' speaks as if he were still alive and in communication with us, so he presents himself as a *jīvan-mukta*, someone who has attained liberation while still living in this world (an extremely rare achievement). The shabad's speaker thus brings us 'living testimony' of the *sahaj sthiti*.

When a human individual enters this simple state, he 'experiences' the *ātmā* or true self within himself in its primordial condition, in which it is identical in 'substance' with godhead or God without attributes. (The Kabir poets consistently refer to the individual bhakta in the masculine gender, and therefore are unapologetically masculist, and even misogynist.) But the attainment of the simple state is not a 'blissful union' with God; so this poem is not an expression of ecstatic or 'intoxicated' mysticism. Moreover, entering the *sahaj sthiti* does not amount to 'knowing' God; He, as such, remains imperceptible and unknowable. God can be 'attained' only through His own grace; as the end of the shabad indicates, He is the ultimate Guru, the True Master, and no human mediator is needed to bring the bhakta to Him. In fact, to 'join' God in the simple state is fully to join the one and only 'true community'. The testimony of a *jīvan-mukta*, of the type represented in this poem, provides the foundation for the 'mystical knowledge' of God without attributes that underlies both the *Ādi Granth* and the Kabir texts in general.

2. Body and Self

TEXT: *Ādi Granth*, Rāga Gauḏī, shabad 54; reproduced in Callewaert 1996, 1:335. VARIANTS: *Pañchavāṇī* Ms. I (1614), pada 158; Rajjabadas, *Sarbañgī* (1620), añga 72, pada 66; *Pañchavāṇī* Ms. III (1658b), pada 166; *Kabīr Granthāvalī*, Tivari 1961, 2:65–66, añga 11, pada 111 (all in Rāga Rāmakalī); *Bījak*, Shukdev Singh 1972, 116, shabda 15. See Callewaert 2000, 316–17, pada 206. TRANSLATIONS: Hess and Singh 1983, 48; Dass 1991, 84; Vaudeville 1993, 237–38. The first sestet in my translation represents the refrain.

Although this poem has six versions in all, it remains grammatically and syntactically obscure; the source-texts all edit it in divergent attempts to make it meaningful and self-consistent. The *Ādi Granth* version seems to have a truncated half-line in its refrain. The other translators (Hess and Singh, Dass and Vaudeville) follow a conventionalized interpretation in which the poem portrays an old woman who seeks out a master-weaver to weave her a new body, but her project fails. (The old woman personifies an 'aged soul' or *jīvātmā*; see the personification of the true self as a girl or young bride in 'Fable' and 'Wedding' below.) Using the Rajasthani variants, I have interpreted the *Ādi Granth* text as a potentially self-consistent allegory of human despair at the decrepitude and mortality of the body, and also of hubris, creativity, transcendence and limitation. In my reading, a human master-weaver attempts vainly 'to play God' and fabricate himself a new body, but even his superior craft does not allow him to do so. In the Sikh and the Kabir traditions, hubris, vanity, pride and egotism are among the worst human shortcomings.

3. Slander

TEXT: *Ādi Granth*, Rāga Gauḏī, shabad 71; reproduced in Callewaert 1996, 1:339 and 2000, 613, pada 543. VARIANTS: None. TRANSLATIONS: Dass 1991, 100–01. Here the first sestet represents the refrain.

This shabad is unique to the *Ādi Granth*, but it articulates a common motif in bhakti poetry, according to which the true devotee is often scorned by society and slandered by his enemies, and therefore ostracized. Bhakti thus projects an exceptionalism upon itself. Early in its history, Sikhism also adopts an exceptionalist stance, as it develops antithetical relations with Hinduism and Islam, both of which institutionally and socially vilify it. This poem is a perfect satiric 'ode' to slander, in which the Kabir poets turn the abuse hurled at them into a source of spiritual strength. The argument moves from a strong opening thesis (I am the child of slander) to an equally strong conclusion (in the quest for mukti, my enemy loses while I win). In this progression, it especially reinforces two ideas: that the bhakta must be prepared for extreme rejection; and that only they attain mukti who are rejected by, and themselves reject, the world. The original poem uses verbal repetition and parallelisms to stress the viciousness of slander; my translation employs variation and divergence to build up a texture that is verbally the 'opposite' of the original.

4. Birth and Light

TEXT: *Ādi Granth*, Rāga Gauḏī, shabad 9; reproduced in Callewaert 1996, 1: 325 and 2000, 604, pada 510. VARIANTS: None. TRANSLATIONS: Dass 1991, 46.

This is one of the most original and subtle poems in the *Ādi Granth* as well as the Kabir tradition. The refrain (the opening stanza here) celebrates absolute fearlessness, a central moral quality in Sikhism; in the religion's later history—after the martyrdom of Guru Arjan and Guru Teg Bahadur, and especially under Guru Gobind Singh—fearlessness becomes militant and militarized; when the Sikhs adopt the common community name of Singh ('lion') for their men, they transform their fearlessness into armed fearsomeness. In contrast, the Kabir tradition upholds a principle of non-violence in conjunction with absolute spiritual and rhetorical fearlessness. The poem suggests that the fearless bhakta should reject both 'light' and 'birth' (a surprising argument, coming from a philosophy of enlightenment); reject all religious ritual; and reject even the binary opposition between good and evil. Its conclusion combines a simple principle with a complex one: find the true touchstone of right and wrong within your (true) self; and do not 'shed light' on the nature of godhead, because human beings ought to know it for what it truly is—imperceptible, unknowable and devoid of such attributes as light and darkness. The latter, an astonishing prescription, is related closely to the argument of 'The Final State' above.

5. The Senses

TEXT: *Ādi Granth*, Rāga Āsā, shabad 11; reproduced in Callewaert 1996, 1:478 and 2000, 615–16, pada 550. VARIANTS: None. TRANSLATIONS: Dass 1991, 132.

This poem, unique to the Sikh tradition, draws its images, symbols and arguments from Nath yoga as well as sufism. As a symbolist poem or a compressed allegory, it adopts the position that an individual's quest for mukti involves three basic steps: he must extinguish the operations of the mind or intellect (in a manner reminiscent of both the Buddhist's 'snuffing out' of the self in nirvana and the sufi's *fana*'); he must put the worldly 'dancer' in himself 'to sleep'; and he must break the circuit of the senses, thus cutting off all engagements with the material-physical world (much as the yogi seeks to disconnect himself from the external world of sensory experience).

6. *The Master Weaver*

TEXT: *Ādi Granth*, Rāga Āsā, shabad 36; reproduced in Callewaert 1996, 1:484. VARIANTS: *Kabīr Granthāvalī*, Tivari 1961, 2:88, aṅga 11, pada 150 (Rāga Āsā); *Bījak*, Shukdev Singh 1972, 90, ramainī 28. Both these versions are very different from the Sikh text; the *Bījak* reclassifies this shabad as a ramainī. See Callewaert 2000, 618, pada 560. TRANSLATIONS: Hess and Singh 1983, 84; Hawley and Juergensmeyer 1988, 55; Dass 1991, 149; Vaudeville 1993, 255–56.

Using symbols from Nath yoga (such as sun and moon), this poem develops its extended metaphor with two interlinked ideas: that God is a master weaver; and that Creation is (like) weaving, so that the created universe is (like) a textile. Thus, God creates the universe by weaving it on His divine loom. Here and in most other occurrences in this book, 'house' represents an individual's self, body or personhood; thus, God and His Creation are actually 'inside' the self. As in the poem 'Body and Self' discussed above, the human weaver in this poem is unable to replicate God's handiwork, which implies that the bhakta must give up hubris and let God do His work.

7. *Trap*

TEXT: *Ādi Granth*, Rāga Soraṭhī, shabad 2; reproduced in Callewaert 1996, 1:654. VARIANTS: Jaipur Ms. I (1660/1669), pada 97; *Pañchavāṇī* Ms. IV (1675), pada 241; Jaipur Ms. II (1681), pada 59; *Kabīr Granthāvalī*, Tivari 1961, 2:40, aṅga 8, pada 68 (all in Rāga Āsāvarī); *Bījak*, Shukdev Singh 1972, 135–36, shabda 73. The last two versions of the poem differ greatly from the first three and from the Sikh text. See Callewaert 2000, 404–05, pada 300. TRANSLATIONS: Hess and Singh 1983, 65–66; Dass 1991, 155–56; Vaudeville 1993, 249–50.

Like 'Body and Self' above, this poem has circulated in six distinct versions since the seventeenth century. It is a satirical attack on human pride, arrogance and vanity; it intensely welds rhythms and patterns in human life to those in nature. For the Kabir poets, the human world as a whole is contained inside the natural world, which, in turn, is contained inside the domain of Māyā. Here, as elsewhere in the Kabir texts, Māyā is a personification in the feminine gender of the illusory nature of the universe created by God; see the poems entitled 'Māyā', 'Deadly Business' and 'The Mystery of Māyā' below.

The Kabir text consistently thinks in terms of *lunar* months (exactly four weeks each); human gestation normally lasts for a period of forty weeks, which equals nine months on a solar calendar but ten months on a lunar calendar. Hence, the 'ten months' in the womb. 'Swan' translates *haṃsa*, which refers equally to swan and goose; *haṃsa* is an Upanishadic, yogic and sufi symbol for the individual soul, *ātmā* or true self. The symbolism of a bird as a personification of the Self or soul appears early in Indo-European texts, such as the Upanishads (starting circa 800 B.C.). It becomes a part of a full-fledged sufi allegory in Fariduddin Attar's *Conference of Birds* in Persian (late twelfth and early thirteenth centuries); in the great mélange of Indian and Persian thought in north India after about 1100, the *ātmā*'s 'progress' towards mukti (a Hindu conception) comes to be identified with a bird's protracted 'journey' or multi-stage flight towards God (now also a sufi conception). The symbol of the *haṃsa*, which I translate as a swan rather than a goose for its many resonances across Indo-European literatures and mythologies, appears in a number of Kabir poems, including 'Fable', 'Parting' and 'Swan' below.

8. Poverty

TEXT: *Ādi Granth*, Rāga Soraṭhī, shabad 11; reproduced in Callewaert 1996, 1:656. VARIANTS: *Kabīr Granthāvalī*, Tivari 1961, 2:27, añga 5, pada 47 (set to Rāga Bhairava); *Bījak*, Shukdev Singh 1972, 146, shabda 108 (which contains only a few echoes of the Sikh text). See Callewaert 2000, 620, pada 566. TRANSLATIONS: Hess and Singh 1983, 77–78; Dass 1991, 161–62; Vaudeville 1993, 268.

In a shift that is surprising for the Kabir corpus as well as the *Ādi Granth*, this shabad adopts a mode of address and discourse typical of saguṇī bhakti, specifically Vaishṇava poetry. Here the speaker directly addresses God as Mādhav, 'the sweet one', an incarnate form of Vishṇu in the Krishṇa literary tradition. The poem is an expression of complete self-abjection, and therefore in the genre of a 'confession', not dissimilar to confessional lyrics in many other religious traditions; roughly contemporaneous parallels in English would include several of John Donne's later sonnets, written in the 1610s. This shabad perfectly defines the bhakti poetics of 'maximum devotion' with the most 'minimal means'; it also records the existential reality of survival in a condition of poverty in middle-period north India with great but unobtrusive precision, with its images of ground wheat, ghee, salt, cot, pillow, thin mattress, sheet, simple rosary and God's Name as the bhakta's sole source of psychological support.

9. Fable

TEXT: Goindval Pothis, Rāga Sūhī, pada 3; reproduced in Callewaert 2000, 527, pada 416. VARIANTS: *Ādi Granth* (1604), Rāga Sūhī, shabad 2 (Callewaert 1996, 1:792); Gopaladas, *Sarbañgī* (1627), añga 109, pada 39; Jaipur Ms. I (1660/1669), pada 139; *Pañchavāṇī* Ms. IV (1675), pada 340; Jaipur Ms. II (1681), pada 26; *Kabīr Granthāvalī*, Tivari 1961, 2:41, añga 8, pada 70 (set to Rāga Bhairava in last four sources); *Bījak*, Shukdev Singh 1972, 145, shabda 106. TRANSLATIONS: Hess and Singh 1983, 76–77; Dass 1991, 169–70; Vaudeville 1993, 161 and 272–73.

One of the earliest Kabir poems in written form, this pada has circulated in at least eight distinct versions since 1570–72. It can be read as a miniature allegory of 'the soul's journey'. Its generalized themes are obvious: time and youth pass quickly; human beings grow old; life is wasted easily; death is always near. But its symbolism is more unusual: the soul or *ātmā* is a young bride, whose husband is God, and who is in a state of foolish ignorance and confusion; the body is a jar of unbaked clay, which disintegrates in water, and allows the soul or self (*haṃsa* or swan) to escape; an unenlightened self, however, wastes its life, loses its chance to attain mukti, and ends up in the domain of mortality. In this compact narrative framework, bumblebees symbolize youth and desire, whereas perched cranes and scavenging crows represent imminent and recent death, respectively. The power of the poem lies in its lyricism, its brevity and suggestiveness, and its enigmatic style as well as message.

'Fable' is one of the five earliest Kabir poems I have included in this book; the other four, also from the 1570–72 notebooks prepared by Guru Amardas, are 'Departure', 'The Way', 'The Jewel' and 'Allāh-Rāma'. If these padas are the most likely to be closest to what the historical Kabir actually composed before his death around 1450, 'Fable' and 'Allāh-Rāma' in particular may be the best examples in the northern textual traditions of the poet's distinctive imagination. Like the latter poem, 'Fable' fuses Upanishadic allusions, sufi symbols and yogic images (self as bird, soul as swan and bride, desire as a bumblebee, body as a clay jar) to create a new lyrical and narrative structure that represents nirguṇa *mat* at the interface of 'Hinduism' and 'Islam'.

10. Departure

TEXT: Goindval Pothis, Rāga Sūhī, pada 4; reproduced in Callewaert 2000, 527–28, pada 417. VARIANTS: *Ādi Granth* (1604), Rāga Sūhī, shabad 3 (Callewaert 1996, 1:792–93). TRANSLATIONS: Dass 1991, 170–71.

One of the earliest Kabir poems recorded in writing; see note on 'Fable' above. This pada is unusual in the Kabir texts for its form and diction. It is noticeably uneven in tone and theme: the refrain (opening pair of lines) and the first two main verses are lyrical and use concrete terms, whereas the last two verses are didactic and employ more abstract terms. My inference is that the first half of the poem survives from an original early-sixteenth-century source; the second half was perhaps added later in the century to 'complete' a valuable fragment. Interestingly, the first main verse identifies God as a Dīvān, a title borrowed from a Muslim socio-political order; in contrast, the third main verse brings a conservative Vaishṇava didacticism into play. With reference to my discussion of textual mediation in the Introduction, 'Departure' may be a vivid instance of a text subjected to ideological containment, using the strategies of re-inscription and composition.

11. Ant

TEXT: *Ādi Granth*, Rāga Rāmakalī, shabad 12; reproduced in Callewaert 1996, 1:972 and 2000, 626–27, pada 585. VARIANTS: None. TRANSLATIONS: Dass 1991, 206–07.

An unusual poem, unique to the Sikh canon. It begins with an outright warning against the corruption of the world and the uselessness of established religion, specifically Hinduism. The shabad then expands its message: not only does the human world deceive and rob us, but the natural world too, which contains the human world, deceives us at many levels, because all is mere appearance and nothing is what it seems. The second half of the poem proceeds with two pairs of contrasts. On the one hand, it suggests that the human mind or personality is like an elephant (large, heavy and clumsy), whereas, given the rigours of mukti, it needs to be like an ant (tiny, light and deft); on the other, it suggests that the world is like granular sand, whereas God is like crystalline sugar, so that the two can mix easily and yet remain completely distinct. This shabad is especially distinguished by the subtlety with which it deals with the general blurring of boundaries between things; and the ease with which it creates the memorable fiction of God as sugar hidden in sand and the bhakta as an industrious ant picking out and savouring crystals of divine sweetness.

12. Mosque with Ten Doors

TEXT: *Ādi Granth*, Rāga Bhairava, shabad 4; reproduced in Callewaert 1996, 1:1158. VARIATIONS: Goindval Pothis (1570–72), Rāga Bhairava, pada 28; Gopaladas, *Sarbaṅgī* (1627), aṅga 55, pada 5; *Pañchavāṇī* Ms. III (1658b), pada 49; *Pañchavāṇī* Ms. IV (1675), pada 59; *Kabīr Granthāvalī*, Tivari 1961, 2:76, pada 129 (assigned to Rāga Gauḏī or Jaṅgalī Gauḏī in last four sources). See Callewaert 2000, 176–77, pada 55. TRANSLATIONS: Dass 1991, 229; Vaudeville 1993, 244–45.

The earliest version of this poem appears in the Goindval Pothis of 1570–72; I have preferred to translate the canonical version of 1604. The shabad offers an aggressive critique of orthodox Muslim practices, systematically arguing for an 'interiorization' of the 'exteriorized' rituals and institutions of Islam, parallel to the interiorization of orthodox Hindu practices that bhakti embodies. A model of the latter process appears in the twelfth-century Kannada *vachanas* of Basavaṇṇā; see Ramanujan 1973. The systematic interiorization that the Kabir poets advocate would transform a mosque into a mullāh's body, the mosque's doors into the body's orifices, Mecca into the mind, the Ka'aba into the body, God into the soul or true self, and animal sacrifice into self-sacrifice (giving up anger, error, impurity and sensory experience). The penultimate verse argues against Islam's institution of conversion: if there is only one true God and He is the God worshipped by people of different faiths, why would one need to convert from one religion to another? The final verse then mocks this irrational element in Muslim orthodoxy by claiming that it is the poet who is crazy and who, in his madness, has slipped into the *sahaj sthiti*, the simple state; see the notes on 'The Final State' above and 'The Simple State' below.

13. The Way

TEXT: Goindval Pothis, Rāga Basanta, pada 21; reproduced in Callewaert 2000, 410–11, pada 308. VARIANTS: *Ādi Granth* (1604), Rāga Basanta, shabad 3 (Callewaert 1996, 1:1194). TRANSLATIONS: Dass 1991, 242.

Perhaps this is the earliest surviving example of a Kabir *ulaṭabāṃsī*, a poem in 'upside-down speech'. The basic codes of the *ulaṭabāṃsī* genre in the middle-period north Indian literary traditions (derived indigenously from Tantric Buddhist precursors) parallel those of what E. R. Curtius once identified as 'the topos of the world upside down' in the Latin middle ages (see Curtius 1953). An *ulaṭabāṃsī* argues that the world is 'upside down' in the present, and therefore irrational and disastrous, and hence to be shunned. It presents the state of affairs in the world as full of unresolvable contradictions; it uses the tropes of paradox and hyperbole to push the illogic of the world to extremes. The working assumption here is that the audience will reflect on the paradoxes in the poem, and so arrive at a true understanding of the nature of human existence and the universe; or that the poem's strategy of dramatic defamiliarization and its aporias will induce enlightenment in the audience's minds. This is likely to happen because an *ulaṭabāṃsī* poses an intriguing puzzle, riddle or mystery before a reader or listener, provoking him or her into searching for a solution, and thereby launching him or her into a process of enlightening self-discovery.

'The Way' is not a polished poem; its beginning and overall organization make it less satisfactory than later *ulaṭabāṃsīs* in the Kabir tradition, such as 'Rāma's Essence' and 'Creation' below. But it defines the basic paradigm of the genre by offering two complementary types of riddles for the reader to solve: a moral riddle, as in the first two quatrains here (which touch upon the extremes of incest and an absurd reversal of generations); and a conceptual riddle, as in the next three quatrains here (which depict impossibly contradictory actions or events). For both types of riddles, an *ulaṭabāṃsī* like this one usually offers a 'theological' solution: God's ways are inexplicable, and only He can lead us to an understanding of such radical disorder.

Besides the two other poems mentioned above, also see 'Debate' and 'Māyā' below. On *ulaṭabāṃsī* poems and related topics, see the commentaries in Ramanujan 1973; Vaudeville 1974; and Hess and Singh 1983.

14. Purity

TEXT: *Ādi Granth*, Rāga Basanta Hiṇḍolā, shabad 7; reproduced in Callewaert 1996, 1:1195. VARIANTS: Goindval Pothis(1570–72), Rāga Basanta, pada

20; Gopaladas, *Sarbañgī* (1627), añga 45, pada 7; *Pañchavāṇī* Ms. IV (1675), pada 248; *Kabīr Granthāvalī*, Tivari 1961, 2:111–12, añga 16, pada 192 (set to Rāga Āsāvarī in last three sources). See Callewaert 2000, 409–10, pada 307. TRANSLATIONS: Dass 1991, 245–46.

Based on an early version in the Goindval Pothis of 1570–72, this poem launches a vital assault on conservative Hindu conceptions of 'purity' and 'pollution'. The poem begins with a provocative question, 'What place is pure?' It then proceeds to answer with an exhaustive list of everyday locations that are demonstrably 'impure', or just cannot be demonstrated to be 'pure'. In effect, the poem rejects all conventional Hindu arguments about physical, material or ritual purity and impurity; in opposition, it proposes the 'mind' or 'thought' as the only true locus of purity, so that all 'exterior' sites are necessarily impure and true purity is only 'interior'. This is a key text in the *Ādi Granth* for the Sikh rejection of Hindu canons of purity and pollution, and in the Kabir tradition as a whole for the dismantling of Hindu orthodoxy.

15. Greed

TEXT: *Ādi Granth*, Rāga Basanta, shabad 1; reproduced in Callewaert 1996, 1:1196 and 2000, 628, pada 590. VARIANTS: None. TRANSLATIONS: Dass 1991, 247.

A poem unique to the *Ādi Granth*, and distinctive because it focuses on a single, specific moral failing: greed. In Hinduism as well as Sikhism, greed is treated as a significant moral defect; although neither religion has such categories as 'vice' or 'sin', their injunctions against greed (in narrative as well as poetic forms) are quite extensive, though perhaps not as severe as in Roman Catholicism. This poem criticises greed for food, or gluttony, because it encroaches on the property of others, invites retaliation, and is potentially uncontrollable. Greed, gluttony and avariciousness, in this perspective, perturb fundamental social relations, causing conflicts and even engendering violence, and hence must be disciplined.

16. The Jewel

TEXT: Goindval Pothis, Rāga Prabhātī, pada 7; reproduced in Callewaert 2000, 397, pada 289. VARIANTS: *Ādi Granth* (1604), Rāga Bibhāsa Prabhātī, shabad 1 (Callewaert 1996, 1:1349). TRANSLATIONS: Dass 1991, 251.

One of the earliest Kabir poems represented in this book, 'The Jewel' draws heavily on sufi imagery and symbolism. The central sufi elements in the pada revolve around two images: one of the lamp, which places light in proximity to God, enlightenment and divine love; and the other of God as a gem or jewel. These sufi symbols are mixed in with several specifically Hindu concepts: thought and meditation as 'roaming'; 'commingling' with reality or the truth; an accumulation of 'wrongs' 'abating'; the heart 'immersed' in the Creator. Like 'Fable' above and 'Allāh-Rāma' below, 'The Jewel' is a textual site for the fusion or hybridization of religions, theologies and cultures. Since it mainly mixes elements associated with Islam and Hinduism, it represents a happy inter-texture of mutually embattled ways of life. This poem is an instance of the 'theological secularism' discussed in the Introduction.

17. Allāh-Rāma

TEXT: Goindval Pothis, Rāga Prabhātī, pada 8; reproduced in Callewaert 2000, 386–89, pada 280. VARIANTS: *Ādi Granth* (1604), Rāga Bibhāsa Prabhātī, shabad 2 (Callewaert 1996, 1: 1349); *Pañchavāṇī* Ms. I (1614), pada 223 (Rāga Āsāvarī); Rajjabadas, *Sarbañgī* (1620), añga 76, pada 11 (Rāga Soraṭhī); Gopaladas, *Sarbañgī* (1627), añga 54, pada 4 (Rāga Āsāvarī); *Pañchavāṇī* Ms. III (1658b), pada 193 (Rāga Āsāvarī); *Pañchavāṇī* Ms. IV (1675), pada 169 (Rāga Rāmakalī); *Kabīr Granthāvalī*, Tivari 1961, 2:103–04, añga 16, pada 177 (Rāga Āsāvarī); *Bījak*, Shukdev Singh 1972, 143, shabda 97. Also see 'Allāh-and-Rāma' below. TRANSLATIONS: Hess and Singh 1983, 73–74; Dass 1991, 251–52; Vaudeville 1993, 217–18.

One of the earliest Kabir poems in the written traditions, 'Allāh-Rāma' (along with 'Debate' and 'Holiness and Hell' below) is also among the most widely disseminated since 1570–72. The poem has ten principal versions spread over the three main textual lines as well as the musical and oral traditions. It is also musically varied, being assigned to at least five distinct ragas: Prabhātī, Bibhāsa Prabhātī, Āsāvarī, Soraṭhi and Rāmakalī. 'Allāh-Rāma' is an influential poem in the Kabir tradition, and is one of the defining moments in the formation of 'Kabir' as a voice, an angle of vision and a discourse.

The poem opens by compounding 'Allāh' and 'Rāma' into a single name, and addressing that compound God directly as a unified divinity. Like 'Mosque with Ten Doors' and 'Purity' above, this pada attacks the 'externalized' rituals and institutions of both Hinduism and Islam. Its main strategy is to question the reasonableness of central Hindu and Muslim beliefs as well as practices; to point to the unacceptable contradictions within the two religions; to highlight the pretension and hypocrisy embedded in their actual practices; and to expose the absurdity of their practices in relation to their professed principles. The poem then rejects the actuality of Hinduism and Islam by proposing an alternative to both, which claims that God 'exists' in the human heart or Self; that all human beings therefore are 'forms' of God; that any human is hence God's 'child'; that we should therefore seek shelter with that one and only true God; and that we should repeat His divine Name as the sole mantra of mukti. Like 'The Jewel' above, 'Allāh-Rāma' is an instance of the 'theological secularism' characteristic of the Kabir poets.

II. 'I've Painted My Body Red': Poems from the Western Texts

18. Wedding

TEXT: *Kabīr Granthāvalī*, Tivari 1961, 2:5–6, añga 2, pada 5 (Rāga Gauḏī). VARIANTS: *Ādi Granth* (1604), Rāga Āsā, shabad 24 (Callewaert 1996, 1: 482); *Pañchavāṇī* Ms. I (1614), pada 1; *Pañchavāṇī* Ms. III (1658b), pada 1; Jaipur Ms. I (1660/1669), pada 1; *Pañchavāṇī* Ms. IV (1675), pada 1; Jaipur Ms. II (1681), pada 86 (placed under Rāga Gauḏī in the last five sources). See Callewaert 2000, 115–16, pada 1. TRANSLATIONS: Dass 1991, 141; Vaudeville 1993, 276–77.

In the course of the seventeenth century, this emerged as a 'defining' pada for the evolving body of Kabir poems in the Rajasthani or western manuscript-line, appearing as the inaugural poem in several major *pañchavāṇī*-style collections. It defines an influential paradigm for 'erotic bhakti' in north Indian nirguṇa poetry, linking this tradition directly to that in saguṇa Vaishṇava literature (especially the poetry attributed to Mirabai [mid-sixteenth century]). More generally and sometimes indirectly, this paradigm is connected to: (*a*) erotic poetry in the sufi tradition; (*b*) erotic poetry associated with women 'saints' in northern as well as southern India, such as Lalla in Kashmiri and Mahadeviyyakka in Kannada (both around the thirteenth century); (*c*) erotic poetry in the Vaishṇava tradition centred around the Braj region after the sixteenth century, which allegorizes Krishṇa as a divine male lover and his human devotees as his female companions; and (*d*) further away, in seventeenth-century Telugu by Kshetrayya and others, erotic poetry in which the male bhakta plays a female courtesan or prostitute, and God appears as a male sexual customer.

In 'Wedding', the human soul or Self is personified as a girl or young woman of marriageable age who, at the moment of enlightenment, becomes or offers to serve as God's bride; the bhakta's Self is thus allegorically 'wedded' to God, who is represented as an 'immortal bridegroom'; and the bhakta's symbolic 'wedding' to God becomes an initiatory ritual into a 'lifelong marriage' that virtually guarantees mukti in this lifetime. The operative contrast here is between a sacred marriage to a deathless, divine 'spouse', and a mundane or profane marriage to a flawed and mortal human husband. The pada elaborates this structure with two ancillary images that stand out in the context of nirguṇa poetry: the bhakta is painted in God's colours, or is drenched in love's festive hues; and he (transformed across gender boundaries into a symbolic 'woman') is giddy with youth and desire, and thus immersed in euphoric or ecstatic devotion. Such images make 'Wedding' a strikingly new type of poem in sixteenth- and seventeenth-century north India because they stress their origins in sufi theory, practice and discourse.

'Wedding' and other poems in the Kabir corpus that employ codes of 'intoxicated' mysticism, especially those that construct an erotic bond between the human and the divine, have many parallels in Christian mystical literature of the late medieval and early Renaissance periods.

19. Fever

TEXT: *Kabīr Granthāvalī*, Tivari 1961, 2:7, aṅga 2, pada 9 (Rāga Gauḏī). VARIANTS: *Ādi Granth* (1604), Rāga Gauḏī, shabad 2 (Callewaert 1996, 1:323–24); *Pañchavāṇī* Ms. I (1614), pada 96; Gopaladas, *Sarbaṅgī* (1627), aṅga 125, pada 35; *Pañchavāṇī* Ms. III (1658b), pada 96; *Pañchavāṇī* Ms. IV (1675), pada 104 (classified under Rāga Gauḏī or Jaṅgalī Gauḏī in the last four sources). See Callewaert 2000, 239–40, pada 123. TRANSLATIONS: Dass 1991, 41–42; Vaudeville 1993, 270–71 and 280. The significant differences between the Sikh and Rajasthani versions are reflected in Vaudeville's translations.

This pada appears, in a different form, early in the *Ādi Granth*; the Rajasthani versions, appearing in *pañchavāṇī*- as well as *sarbaṅgī*-style collections, share a poetic structure that offers five distinct sliding metaphors for the bhakta-God relationship in its four verses. (*a*) The bhakta-God bond is that between lovers; hence, the bhakta burns in a feverish desire for God, or suffers from 'love-sickness' in God's absence. (*b*) The bond is that between creature and nature; the bhakta is therefore like a fish in an ocean; here God contains the natural universe, which, in turn, contains the bhakta. (*c*) The bond is that between domestic pet and owner or guardian; here the bhakta is like a bird in a cage; God is now a different kind of 'container', protecting the vulnerable bird from death, personified as a voracious and aggressive cat. (*d*) The bhakta-God bond is that between master and pupil. (*e*) The bond is that between child and parent. The implicit argument of the poem is that the human-divine relationship is multifaceted, can be represented only figuratively, and needs to be characterized with a range of metaphors or tropes.

20. *The Provider*

TEXT: *Kabīr Granthāvalī*, Tivari 1961, 2:9, añga 2, pada 12 (Rāga Gauḏī). VARIANTS: *Ādi Granth* (1604), Rāga Gujarī, shabad 2; *Pañchavāṇī* Ms. I (1614), pada 22; Gopaladas, *Sarbañgī* (1627), añga 92, pada 10; *Pañchavāṇī* Ms. III (1658b), pada 100; Jaipur Ms. I (1660/1669), pada 32; *Pañchavāṇī* Ms. IV (1975), pada 25; Jaipur Ms. II (1681), pada 97. Gopaladas places this pada under Rāga Bilāvala; the other five texts set it to Rāga Gauḏī. See Callewaert 2000, 145–46, pada 123. TRANSLATIONS: Hawley and Juergensmeyer 1988, 53; Dass 1991, 152–53; Vaudeville 1993, 209–10.

One of the more widely disseminated poems in the northern and western texts, 'The Provider' is a quasi-minimalist pada that presents us with the bare facts about Kabir's bhakti and his domestic and occupational existence. In this compressed dramatic lyric, the poet's mother despairs about his impractical devotion to God, and frets about the survival of the dependents in his household. Kabir himself intervenes, only to deepen her anxieties, but then also to lighten them: though his mother sees him (on the outside) as totally immersed in bhakti, his devotion (on the inside) is still very fragile and inadequate; in fact, the poet is totally at God's mercy, because he has nothing else to offer; but it is precisely God's mercy that provides an absolute guaranty of survival, for by definition He is 'the provider of the world'.

21. *Debate*

TEXT: *Kabīr Granthāvalī*, Tivari 1961, 2:17, añga 4, pada 27 (Rāga Gauḏī). VARIANTS: *Ādi Granth* (1604), Rāga Gauḏī, shabad 42 (Callewaert 1996, 1: 331); *Pañchavāṇī* Ms. I (1614), pada 25; Rajjabadas, *Sarbañgī* (1620), añga 97, pada 5; Gopaladas, *Sarbañgī* (1627), añga 17, pada 32; *Pañchavāṇī* Ms. III (1658b), pada 23; Jaipur Ms. I (1660/1669), pada 36; *Pañchavāṇī* Ms. IV

(1675), pada 30; Jaipur Ms. II (1681), pada 101; *Bījak*, Shukdev Singh 1972, 147, shabda 112. All the Rajasthani texts classify this pada under Rāga Gauḏī. See Callewaert 2000, 147–48, pada 30. TRANSLATIONS: Hess and Singh 1983, 78; Dass 1991, 67; Vaudeville 1993, 264–65.

An early poem like 'Allāh-Rāma' and 'Holiness and Hell', 'Debate' is among the most widespread Kabir poems in the written mode, with ten versions placing it in equally central roles in the northern, western and eastern manuscript-lines. Paradigmatically, it poses a series of fundamental conceptual puzzles, each of which highlights an unresolvable dilemma in Hindu or Muslim theology and ritual practice. It articulates each dilemma as a question without an answer, challenging the audience to think afresh and hence to arrive at a moment of illumination. The irrepressible irony of the poem is that it addresses its questions directly to God, thus preventing them from degenerating into merely rhetorical questions. The successive riddles in the poem alternate between two basic structures: (*a*) which is greater, an effect or a cause? and (*b*) which is greater, a knowing subject or an object of knowledge?

22. Mother and Son

TEXT: *Kabīr Granthāvalī*, Tivari 1961, 2:22, aṅga 5, pada 37 (Rāga Gauḏī). VARIANTS: *Ādi Granth* (1604), Rāga Āsā, shabad 12 (Callewaert 1996, 1:478); *Pañchavāṇī* Ms. I (1614), pada 95; Rajjabadas, *Sarbaṅgī* (1620), aṅga 39, pada 11; Gopaladas, *Sarbaṅgī* (1627), aṅga 78, pada 82; *Pañchavāṇī* Ms. III (1658b), pada 89; Jaipur Ms. I (1660/1669), pada 72; *Pañchavāṇī* Ms. IV (1675), pada 103; Jaipur Ms. II (1681), pada 143. Rajjabadas and Gopaladas place this pada under Rāga Sāraṅga; the other five Rajasthani source set it to Rāga Gauḏī or Jaṅgalī Gauḏī. See Callewaert 2000, 238–39, pada 121. TRANSLATIONS: Dass 1991, 132–33; Vaudeville 1993, 269.

Like 'Wedding', 'Fever' and 'The Provider' (above), this is a relatively early poem, but it is more widespread in the northern and western texts than any of them. It is representative of bhakti poems that assign God a feminine gender, and make Him maternal rather than paternal. In nirguṇa as well as saguṇa traditions, when the parent-child relationship serves as an analogue for the divine-human bond, it is usually polarized as a *mother-son* relationship; Indian bhakti, in this context, 'reverses' the 'God-Man' relationship in Judaism, Christianity and Islam, in which the human metaphor is often that of *father and son.* When bhakti poems temporarily assign God the feminine gender and a maternal role, they usually underscore the element of 'tender love' between deity and devotee. The unusual feature of this Kabir poem is that it highlights the potential violence in the relationship, with the son (bhakta) physically abusing the mother (God). The importance of this lyric since the early seventeenth century lies precisely in its realism about love: love is not merely beatific or euphoric, it is invariably implicated in error, violence, transgression and pain; it cannot surmount the necessity of forgiveness, both in the asking and the giving; and it is inescapably embattled with its own object and the contrary elements that arise from itself. For another example of God in a transient motherly role, see the saguṇa Vaishṇava poetry of Tukaram in Marathi (Dharwadker 1995b).

23. Banaras and Magahar

TEXT: *Kabīr Granthāvalī*, Tivari 1961, 2:27, añga 4, pada 46 (Rāga Gauḏī). VARIANTS: *Ādi Granth* (1604), Rāga Gauḏī, shabad 15 (Callewaert 1996, 1: 326 and 2000, 604, pada 512); *Bījak*, Shukdev Singh 1972, 146, shabda 108 (very different from the Sikh version). TRANSLATIONS: Hess and Singh 1983, 77–78 (*Bījak* text); Hawley and Juergensmeyer 1988, 53 (*Granthāvalī* text); Dass 1991, 49–50 (*Ādi Granth* text); Vaudeville 1993, 156–57 (*Bījak* text) and 212–13 (*Granthāvalī* text).

Not widely circulated, this poem has three rather divergent versions that appear in the three main lines of sources; nevertheless, modern scholars, both Indian and Western, have quoted it frequently, primarily in the form fixed in the *Ādi Granth*. As a result, it has emerged as a paradigmatic 'autobiographical' poem, which commentators use to explicate the mutual relations among author, text, location and biography in the case of 'Kabir'. But the poem, in any of its three interdependent versions, gives us only an archetyped moral-spiritual life-history rather than a factual autobiography, with four stock elements: a regrettable but irreversible decision late in life; a squandering of past goodness; a moment of spiritual danger; and a quest for salvation in the marginal and the oppositional. Like 'Debate', this poem is addressed directly to God in a condition of confusion; it grasps at the straws of an unpredictable future and a lost past; and it attempts to undercut the disorienting differences between past and future by erasing the differences between Banaras and Magahar. The vividness and immediacy of the pada attests to its skilful artifactuality, and not to its supposed basis in biographical fact.

24. Let Me See You

TEXT: *Kabīr Granthāvalī*, Tivari 1961, 2:27, aṅga 4, pada 47 (Rāga Bhairava). VARIANTS: *Pañchavāṇī* Ms. I (1614), pada 327; Gopaladas, *Sarbaṅgī* (1627), aṅga 61, pada 10; *Pañchavāṇī* Ms. III (1658b), pada 283; Jaipur Ms. I (1660/1669), pada 127; *Pañchavāṇī* Ms. IV (1675); Jaipur Ms. II (1681), pada 16; *Bījak*, Shukdev Singh 1972, 146, shabda 108 (a partial version). All the Rajasthani variants place this pada under Rāga Bhairava. See Callewaert 2000, 536, pada 429. TRANSLATIONS: Vaudeville 1993, 156–57 (a partial rendering).

There are eight versions of this pada in the three textual traditions, so it is one of the widely circulated poems translated here. It is a poem entirely in the saguṇa style, and therefore defines a limit of the articulation of nirguṇa *mat* in the Kabir texts. It models the relationship between God and bhakta as a master-servant relationship in the human world, a trope that appears frequently in conservative Vaishṇava bhakti, from Nammāḻvār in Tamil to Surdas in Braj, Tulsidas in Avadhi, and Tukaram in Marathi. See, for example, Ramanujan 1981; Bryant 1978; Allchin 1966; Dharwadker 1995b.

25. Storm

TEXT: *Kabīr Granthāvalī*, Tivari 1961, 2:30, aṅga 5, pada 52 (Rāga Gauḏī). VARIANTS: *Ādi Granth* (1604), Rāga Gauḏī Chetī, shabad 43 (Callewaert 1996, 1:331–32); *Pañchavāṇī* Ms. I (1614), pada 173; Rajjabadas, *Sarbaṅgī* (1620), aṅga 73, pada 1; Gopaladas, *Sarbaṅgī* (1627), aṅga 7, pada 9; Jaipur Ms. I (1660/1669), pada 6; Jaipur Ms. II (1681), pada 95. The earliest Rajasthani text places this pada under Rāga Rāmakalī, whereas the other four sources classify it under Rāga Gauḏī or Mālī Gauḏī. See Callewaert 2000, 338, pada 224. TRANSLATIONS: Dass 1991, 69; Vaudeville 1993, 286.

Quite widely circulated since the early seventeenth century, but confined to the northern and western manuscripts. One of the famous 'allegorical lyrics' in the Kabir tradition, this pada equates knowledge with a storm or a hurricane, and then expands the analogy into a conceit, thus producing a miniature allegory of enlightenment. The poem's first two stanzas (in my English version) use a very specific type of metaphor, in which the vehicle is a concrete object whereas the tenor is an abstract term. (This is the type of metaphor that twentieth-century magical realists, from Gabriel García Márquez in *One Hundred Years of Solitude* and *Autumn of the Patriarch* to Salman Rushdie in *Midnight's Children* and *The Satanic Verses*, use to construct their allegorical narratives.) The final stanza, however, employs images without the concrete-abstract double structure, combining 'rain', 'storm', 'sun' and 'radiance' to bring the allegory to a beautiful and memorable close.

26. The Love of King Rāma

TEXT: *Kabīr Granthāvalī*, Tivari 1961, 2:50–51, aṅga 8, pada 86 (Rāga Soraṭhī). VARIANTS: *Ādi Granth* (1604), Rāga Soraṭhī, shabad 3 (Callewaert 1996, 1:654–55); *Pañchavāṇī* Ms. I (1614), pada 239; Gopaladas, *Sarbaṅgī* (1627), aṅga 47, pada 3; *Pañchavāṇī* Ms. III (1658b), pada 241; Jaipur Ms. II (1681), pada 165 (all in Rāga Soraṭhī). TRANSLATIONS: Dass 1991, 156–57.

This is a typical Kabir poem that attacks Hindu 'orthodoxy'. It argues that the means of attaining mukti that had become entirely conventional in Hinduism by the middle of the middle period (around 1500) cannot succeed because they are deceptive, contain contradictions, and fail to transcend the domain of mortality. Only true bhakti can help its practitioner to attain mukti, and it has to be modelled on Nāradī bhakti—devotion based on unswerving love and absolute loyalty to God, as exemplified by a seer or sage named Nārada in the ancient period, frequently identified as the 'first bhakta' in Indian history. The bhakta must be a 'true seer'; for the Kabir poets, a true seer is never a person who obeys brahminical authority, or who follows the ritual texts of Hinduism in normal society, or who renounces the everyday world to become an ascetic in the wilderness. Rather, the true seer is a devotee of 'King Rāma', who, as numerous other poems in the tradition explain, is not the epic hero of the *Rāmāyaṇa* (there a saguṇa incarnation of Vishṇu), but nirguṇa Rāma, God without predicable qualities.

27. Doer and Deed

TEXT: *Kabīr Granthāvalī*, Tivari 1961, 2:92, aṅga 12, pada 158 (Rāga Āsāvarī). VARIANTS: None. TRANSLATIONS: None.

Among the least well known poems in the tradition, this pada nevertheless is important for its particular philosophical argument. It adopts a position of *dvaita* or dualism to confront the question of whether the categories of 'agent' and 'action' are the same or different, and selects the latter option. As a result, its argument here is that an individual's Self is his or her ultimate principle of identity as an agent of action; but that the Self is essentially different in nature from the actions he or she performs in the world, as also from the fruits or consequences of those actions. The doer is thus fundamentally distinct from his or her deeds. In the realm of causality, this principle means that cause is different from effect, which, in turn, implies that parent is distinct from child, and creator is distinct from created object or creation. Consequently, an individual's 'phenomenal self' or personality in the world may be a 'slave' to his or her deeds, but his or her 'true self' is not. The dualistic argument in 'Doer and Deed' about the ontological difference between agent and action is a variation on that found, for example, in the *Bhagavad-gītā*.

The philosophical dualism of this piece is important because, in the conventional theory of karma, doer is identical to deed. This identity is the basis for the Hindu theory of purity and pollution (and hence of untouchability); the older Vedic theory of ritual sacrifice; the saguṇa theory of the avatars or incarnations of Vishṇu; and even the general theory of 'character' or *charitra*. 'Doer and Deed' breaks that identity by arguing that cause is not the same as effect, God is not identical with His so-called avatars, and therefore agent is not in the same category as action (and hence also not in the same class as the fruits of action). Also see the poem 'Warrior' below.

28. Māyā

TEXT: *Kabīr Granthāvalī*, Tivari 1961, 2:95–96, aṅga 13, pada 163 (Rāga Bihāga). VARIANTS: *Bījak*, Shukdev Singh 1972, 131, shabda 59. TRANSLATIONS: Hess and Singh 1983, 60–61; Vaudeville 1993, 253–54.

This is probably a relatively late composition in the western and eastern manuscript-lines (with no precursor in the Sikh tradition), but in the twentieth century it became popular in its musical form; in the past fifty years it has become one of the best-known Kabir songs among urban, educated audiences. Māyā is a personification (in the feminine gender) of 'universal illusion': at the level of ordinary human experience, the universe consists of nothing but a series of appearances that create the illusion that they constitute reality. God creates Māyā playfully and perhaps even perversely; the illusory nature of everything in our everyday experience of the world is part of His 'design' and 'play' as creator, sustainer and master of the universe. This poem catalogues the multiple levels of existence at which Māyā deceives human beings by simulating reality; the surprising element in the pada may be that even the saguṇa gods and their consorts are part of the pervasive illusion. The poem's simple argument is that if and when a person realizes that what he or she has been dealing with in the world is merely illusory, mere māyā, then he or she has already broken through the layer of appearances, and is ready to grasp the truth and the reality that lie beyond the illusions. Recognizing Māyā for what she is marks the beginning of 'enlightenment', and hence a crucial stage in the progress towards mukti.

29. Meditation

TEXT: *Kabīr Granthāvalī*, Tivari 1961, 2:118, ramainī 2 (*bārahapadī* ramainī). VARIANTS: *Bījak*, Shukdev Singh 1972, 106, ramainī 77 (very different from the Rajasthani version). TRANSLATIONS: Vaudeville 1993, 148.

Like 'Doer and Deed' and 'Māyā', probably a late composition, and not widely distributed in the western and eastern texts; moreover, in this case, the *Granthāvalī* and *Bījak* versions diverge markedly. The significance of this poem is that it complements 'The Final State' (the opening piece in my selection); the terms used for evoking the *sahaj sthiti* in 'The Final State' are employed in 'Meditation' to describe nirguṇa Brahman directly. The poem explicitly equates 'nirguṇa Rāma', a conception of the post-classical period in north India, with 'Brahman', the conception of godhead and ultimate reality that was formulated in the early Upanishads by about 800 B.C. Thus, 'Meditation' seems to take nirguṇa *mat*, as formulated around the seventeenth and eighteenth centuries, back to its 'theological roots' in Upanishadic philosophy (as mediated in part by Advaita Vedānta in the eighth to tenth centuries). But, very importantly, the last stanza of the poem also does the exact *opposite*: it actually absorbs and therefore 'updates' the old concept of Brahman into the late-middle-period concept of nirguṇa Rāma. In this compact but decisive lyric, nirguṇa *mat* 'trumps' the older theological and philosophical systems of thought.

30. Sapling and Seed

TEXT: *Kabīr Granthāvalī*, Tivari 1961, 2:120–21, ramainī 7 (*ashṭapadī* ramainī). VARIANTS: *Bījak*, Shukdev Singh 1972, 62, ramainī 35. TRANSLATIONS: Hess and Singh 1983, 85–86.

Another little-known poem that mounts a direct attack on brahmins and their 'orthodox' practices. Its specific targets are the Vedas and Vedic learning, and the hypocrisy involved in the latter; the theory of karma, which provides the ideological foundation of the caste system; and the institution of *varṇāśrama* dharma, the ideology of the 'natural' division of society into *varṇas* (caste-groups, large 'classes' of actual castes or jātīs) and the prescriptive code of conduct for a series of *āśramas* or four main 'stages of life' within the order of *varṇas*. The poem also attacks the notions that Vedic formulas (such as the *gāyatrī* mantra, the most famous of the ancient formulas) are sufficient means to attain mukti; and that 'pollution' among the castes is real and can be reversed by 'ritual purification'. Like many other poems in this volume, 'Sapling and Seed' demonstrates that each of its targets involves hypocrisy and self-contradiction; and it offers an 'anti-originary' argument to 'deconstruct' the ideological scaffolding of orthodox Hinduism. Thus, the key point is that 'the sapling' (the effect, consequence or product of any process) is not and cannot be contained, controlled or regulated by 'the seed' (source, cause or origin) from which it emerges. To be what it is, to become what it needs to become, the sapling must discard the seed out of which it has grown, allowing its progenitor to wither, rot away, fall off, disintegrate. Interestingly, 'Sapling and Seed' overtly rejects the classical Hindu notion of *mokśa* (the direct precursor of the bhakti notion of mukti), and advocates the Buddhist concept of nirvana (a total 'snuffing out' of the [non-existent] 'self') and the Natha yogic ideal of 'eternal bodilessness' or 'disembodied immortality' as the true alternatives.

31. Moth

TEXT: *Kabīr Granthāvalī*, Tivari 1961, 2:126, ramainī 15 (*baḍī ashṭapadī* ramainī). VARIANTS: *Bījak*, Shukdev Singh 1972, 88, ramainī 23. TRANSLATIONS: Hess and Singh 1983, 82; Vaudeville 1993, 150.

'Moth' is little known, but it is one of the most original poems in the Kabir tradition. It offers a 'direct treatment' of its themes, almost along the lines advocated by Ezra Pound and the Imagist poets of the early twentieth century. Its main framework consists of a series of familiar binary oppositions—joy and sorrow, truth and falsehood, youth and age, life and death. But against that frame, it develops a series of surprising and surprisingly intricate images: the mind as a crazed and amnesiac elephant; the moth that plunges suicidally into the flame of a lamp (a typical sufi motif); and the abstract 'process' that is 'always in motion'. The second main verse is especially exceptional: it proposes a parallel between the 'unity' with which the moth's wing burns in the fire of the lamp, and the 'unity' with which air and flame come together in the process of combustion. The final verse is also masterly; the poem concludes with direct general statements that, in the hands of lesser poets, would have deteriorated into sentimental clichés. The miraculous poetic balance here is between the intricacy of the multilayered metaphors in the first two verses (centred around the elephant and the moth), and the unembellished statements in the rest of the poem.

32. Deadly Business

TEXT: *Pañchavāṇī* Ms. IV (1675), pada 72 (Rāga Gauḏī). VARIANTS: Rajjabadas, *Sarbañgī* (1620), añga 118, pada 3; Gopaladas, *Sarbañgī* (1627), añga 85, pada 2; *Pañchavāṇī* Ms. III (1658b), pada 69; Jaipur Ms. II (1681), pada 124. All four sources place the poem under Rāga Gauḏī or Jañgalī Gauḏī. TRANSLATIONS: None.

A poem that belongs exclusively to the Rajasthani tradition, and has been in circulation since the early seventeenth century; one of the two or three clearly Niranjani padas represented in this book, but not included in the three dominant sources (the *Ādi Granth*, the modern *Granthāvalī*, and the *Bījak*). Like other Niranjani poems, 'Deadly Business' presents a starkly theological and philosophical argument in a catalogue or list form, with little or no poetic embellishment. For two important poems on the same theme but with different approaches, see 'Māyā' above and 'The Mystery of Māyā' below.

III. 'The Ganga Drains the Ocean': Poems from the Eastern Texts

33. Warrior

TEXT: *Bījak*, Shukdev Singh 1972, 108, ramainī 83. VARIANTS: None. TRANSLATIONS: None.

Like 'Doer and Deed' above, 'Warrior' dismantles the conventional Hindu logic of karma, but it does so by using more obscure concepts from the Tantric and Natha yogic traditions, in which the process of controlling the mind (*manas* in Sanskrit, *man* in Hindi) is sometimes called the process of 'killing the mind', and the yogi's final victory over this 'enemy' coincides with his attainment of the *sahaj sthiti*, the final simple state. The ramainī therefore personifies the bhakta's *ātmā* or true self as a warrior who has to kill the mind in order to achieve mukti. What transforms this Tantric-yogic topos into a bhakti poem is the final verse, which insists that the 'love' at the heart of the enterprise is linked indissolubly to nirguṇa Rāma, the only ultimate object of disciplined devotion.

34. Rāma's Essence

TEXT: *Bījak*, Shastri 1989, 370–78, shabda 2. VARIANTS: *Pañchavāṇī* Ms. I (1614), pada 138; Rajjabadas, *Sarbaṅgī* (1620), aṅga 72, pada 67; *Pañchavāṇī* Ms. III (1658b), pada 154; *Pañchavāṇī* Ms. IV (1675), pada 157; *Kabīr Granthāvalī*, Tivari 1961, 2: 72, aṅga 11, pada 122 (all in Rāga Rāmakalī). See Callewaert 2000, 293–95, pada 185. TRANSLATIONS: Hess and Singh 1983, 41 (which uses the Shukdev Singh 1972 version of the shabda).

'Rāma's Essence', distributed quite widely among the major manuscript-lines since the early seventeenth century, is a major instance of the *ulaṭabāṃsī* form in the Kabir tradition. For an early example, and a discussion of the form, see 'The Way' above; also see 'Creation' below. 'Rāma's Essence' proceeds with a specific two-part logic: seek enlightenment, because it leads to a transcendence of death and hence to mukti; and, to reach enlightenment, resolve the paradoxes that beset the rhythms and patterns of existence in the created universe. Under the ubiquitous power of Māyā, the universe is in a state of being completely 'upside down': its extreme disorder is characterized by an inversion of all the processes and phenomena we expect to encounter in it. 'Reversal' thus becomes the dominant trope that shapes this shabda as it enumerates a large number of paradoxes and internal contradictions in the human and natural worlds and the larger cosmos that contain us. Interestingly, the explicit goal (for which enlightenment is the means) that 'Rāma's Essence' sets before the audience is the attainment of 'immortality', a characteristically yogic (rather than bhakti) objective. This may be explained by the fact that the version of the poem I have translated here is from the *Bījak*, which often represents a division within the Kabir tradition that valorizes yogic asceticism over householder *upāsanā* and bhakti.

35. The Simple State

TEXT: *Bījak*, Shukdev Singh 1972, 111, shabda 4. VARIANTS: None. TRANSLATIONS: Hess and Singh 1983, 42–43.

Like 'Warrior' above, this shabda is unique to the eastern tradition and the *Bījak*, and probably emerges quite late (in the nineteenth century) in the

Kabir corpus. 'The Simple State' is a masterful and comprehensive satire, which mocks pious brahmins, Hindu ritualists and idol-worshippers, Muslim scholars and teachers, yogis, pilgrims, itinerant sādhus and fakirs, and an assortment of other spiritual practitioners in middle-period and early modern India. The poem deploys a classic topos of satire: am I crazy, as the world claims, or is the world actually the crazy one? In answer, the shabda carefully catalogues the principal forms of irrationality evident in the 'religious' culture all around it, which are reflections of the underlying fact that the world is completely 'upside down'. The world's disorder manifests itself in its contradictions and absurdities, its hypocrisy and fraudulence, its vanity and greed and its hatred and violence: all the practitioners we actually find around us perpetrate 'mere complexities' (in W. B. Yeats' sense of the phrase) in the name of religion and salvation that directly contradict the simplicity, spontaneity, naturalness and easy accessibility of the *sahaj sthiti*, which is the one true goal of all spiritual striving. The rest is all 'vanity', virtually in the Biblical sense of the word.

36. The Ten Avatars

TEXT: *Bījak*, Shastri 1989, 402–12, shabda 8. VARIANTS: None. TRANSLATIONS: Hess and Singh 1983, 45–46 (based on the text in Shukdev Singh 1972).

This long pada is unique to the *Bījak* tradition, and is probably an early modern composition. It thoroughly anatomizes the ideology of avatars in Vaishṇava mythology, with the argument that the saguṇa incarnations of Vishṇu cannot possibly be manifestations of godhead. This poem is designed to clinch the nirguṇa position that the true creator, sustainer, guardian and master of the universe is not part of the traffic of Māyā; is strictly non-violent; is deeply compassionate towards His creatures; is neither indiscriminate nor unjustly discriminating; is detached from all wars and contests, with no interest in victory or defeat; and is gracious to all. The ten avatars that Vaishṇavas promulgate constitute a 'masterful illusion', and are part of the mystifying and mystified ebb and flow of 'life' within the limits of Creation.

The incarnations of Vishṇu to which the poem refers, in their canonical order, are: Matsya (fish), Kashyapa (tortoise), Varāha (boar), Narasiṃha (man-lion), Vāmana (dwarf), Parashurāma, Rāma, Krishṇa, the Buddha, and Kalki. In this set, the first four involve an animal form, alone or in combination with a human form; the fifth is a 'reduced' human form; the next four are fully realized human forms; and the last is an unmanifest future form. These ten avatars are the most important of a larger set of twenty-four avatars in Vishṇu's mythology; the other fourteen are: Brahmā, Nārada, Naranārāyaṇa, Kapila, Dattātreya, Yajñya, Rishabha, Prithu, Dhanvantari, Mohinī, Vedavyāsa, Balarāma, Haṃsa and Hayagrīva. The Vaishṇava verbal and performative arts celebrate the ten main avatars of Vishṇu in a form called the *dashāvatār*, 'the ten incarnations'. This pada adopts that poetic form but turns it 'upside down' by using it to 'deconstruct' the avatars.

37. Parting

TEXT: *Bījak*, Shukdev Singh 1972, 123, shabda 33. VARIANTS: None. TRANSLATION: Hess and Singh 1983, 52.

Like 'Fable' above and 'Swan' below, this pada uses the symbolism of the *haṃsa* or swan to dramatize the 'journey of the soul' in a highly lyrical form. The unusual reasoning in this poem is as follows. The poem's speaker represents the everyday, epiphenomenal human self; he addresses the *haṃsa* or true self as a distinct entity, thus splitting the *jīvātmā* or living creature into two 'selves', one mortal and the other immortal. In the course of a lifetime, the two together have inhabited the world of sensory experience, pleasure and pain, or Māyā, as symbolized by the lake in the poem. The epiphenomenal or perishable self knows already that, at the moment of death, the immortal *haṃsa* will part from it and proceed on its own journey towards God and mukti. For the mortal self, that parting from its 'better half' promises to be a painful and sorrowful one, with no hope of being attached to the *haṃsa* again. The mortal self's sorrow at its imminent parting with the swan is multifold: it understands that it, as such, faces extinction; it comprehends that the *haṃsa* with which it has been paired so far is now ready for mukti or liberation; and it grasps the impossibility of finding a means of survival for itself. The speaker's grief in the poem is thus the grief of the most human part of himself in the face of the absoluteness of mortality.

38. A City Ablaze

TEXT: *Bījak*, Shastri 1989, 622–25, shabda 58. VARIANTS: None. TRANSLATIONS: Hess and Singh 1983, 60 (based on the text in Shukdev Singh 1972).

Taken in its entirety, one of the most obscure and intriguing poems in the *Bījak* and the Kabir tradition. The difficulty lies in its poetic argument as well as its esoteric symbolism; Kabir Panthi interpreters therefore allegorize it using specialized codes. A 'commonsensical' interpretation might run as follows. At the beginning of the poem, the fire represents a conflagration in the domain of sensory experience; the senses are 'inflammatory', and their fire consumes the nine bodily orifices ('nine women') at which human individuals experience much of their sensory interaction with the physical-material world. The body itself is a 'city with nine gates', and its 'guard' is the *antahkaraṇa*, literally 'the inner agent of action', the mind or everyday self that controls its sensory capacities and motor organs, and hence its basic actions in the world. The 'hunchback' who 'clings / around one's neck' is the warped intellect that tries to solve problems merely by thinking or reasoning through them; it fails to find a way to put out the fire of the senses that consumes the body, and the body itself remains deeply unsatisfied. 'Woman' in general is Māyā, universal illusion that deceives human subjects. From the point of view of a true bhakta, however, only fools and liars fall into the trap of Māyā or Woman; his task is to resist being consumed by the senses and being deceived by illusory effects, and to state the truth as he perceives it. God Himself rejects the world governed by Māyā, and the bhakta must do likewise. In the final analysis, this is a remarkable but unapologetically misogynistic poem; its misogyny derives, for the most part, from the Kabir Panth's valorization of a male order of devotees (sādhus, *avadhūts*, and yogis), largely to the exclusion of women.

39. Holiness and Hell

TEXT: *Bījak*, Shastri 1989, 675–78, shabda 75. VARIANTS: *Pañchavāṇī* Ms. I (1614), pada 57; Rajjabadas, *Sarbañgī* (1620), añga 77, pada 4; Gopaladas, *Sarbañgī* (1627), añga 53, pada 15; *Pañchavāṇī* Ms. III (1658b), pada 45; Jaipur Ms. I (1660/1669), pada 44; *Pañchavāṇī* Ms. IV (1675), pada 55; Jaipur Ms. II (1681), pada 112; *Kabīr Granthāvalī*, Tivari 1961, 2:105–06, añga 16, pada 181. TRANSLATIONS: Hess and Singh 1983, 67 (based on Shukdev Singh 1972); Vaudeville 1993, 216–17.

With 'Allāh-Rāma' and 'Debate', this is the most widely distributed of the poems included in my selection. In this pada, the Kabir poets bluntly attack Hindu orthodoxy, with a sideways thrust at Islam. The illusion mentioned in the opening verse is the false belief among Hindus (and Muslims) that, somehow, the Vedas are fundamentally different from the Qur'ān; that 'heaven' is not the same as 'hell'; and that 'male' and 'female' are essentially distinct categories. The poem implies that such a belief is false because there are no true differences separating these so-called opposites. Another erroneous belief is that the body can be used merely as a means to an end; this belief arises from a confusion between cause and effect: in reality, the body is not a cause but an effect, and therefore cannot serve as a 'cause' leading to some further end. Moreover, all created things come from a common source or origin; so there cannot be any 'real' differences among them. The distinctions that arise among things in society are merely of social origin, and therefore false; as a consequence, there can be no essential difference between a brahmin and a shūdra, or one caste and another. (The poem, in effect, argues that our fundamental categories and binary oppositions are all social or ideological 'constructions'.) Finally, the three main gods of Hinduism—Brahmā, Shiva, and Vishṇu—are all saguṇa gods, deities distinguished by their specific attributes. But such qualities are 'man-made', as are all religious differences: so there can be no true differences between Hindus and Muslims, or one god and another. The only possibility then is to immerse oneself in nirguṇa Rāma, the God without qualities, who is the sole source of everything in the universe.

IV. 'Neither Line Nor Form': A Selection of Aphorisms

Shaloks from the Ādi Granth

40. Aphorism 1

TEXT: *Ādi Granth*, shalok 2 (Callewaert 1996, 1:1364). VARIANTS: None. TRANSLATIONS: Vaudeville 1974, 314 and 1993, 297.

This is a much-cited aphorism, in which the poet rejects the common social mockery of the julāhās; and affirms that julāhās, too, have access to God and are devoted to Him.

41. Aphorism 2

TEXT: *Ādi Granth*, shalok 26 (Callewaert 1996, 1:1365). VARIANTS: See Vaudeville 1993, 203. TRANSLATIONS: Vaudeville 1974, 277 and 1993, 300.

This piece defines the social and spiritual mission of the true bhakta, which is to establish solidarity with those who manage to break away from the everyday world and undertake the quest for mukti.

42. Aphorism 3

TEXT: *Ādi Granth*, shalok 37 (Callewaert 1996, 1: 1366). VARIANTS: See Vaudeville 1993, 188. TRANSLATIONS: Vaudeville 1974, 232 and 1993, 301.

This aphorism strikes a universalist note by asserting a fundamental equality among all human beings, regardless of their socio-economic rank or status. The theme is virtually 'Shakespearean', especially as articulated in *King Lear*. Also see 'Holiness and Hell' above.

43. Aphorism 4

TEXT: *Ādi Granth*, shalok 58 (Callewaert 1996, 1: 1367). VARIANTS: See Vaudeville 1993, 206. TRANSLATIONS: Vaudeville 1974, 290 and 1993, 304.

This couplet uses the motif of the human mind as an elephant, too unruly to attain mukti. See the pada entitled 'Moth' above. This aphorism also stresses a theme that appears frequently in the Kabir poems: that mukti is very difficult and is attained very rarely.

44. Aphorism 5

TEXT: *Ādi Granth*, shalok 115 (Callewaert 1996, 1:1370). VARIANTS: None. TRANSLATIONS: Vaudeville 1974, 322 and 1993, 308.

This aphorism is quoted often in modern times as biographical evidence of Kabir's domestic life. The inference usually is that Kabir had a son named Kamāl, who rejected his father's spirituality and unworldliness, and became a successful and wealthy merchant.

45. Aphorism 6

TEXT: *Ādi Granth*, shalok 172 (Callewaert 1996, 1: 1373). VARIANTS: *Kabīr Granthāvalī*, Tivari 1961, 2:112, añga 21, sākhī 11; see Vaudeville 1993, 200. TRANSLATIONS: Vaudeville 1974, 266; Hawley and Juergensmeyer 1988, 60; Vaudeville 1993, 311.

The implicit idea here is that a wooden house burns down, but a stone building would not; in real life, learned people perish, whereas scoundrels always succeed in saving themselves.

46. Aphorism 7

TEXT: *Ādi Granth*, shalok 197 (Callewaert 1996, 1:1375). VARIANTS: See Vaudeville 1993, 174. TRANSLATIONS: Vaudeville 1974, 180–81 and 1993, 313.

Another frequently-quoted couplet, in which we hear God speak, and in which He indicates that He does not inhabit 'holy sites' and does not accept orthodox rituals. In fact, God Himself rejects organized religion as it has been established in the human world.

47. Aphorism 8

TEXT: *Ādi Granth*, shalok 200 (Callewaert 1996, 1: 1375). VARIANTS: See Vaudeville 1993, 200. TRANSLATIONS: Vaudeville 1974, 265 and 1993, 313.

This aphorism offers a direct statement of the principle of non-violence adopted consistently in the Kabir tradition. It also explains that God alone can exercise retributive justice ('an eye for an eye').

48. Aphorism 9

TEXT: *Ādi Granth*, shalok 229 (Callewaert 1996, 1:1376). VARIANTS: See Vaudeville 1993, 194. TRANSLATIONS: Vaudeville 1974, 253–54 and 1993, 314.

This is one of the most beautiful couplets in the Kabir tradition: a perfect miniature scene of 'the tree of life'. The image of the birds here resonates with the Upanishadic symbol of the *haṃsa* or swan as the soul or true self on a journey towards God, used often by the Kabir poets; and with the metaphor of two birds for a 'split' human self, also found in the early Upanishads.

49. Aphorism 10

TEXT: *Ādi Granth*, shalok 236 (Callewaert 1996, 1:1377). VARIANTS: None. TRANSLATIONS: Vaudeville 1974, 330 and 1993, 314.

In tone, texture and symbolism, this is a sufi-style couplet. If God is the Belovèd, and the Self and its body are both involved in the relationship with Him, the question is: which contains which, and which is contained by the others? Functioning as a riddle, the aphorism deliberately poses a metaphysical and theological conundrum. Also see 'Debate' and 'Holiness and Hell' above; and especially aphorism 22 below.

Sākhīs from the **Kabīr Granthāvalī**

50. Aphorism 11

TEXT: *Kabīr Granthāvalī*, Tivari 1961, 2:161, aṅga 6, sākhī 2. VARIANTS: None. TRANSLATIONS: Vaudeville 1974, 190 and 1993, 176.

This aphorism employs reasoning that is widespread in religious poetry in many parts of the world: everything 'mine' already belongs to God, so I cannot really give anything to God that is not already His.

51. Aphorism 12

TEXT: *Kabīr Granthāvalī*, Tivari 1961, 2:164, aṅga 8, sākhī 2. VARIANTS: None. TRANSLATIONS: Vaudeville 1974, 195 and 1993, 177.

The argument here is familiar: the world is not large enough to contain all of God's good qualities, because they are infinite in number. This aphorism offers a theological definition of infinity.

52. Aphorism 13

TEXT: *Kabīr Granthāvalī*, Tivari 1961, 2:166, aṅga 9, sākhī 1. VARIANTS: None. TRANSLATIONS: Vaudeville 1974, 199 and 1993, 178.

A sufi-style couplet, which suggests the opposite of aphorism 10 above. Here, God and human self are mutually exclusive; God becomes manifest when the self is extinguished (the sufi concept of *fana*' may underlie this suggestion). The lamp serves as a sufi trope for enlightenment and mystical understanding. The surprising feature is that the couplet applies its sufi symbolism to 'Hari', a very conventional Vaishṇava name for God.

53. Aphorism 14

TEXT: *Kabīr Granthāvalī*, Tivari 1961, 2:190, aṅga 15, sākhī 32. VARIANTS: None. TRANSLATIONS: Vaudeville 1974, 234.

An unusual piece in the Kabir corpus, with its focus on self-abasement. But it places a sincere emphasis on humility as the basis of vital human bonds: friendship and solidarity in a community.

54. Aphorism 15

TEXT: *Kabīr Granthāvalī*, Tivari 1961, 2:205, aṅga 18, sākhī 11. VARIANTS: See Hess and Singh 1983, 112–13. TRANSLATIONS: Vaudeville 1974, 257 and 1993, 195.

A couplet quoted often in the context of Kabir's biography. But its meaning remains ambiguous; it may not be literally true at all. 'East' is frequently a symbol of esoteric spiritual knowledge; so the statement may well mean that Kabir's speech is esoteric, and whoever is able to decode it qualifies as a true bhakta.

***Sākhīs from the* Bījak**

55. Aphorism 16

TEXT: *Bījak*, Shastri 1989, 1002, sākhī 29. VARIANTS: *Kabīr Granthāvalī*, Tivari 1961, 2:186, aṅga 15, sākhī 11; also see Vaudeville 1993, 186. TRANSLATIONS: Hess and Singh 1983, 92 (based on Shukdev Singh 1972).

This couplet, quite 'Socratic' in a comparative context, uses the sufi symbol of the mirror in the heart to reinforce the points that self-knowledge is the primary basis of enlightenment, and that doubt, especially self-doubt, is a major obstacle to it.

56. Aphorism 17

TEXT: *Bījak*, Shastri 1989, 1003, sākhī 31. VARIANTS: *Kabīr Granthāvalī*, Tivari 1961, 2:209, aṅga 20, sākhī 4. See also Vaudeville 1993, 197–98. TRANSLATIONS: Vaudeville 1974, 262; Hess and Singh 1983, 92–93 (based on Shukdev Singh 1972); Hawley and Juergensmeyer 1988, 61.

A critique of orthodox Hindu practice, according to which brahmins take the easy, common path (and therefore attract huge, lucrative followings), whereas Kabir takes the hard, rare and solitary path. The difficulty of Kabir's 'method' and the infrequency with which human beings actually attain mukti ('one in a million') are major themes throughout the tradition.

57. Aphorism 18

TEXT: *Bījak*, Shastri 1989, 1005, sākhī 34. VARIANTS: None. TRANSLATIONS: None.

An attack on religious hypocrisy using the metaphor of the marketplace; the 'heartless man' is a spiritual pretender or con-man, 'that country' is mukti, 'salt' represents a spiritually impoverished diet, and 'camphor' is a distracting illusion, an expensive luxury-item that promises something it cannot deliver.

58. Aphorism 19

TEXT: *Bījak*, Shastri 1989, 1008, sākhī 38. VARIANTS: None. TRANSLATIONS: Hess and Singh 1983, 93 (based on Shukdev Singh 1972 version).

The sandalwood tree is a frequent image in Kabir poems, and is associated with mukti; see aphorism 9 above, and the pada entitled 'Creation' below. The snake or serpent as a symbol of 'evil' is quite widespread in bhakti poetry; see Tukaram's 'Viṭṭhala' in Dharwadker 1995b, 101.

59. Aphorism 20

TEXT: *Bījak*, Shastri 1989, 1031, sākhī 64. VARIANTS: None. TRANSLATION: Hess and Singh 1983, 95 (using text in Shukdev Singh 1972).

This can be read 'straight' as a proverb or statement of common folk wisdom, and also more 'technically' as a symbolist aphorism in which 'truth' is knowledge of nirguṇa God and 'happiness' is mukti. It stresses an important motif in the Kabir corpus: the mutual incompatibility of truth and the created world, and of happiness and illusion (or falsehood).

60. Aphorism 21

TEXT: *Bījak*, Shastri 1989, 1032, sākhī 65. VARIANTS: None. TRANSLATIONS: None.

A didactic statement of the principles of independence of judgement; complete honesty with oneself and others; and absolute truth. 'Falsehood' obliquely refers to Māyā, the universal illusion that deceives human subjects in the absence of enlightenment.

61. Aphorism 22

TEXT: *Bījak*, Shastri 1989, 1035, sākhī 69. VARIANTS: None. TRANSLATIONS: Hess and Singh 1983, 96 (using Shukdev Singh 1972).

A perfect sufi poem in a nutshell. The 'single drop' represents the individual soul or self, whereas the 'ocean' represents God. The usual logic of salvation, familiar also in Christianity, is that the single drop mingles with the ocean, or the individual soul merges with God. The inverted mystical logic here is that mukti occurs when the ocean (God) merges into the drop (the individual soul). See the comparable sufi 'paradox' in aphorism 10 above.

62. Aphorism 23

TEXT: *Bījak*, Shastri 1989, 1045, sākhī 83. VARIANTS: None. TRANSLATIONS: Hess and Singh 1983, 98 (based on Shukdev Singh 1972).

Like aphorism 20, this can be interpreted as a straightforward, commonsensical proverb, or as a statement of nirguṇa principle; but whereas aphorism 20 has an earnest tone, this piece is witty and satirical.

63. Aphorism 24

TEXT: *Bījak*, Shastri 1989, 1054, sākhī 95. VARIANTS: None. TRANSLATIONS: Hess and Singh 1983, 100 (based on text in Shukdev Singh 1972).

This aphorism offers a remarkable ratio (in the original Latin sense of the term), in which the street-entertainer is to his performing monkey as a man is to his own mind. A merely clever person is no more than a cheap performer; the injunction in the aphorism is: do not be overly impressed with an intellect that jumps through hoops like a dancing monkey. This theme of resisting trickery, deception and money-making gambits recurs throughout the Kabir tradition, and broadens out into its theological critique of Māyā as a con-woman or trickster (see 'Māyā' above).

64. Aphorism 25

TEXT: *Bījak*, Shastri 1989, 1062, sākhī 105. VARIANTS: None. TRANSLATIONS: Hess and Singh 1983, 101 (based on Shukdev Singh 1972).

The claims that no one is naturally free of Māyā, and that the individual who has freed himself of all illusion is a rare and isolated one, are central to the Kabir position. This aphorism stresses the exceptional status of enlightenment with the help of a 'logical' witticism, the form of which is a model of its kind. (The best modern example in this form is the American poet W. S. Merwin's 'Elegy', in which the entire poem consists of the single line: 'who would I show it to'.)

65. Aphorism 26

TEXT: *Bījak*, Shastri 1989, 1070, sākhī 115. VARIANTS: *Kabīr Granthāvalī*, Tivari 1961, 2:185, aṅga 15, sākhī 5. TRANSLATIONS: Vaudeville 1974, 228–29 and 1993, 185; Hess and Singh 1983, 102 (using Shukdev Singh 1972); Hawley and Juergensmeyer 1988, 58.

An unusual twist on the theology of karma, but the variation is commonsensical in that a human individual is born only once, and therefore has only one chance to attain mūkti.

66. Aphorism 27

TEXT: *Bījak*, Shastri 1989, 1081, sākhī 129. VARIANTS: *Kabīr Granthāvalī*, Tivari 1961, 2:198, añga 16, sākhī 5. TRANSLATIONS: Vaudeville 1974, 246 and 1993, 191; Hess and Singh 1983, 104 (based on Shukdev Singh 1972).

This has the structure and texture of a proverb in the oral-folk tradition. Its theological significance lies in the fact that the grinding mill is a significant motif in bhakti poetry throughout the subcontinent.

67. Aphorism 28

TEXT: *Bījak*, Shastri 1989, 1083, sākhī 131. VARIANTS: None. TRANSLATIONS: Hess and Singh 1983, 104 (using Shukdev Singh 1972).

Poetically a superb denunciation of Vedic authority: all that the ancient canon amounts to is a mountain of rituals celebrating milk and the ghee it produces. This aphorism may be the most perfect instance of the satirical wit at the core of the Kabir corpus.

68. Aphorism 29

TEXT: *Bījak*, Shastri 1989, 1090, sākhī 139. VARIANTS: None. TRANSLATIONS: Hess and Singh 1983, 105–06 (based on text in Shukdev Singh 1972).

An aphoristic rejection of the logic of caste in Hindu society. The condensed two-part argument is that social status and rank are mere vanity; and that, without an understanding of the true nature of God, all four principal caste-groups are no better than the caste-group of untouchables they malign. The approach in this aphorism is exactly the opposite of that in 'The Bhakta's Caste' below.

69. Aphorism 30

TEXT: *Bījak*, Shastri 1989, 1120, sākhī 174. VARIANTS: *Kabīr Granthāvalī*, Tivari 1961, 2:186, añga 15, sākhī 7. TRANSLATIONS: Hess and Singh 1983, 110 (based on Shukdev Singh 1972); Hawley and Juergensmeyer 1988, 59; and Vaudeville 1993, 185–86.

The key images in this aphorism—bone, wood, hair, grass, cotton, house, fire—reappear in many other Kabir poems. On houses and conflagrations especially, see aphorism 6 and the pada entitled 'A City Ablaze' above.

70. Aphorism 31

TEXT: *Bījak*, Shastri 1989, 1132, sākhī 188. VARIANTS: None. TRANSLATIONS: Hess and Singh 1983, 112 (based on Shukdev Singh 1972).

Besides aphorism 9, perhaps the best aphorism in the Kabir tradition. In the space of two verses it gives us a remarkable typology of knowledge; a precise articulation of the self-reflexive dimension of knowledge; and a witty conception of transcendent knowledge. The Kabir poets are philosophically exact to an astonishing degree: as G. W. F. Hegel points out in the European tradition, what distinguishes human consciousness is its self-consciousness; this 'double consciousness' (which later gave W. E. B. Dubois his key term) entails that we cannot construct knowledge as such without also constructing an epistemology, or a knowledge of what knowledge is (which is the basis for 'the philosophical turn' of the human mind).

71. Aphorism 32

TEXT: *Bījak*, Shastri 1989, 1132, sākhī 189. VARIANTS: *Kabīr Granthāvalī*, Tivari 1961, 2:209, aṅga 20, sākhī 6. TRANSLATIONS: Vaudeville 1974, 262; Hess and Singh 1983, 112 (using the Shukdev Singh 1972 text).

Among the most radical in the *Bījak* and the Kabir tradition, this aphorism initially distinguishes between those who stay within prescribed limits (ordinary people) and those who do not ('saints'). But its real goal is to dismantle both limits and limitlessness, and in doing so it defines the space of what in English we might call 'the total freedom of the spirit'. Much of the deepest 'thinking' in the Kabir tradition takes place in this sphere of 'total freedom'. See aphorism 33 below.

72. Aphorism 33

TEXT: *Bījak*, Shastri 1989, 1142, [*chaupāī*] 200. VARIANTS: None. TRANSLATIONS: Hess and Singh 1983, 113 (following the version in Shukdev Singh 1972).

A radical aphorism like aphorism 32 above, this piece asserts the absoluteness of the nirguṇa bhakta's knowledge of God. Once a person has acquired such knowledge, he does not need to follow either Vedic prescriptions or worldly codes of conduct. Knowledge of God thus creates a sphere of 'total freedom' of action in the world.

73. Aphorism 34

TEXT: *Bījak*, Shastri 1989, 1149, sākhī 208. VARIANTS: None. TRANSLATIONS: Hess and Singh 1983, 114 (based on Shukdev Singh 1972).

A didactic couplet with a simple, 'folksy' touch, this piece suggests, through echoes in the concept of 'true community', that happiness lies only in the company of God.

74. Aphorism 35

TEXT: *Bījak*, Shastri 1989, 1149, sākhī 209. VARIANTS: See Vaudeville 1993, 186. TRANSLATIONS: Hess and Singh 1983, 114 (following Shukdev Singh 1972).

An 'allegorical' aphorism. On the concrete level, it formulates the principle of accumulation with reference to money and capital. On the abstract level, each 'cowrie' represents a good deed, and the accumulated capital represents one's 'stock of goodness'. The argument thus is one from the classical theory of karma, and what the *Bhagavad-gītā* calls karma-yoga: mukti can be attained only by a slow, incremental process of accumulating *puṇya*, merit or goodness.

75. Aphorism 36

TEXT: *Bījak*, Shastri 1989, 1202, sākhī 272. VARIANTS: None. TRANSLATIONS: Hess and Singh 1983, 121–22 (using Shukdev Singh 1972).

Although only a couplet, this piece effortlessly amalgamates sufism, nirguṇa *mat*, and Advaita Vedānta or Uttar Mīmāṃsā. The first verse establishes a 'commutative' equation between God as One (a version of the Qur'ānic concept of the unity of Allāh) and God as All, the origin and foundation of everything that exists in the universe. The second verse then argues, implicitly, that God is the object of true knowledge, and since God is One (even though He is also All), true knowledge can only be knowledge 'without duality'. In the epistemology of nirguṇa *mat*, true knowledge is knowledge without dualism or duality; this system of thought therefore often resembles Uttar Mīmāṃsā or Advaita Vedānta (most famously represented by the eighth-century philosopher Shankarācharya), which espouses an intricate epistemology of 'non-dualist' knowledge. The brilliance of the Kabir aphorism lies in the ease with which it compresses this nexus of ideas into a single, lucid verse.

76. *Aphorism 37*

TEXT: *Bījak*, Shastri 1989, 1149, sākhī 273. VARIANTS: *Kabīr Granthāvalī*, Tivari 1961, 2:187, anga 15, sākhī 14. TRANSLATIONS: Hess and Singh 1983, 122 (using Shukdev Singh 1972).

A proverb-like couplet, a piece of folk wisdom. The structure of this aphorism moves from a statement of general principle to an example that clinches the principle with the help of a precise, memorable image. This structure recurs frequently in the Kabir texts.

77. *Aphorism 38*

TEXT: *Bījak*, Shastri 1989, 1205, sākhī 276. VARIANTS: None. TRANSLATIONS: Hess and Singh 1983, 122 (based on Shukdev Singh 1972).

Like aphorism 37, this couplet offers commonsensical advice in the style of a proverb. Its specific concern is with the moral quality and social effect of human speech, a recurrent theme in the Kabir tradition.

78. *Aphorism 39*

TEXT: *Bījak*, Shastri 1989, 1218, sākhī 291. VARIANTS: None. TRANSLATIONS: Hess and Singh 1983, 124 (based on Shukdev Singh 1972).

This piece bluntly describes everyday life in the human world as a unilateral 'looting spree', without the 'give and take' that might enhance reciprocity, equal opportunity, sharing of resources and fair exchange. The recognition of this as the primary dynamic of worldly life is itself a function of 'waking' or enlightenment.

79. *Aphorism 40*

TEXT: *Bījak*, Shastri 1989, 1227, sākhī 301. VARIANTS: None. TRANSLATIONS: Hess and Singh 1983, 125 (using Shukdev Singh 1972).

Like aphorism 38, this couplet focuses on speech, but here the specific concern is with the destructive and potentially violent effect of harsh words.

80. Aphorism 41

TEXT: *Bījak*, Shastri 1989, 1239, sākhī 316. VARIANTS: None. TRANSLATIONS: Hess and Singh 1983, 126 (using Shukdev Singh 1972).

Proverb-like and folksy, this aphorism valorizes discrimination, the ability to distinguish right from wrong and to make good choices—a moral dimension that the *Bhagavad-gītā* (a text often in the backdrop of the Kabir poems) identifies as *viveka* and values very highly.

81. Aphorism 42

TEXT: *Bījak*, Shastri 1989, 1251, sākhī 330. VARIANTS: *Kabīr Granthāvalī*, Tivari 1961, 2:187, aṅga 15, sākhī 17. TRANSLATIONS: Hess and Singh 1983, 128 (based on Shukdev Singh 1972).

Like aphorisms 23, 38 and 40, this piece returns to speech as a theme, but this time using the quality of speech as a signifier of character and moral quality.

82. Aphorism 43

TEXT: *Bījak*, Shastri 1989, 1252, sākhī 333. VARIANTS: None. TRANSLATIONS: Hess and Singh 1983, 129 (using Shukdev Singh 1972).

'Ready-made man' refers to the stereotypical human being, who is unintelligent and morally weightless. The structure of this aphorism is the same as that of aphorism 37 above.

83. Aphorism 44

TEXT: *Bījak*, Shastri 1989, 1257, sākhī 338. VARIANTS: None. TRANSLATIONS: Hess and Singh 1983, 129 (based on the text in Shukdev Singh 1972).

Another proverb-like couplet, devoted to the folk-theme that death devours all human beings equally, regardless of their stations in life. The structure, however, is an inversion of the structure in aphorisms 37 and 43 above, because the example now precedes the statement of general principle.

84. Aphorism 45

TEXT: *Bījak*, Shastri 1989, 1266, sākhī 347. VARIANTS: None. TRANSLATIONS: Hess and Singh 1983, 130 (based on Shukdev Singh 1972).

A miniature *ulaṭabāṃsī* (see note on 'The Way' above). The riddle presents us with a wondrous image of a perfect yogi, who has transcended bodily existence as well as the force of gravitation and now floats in middle space, the 'mandala of the sky'.

85. Aphorism 46

TEXT: *Bījak*, Shastri 1989, 1271, sākhī 353. VARIANTS: None. TRANSLATIONS: Hess and Singh 1983, 131 (based on the text in Shukdev Singh 1972).

'Sākhī' is derived from *sākśī*, which in Sanskrit denotes witness or ('eye-witness') testimony; a sākhī in Hindi and other languages is thus a poem (usually an aphoristic 'couplet') of true witness and testimony. As a genre, the sākhī offers a 'true' or knowledgeable vision to an audience, but its knowledge comes from its author's actual experience and self-reflection, often with God as the object of experience and knowledge. This piece affirms the textual power of the genre: the true testimony embodied in a sākhī is capable of resolving the quarrels and conflicts that erupt in the world of everyday existence, as also in the long cycle of birth, death and rebirth in this world.

V. 'This Sheet, So Fine, So Fine': A Selection of Songs

86. Sheet

TEXT: Upadhyaya 1964, 251, *bhajan* 223. VARIANTS: Gandharva 1985, cassette 1. TRANSLATIONS: Lorenzen 1996, 208.

This pada projects God as a divine weaver, but its conception is different from that in 'The Master Weaver' above. God weaves human bodies as sheets on a loom, on which the yarn is the Sushumnā, the warp is the Iñgalā, and the weft is the Piñgalā. All three terms come from the terminology of classical yoga, where they are the names of three major *nāḍī*s or cord-like channels that are said to carry 'vital airs' through the 'subtle body'. God spins the yarn for his loom on a spinning-wheel that is an eight-petalled lotus; this refers to one of the *chakra*s or 'wheels' in the 'subtle body' in yogic physiology. The thread he produces on this wheel is made of the five elements (earth, water, fire, air and space), identified in classical yoga as the constituents of the 'subtle body'; and three great qualities (*tamas* or darkness and inertia; *rajas* or energy and momentum; and *sattva* or light and truth), identified in the *Bhagavad-gītā*, for example, as the three qualitative 'strands' out of which all existence in the universe is 'woven'. Beneath the elaborate metaphor of this poem lies the ancient Hindu conception that the individual *ātmā*, when embodied, is enclosed in a series of *kosha*s or envelopes, which constitute a *sūkshma sharīra* or 'subtle body'; and that this imperceptible body around the self, in turn, is enclosed in a *sthūla sharīra* or 'gross body', the structure of bone, blood and flesh one normally identifies as one's 'body'. In 'Sheet', God weaves all the layers of a human being's subtle and gross bodies as a flawless, diaphanous sheet, which we ought to 'wear' for life with the care and reverence due to such a beautiful thing.

87. The Flawless One

TEXT: Gopaladas, *Sarbañgī* (1627), añga 45, pada 2 (Rāga Bhairava); see Callewaert 2000, 537, pada 430. VARIANTS: Jaipur Ms. II (1681), pada 17 (also Rāga Bhairava); Gandharva 1985, cassette 2. TRANSLATIONS: None.

This early seventeenth-century song is of Niranjani origin. It characterizes Rāma not only as nirguṇa (without attributes) but also as *nirañjan* (absolutely pure, flawless). Everything that exists in the created universe is the opposite of *nirañjan* Rāma: the Vedas and their mantras, the saguṇa gods of the Hindu pantheon, Vishṇu's various avatars, speech itself, learning, knowledge and books, and the materials of sacrificial ritual are all marred by flaws. Impurity and pollution dominate the universe, destroying all that is good and right. In such circumstances, enlightenment consists of recognizing the sullied nature of everything around oneself and seeking a union with absolute purity, which alone can lead to mukti. As 'The Flawless One' implies, in this Niranjani version of the metaphysics of salvation, knowledge (*jñāna*) rather than love or devotion (bhakti) provides the basis for liberation from karma and rebirth.

88. Breath

TEXT: Dvivedi 1990, 179, pada 1. VARIANTS: None. TRANSLATIONS: Tagore 1915, 45.

This is a rare type of poem in the Kabir tradition, in which God speaks in His own voice directly to the audience; the only other example in my selection is aphorism 7 above. According to God's own account, He 'inhabits' the human self; as a consequence, we can find Him quickly and easily within ourselves, and we do not need rituals, sacred places, pilgrimages or other means to reach Him. The reference to breath in the concluding verse is important: in the early Upanishads (composed around 800 B.C.), the enduring self or *ātmā* is identical with *prāṇa*, breath. (In the less well known Upanishads, *haṃsa* is also equated with *prāṇa*.) The *ātmā* departs from the body in the last exhalation at the moment of death.

89. The Bhakta's Caste

TEXT: Dvivedi 1990, 179, pada 2. VARIANTS: None. TRANSLATIONS: Tagore 1915, 45–46.

This pada is unusual because, instead of denouncing the whole logic of caste, it embraces that rationale—but only to turn it against itself, by praising famous bhaktas for belonging to the lowest of castes and caste-groups. The argument here is that, if the caste system is good, as its proponents claim, then all its parts must be equally good, which means that even the shūdras and the untouchables must be as good as the brahmins and other upper-caste groups. The poem thus pushes the apparent self-consistency of the ideology of caste to its logical limit, and thereby forces it to revalue its outcastes. The negative implication is that, if Hindus and Muslims establish internally differentiated societies, but fail to apply their principles of differentiation consistently, their principles as well as their social orders must be debased, in which case their systems of inequality must be fundamentally wrong.

In its list of castes or groups that are members of the Hindu system, the pada mentions several important components: the 'thirty-six clans' are the clans of the epic period of ancient Indian history, from which all subsequent upper-caste groups on the subcontinent are theoretically supposed to have derived; the barbers, washermen and carpenters are shūdras; whereas the 'scavengers' are *atishūdras* or untouchables. The poem is grounded in the historical fact that, over time, many (but not all) of the famous bhaktas have come from the low castes and from untouchable groups. Also see note on aphorism 29 above.

90. Garden

TEXT: Dvivedi 1990, 181, pada 4. VARIANTS: None. TRANSLATIONS: Tagore 1915, 47.

This short, intensely lyrical poem offers a perfect amalgam of sufi and broadly Hindu conceptions. The garden and the bower in bloom are both sufi images, whereas the thousand-petalled lotus is an image from classical yoga (the *sahasrāra chakra*, where the *ātmā* unites with Brahman). In contrast, the notion that God is 'inside' oneself refers to classical Hindu as well as middle-period nirguṇa conceptions of God and Self. 'Garden' is like a perfect miniature painting of the 'interiorization' of both God and the process of attaining mukti that characterizes the work of the Kabir poets.

91. The Mystery of Māyā

TEXT: Dvivedi 1990, 181, pada 5. VARIANTS: None. TRANSLATIONS: Tagore 1915, 48.

This late pada from the eastern oral-musical tradition parallels 'Māyā' and 'Deadly Business', both from the western manuscript-lines discussed above. In 'The Mystery of Māyā', the Kabir poets suggest that trying to step outside the domain of Māyā is like peeling off a series of impossible layers. When the process is finally complete, the bhakta achieves a pure state of consciousness, memory and self-expression.

92. Swan

TEXT: Dvivedi 1990, 186, pada 12. VARIANTS: None. TRANSLATIONS: Tagore 1915, 55–56.

This poem has close affinities with 'Parting' above, and connects also with 'Fable' and 'Trap'. As in 'Parting', the speaker in 'Swan' represents the everyday self addressing the true self; and the true self's attainment of mukti is through a journey. In both poems, the interesting poetic emotion revolves around the mortal self's desire to cling to the imperishable *ātmā*. See the note on 'Parting' for further details.

93. Fish

TEXT: Dvivedi 1990, 203, pada 43. VARIANTS: None. TRANSLATIONS: Tagore 1915, 91.

A poem with a disarmingly vivid and personal opening. The stress here, as in many other Kabir poems, is on knowledge and self-knowledge as the keys to salvation. Mathura is associated with the child-god and adult erotic god Krishṇa, an avatar of Vishṇu, and is a city associated primarily with conservative Vaishṇava devotion. Kashi (Banaras or Varanasi) is known chiefly as Shiva's city, and hence is a centre of Shaiva devotion, though it also serves all Hindus in a greater variety of ways than Mathura. Both cities are linked to saguṇa conceptions of God, and hence, in the eyes of the Kabir poets, they are part of Māyā. As in 'The Mystery of Māyā' above, the argument in the final verse here is that knowledge and self-knowledge provide the only means of overcoming the effects of Māyā.

94. The Ineffable

TEXT: Dvivedi 1990, 204, pada 49. VARIANTS: None. TRANSLATIONS: Tagore 1915, 95–96.

Perhaps intellectually one of the most complex poems in this book and in the Kabir tradition, this poem presents its philosophical argument with astonishing ease and brevity. Ultimate reality is nirguṇa, without predicable attributes, which means that it is invisible and imperceptible; what is visible must therefore be unreal. Nirguṇa reality is also indescribable, so what is real in the universe is also ineffable. But in ordinary human terms, what is unseen is unknowable, and what cannot be expressed cannot be an object of belief. And yet the man who is truly knowledgeable is able to express himself, whereas only the ignoramus gapes speechlessly at reality. The world is populated by believers who worship either a formless god or a god with an outward shape; the man who knows the truth understands that God is neither without form nor with a qualified shape. God is invisible to human eyes, and His words are inaudible to human ears. Given this, only the man who understands both love (of God) and renunciation (of the world) is able to attain mukti.

95. Apostasy

TEXT: Dvivedi 1990, 209, pada 67. VARIANTS: None. TRANSLATIONS: Tagore 1915, 110–11.

This satire is aimed equally at Muslim mullāhs and Hindu sādhus and yogis, on the grounds that practitioners of both religions wear the outward marks of devotion, but deep inside are actually 'apostates' or hypocritical unbelievers.

96. Allāh-and-Rāma

TEXT: Dvivedi 1990, 210, pada 69. VARIANTS: See the note on 'Allāh-Rāma' above. TRANSLATIONS: Tagore 1915, 112.

This is a late version, probably produced in the late nineteenth or the early twentieth century, of one of the earliest and more widely known of the poems in the Kabir tradition, 'Allāh-Rāma', which I have discussed in the notes above and also in the Introduction.

97. Neither This Nor That

TEXT: Dvivedi 1990, 214–15, pada 79. VARIANTS: None. TRANSLATIONS: Tagore 1915, 125.

As noted in the Introduction, this poem offers a version of the 'middle path' or the 'golden mean', with negative disclaimers rather than positive definitions. The pada rejects conventional binary oppositions in relation to morality and ethics; at the same time, it claims both agency and responsibility for the bhakta, even while advocating the ideal of detachment. (Compare the argument in 'Doer and Deed' above.) The final verse is particularly interesting because it explicitly characterizes the creed of 'Kabir' as one that combines constructive and de(con)structive positions.

98. Rain

TEXT: Dvivedi 1990, 217, pada 87. VARIANTS: None. TRANSLATIONS: Tagore 1915, 133–34.

This is a particularly lyrical piece, with the first two verses structured like verses in a song celebrating the beauty of the rainy season. In verses three to six, 'Rain' develops allegorical parallels between various aspects of farming and various stages of spiritual practice. It proposes that the activities of the diligent bhakta correspond quite exactly to those of the industrious farmer; like the farmer who does all that is needed to cultivate his crops, the bhakta should do whatever is necessary for the attainment of mukti. Thus, figuratively, the bhakta should plough and prepare the ground for salvation, sow the right seed for it, and then reap it as the farmer reaps his harvest. If they follow this model, both holy man and scholar can reap the right rewards for their labours at the end.

This pada, also probably a late composition in the Kabir corpus, resonates with an *abhang* ('unbroken song') in Marathi attributed to the seventeenth-century poet Tukaram, who belonged to the saguṇa Vaishṇava tradition of bhakti in Maharashtra. For a translation, entitled 'The Harvest', and commentary, see Dharwadker 1995b.

99. Creation

TEXT: Dvivedi 1990, 227, pada 112. VARIANTS: *Kabīr Granthāvalī*, Tivari 1961, 2:91, aṅga 12, pada 157; *Bījak*, Shukdev Singh 1972, 119, shabda 23; Gandharva 1985, cassette 1. TRANSLATIONS: Hess and Singh 1983, 49 (based on Shukdev Singh 1972).

This is another important example of a Kabir *ulaṭabāṃsī*; for an explanation of the term, and for other instances of the form in this book, see the notes on 'The Way' and 'Rāma's Essence' above. 'Creation' is common to the Rajasthani, *Bījak*, and oral-musical traditions, but it is mostly a variation in the Niranjani style of composition (see 'The Flawless One' above). Its driving topos is that the created universe is fundamentally 'upside down', and therefore has the structure of a multilayered paradox or riddle. All the elements of the universe are interchangeable with their opposites; everything does the opposite of what it can or is supposed to do; and the universe itself constantly reverses or inverts itself and its basic order. This disorder in Creation is incomprehensible to human reason; God controls His Creation, so He must have His reasons for this state of affairs; whatever He chooses to do, however, is inherently beautiful. The poem, unawares, thus echoes the Biblical notion that the ways of God are incomprehensible to human beings, or that God works in mysterious ways.

100. Don't Stay

TEXT: Dvivedi 1990, 235, pada 130. VARIANTS: None. TRANSLATIONS: None.

One of the best-known Kabir lyrics among urban, educated Indian audiences at the end of the twentieth century, 'Don't Stay' is a plaintive song of renunciation. It suggests that we ought to 'renounce' the world because it is perishable, painful, transient and dangerous. In contrast to the world, 'God's name' is imperishable, a source of happiness and freedom, a safe and permanent abode.

NOTE ON TRANSLITERATION

In this book, I have used the following symbols for the transliteration of words from languages other than English.

a pronounced like the *u* in English 'b*u*t' (short simple vowel)
ā pronounced like the *a* in English 'f*a*ther' (long simple vowel)
i pronounced like the *i* in English 's*i*t' (short simple vowel)
ī pronounced like the *ee* in English 'f*ee*t' (long simple vowel)
u pronounced like the *u* in English 'p*u*t' (short simple vowel)
ū pronounced like the *oo* in English '*coo*l' (long simple vowel)
ṛ pronounced approximately like the *ri* in English '*ri*g' (short syllabic liquid)
ṝ pronounced like the *ṛ* but lengthened out, approximately like the *rea* (sounded like *ree*) in the American 'P*rea*kness' (long syllabic liquid)
e pronounced like the *a* in English 'm*a*ke' (diphthong)
ai pronounced by gliding from the *a* sound into the *i*, keeping both vowels short (diphthong)
o pronounced like the *o* in English 'h*o*pe'
au pronounced by gliding from the *a* sound into the *u*, keeping both vowels short (diphthong)
ṃ pronounced like the *m* in English 'hi*m*', nasalising the vowel that precedes it
k pronounced like the *k* in English '*k*ite' (unvoiced unaspirated velar)
kh pronounced like the *kh* that should be used in Indian-English 'la*kh*' (unvoiced aspirated velar)
g pronounced like the *g* in English 'ba*g*' (voiced unaspirated velar)
gh pronounced like the *gh* that should be used in Indian-English '*gh*ee' (voiced aspirated velar)
ṅ pronounced like the *n* in English 'thi*n*g' (velar nasal)
ch pronounced like the *ch* in English '*ch*air' (unvoiced unaspirated palatal)
chh pronounced more like the *ch* in English '*ch*ew', but with a stronger aspiration (unvoiced aspirated palatal)
j pronounced like the *j* in English '*j*oke' (voiced unaspirated palatal)
jh no English equivalent; pronounced with a strong aspiration of *j* (voiced aspirated palatal)
ñ pronounced like the *n* in English 'pi*n*ch' (palatal nasal)
ṭ pronounced like the *t* in English '*t*op' (unvoiced unaspirated retroflex)
ṭh no English equivalent; pronounced with a strong aspiration of *ṭ*, stronger than in the first *t* in American '*t*art' (unvoiced aspirated retroflex)

ḍ pronounced like the *d* in English '*d*o' (voiced unaspirated retroflex)

ḍh no English equivalent; pronounced with a strong aspiration of *ḍ* (voiced aspirated retroflex)

ṇ pronounced approximately like the *n* in English 'ti*n*t', but with stronger retroflexion (retroflex nasal)

t pronounced like the first *t* in French '*t*out' (unvoiced unaspirated dental)

th no English equivalent; *not* pronounced like the *th* in English '*th*ing' (unvoiced aspirated dental)

d pronounced approximately like the *th* in 'ba*th*e' (voiced unaspirated dental)

dh no English equivalent; pronounced with a strong aspiration of *d* (voiced aspirated dental)

n pronounced like the *n* in English 'si*n*' (dental nasal)

p pronounced like the *p* in English '*p*op' (unvoiced unaspirated labial)

ph pronounced like the *p* and *h* together in English 'u*ph*eaval', when the two sounds are articulated in rapid succession (unvoiced aspirated labial)

b pronounced like the *b* in English '*b*ib' (voiced unaspirated labial)

bh no English equivalent; pronounced with a strong aspiration of *b* (voiced aspirated labial)

m pronounced like the *m* in English '*m*an' (labial nasal)

ya pronounced like the *yu* in English slang '*yu*p' (palatal semi-vowel)

ra pronounced like the *ru* in English '*ru*n' (retroflex semi-vowel)

la pronounced like the *lu* in English '*lu*g' (dental semi-vowel)

va pronounced so that the *va* sound lies between the *wo* in English '*wo*rse' and the *ve* in '*ve*rse' (labial semi-vowel)

ś pronounced like the *sh* in English '*sh*ock' (palatal sibilant); used to transliterate Sanskrit, but replaced by *sh* for Hindi here

ṣ very similar to *ś* but retroflexed (retroflex sibilant); used to transliterate Sanskrit, but replaced by *sh* for Hindi here

sh used for both *ś* and *ṣ* in Hindi here; pronounced like the *sh* in English '*sh*ock' (palatal sibilant)

s pronounced like the *s* in English '*s*ip' (dental sibilant)

ha pronounced like the *hu* in English '*hu*lk' (voiced aspirate)

k̲a pronounced approximately like *qa*; the same consonantal sound as at the beginning of 'Qur'ān'(Arabic unvoiced unaspirated uvular)

k̲h̲a pronounced like the *ch* in Scottish 'lo*ch*' or German 'Ba*ch*'; the consonantal sound that should be used at the beginning of Anglicized '*kh*aki'; distinct from *kh* (Persian-Arabic unvoiced fricative)

g̲ pronounced like *k̲h̲a*, but voiced; the consonant that should be used at the beginning of Anglicized 'ghazal', more precisely transliterated as 'gazal' (Persian-Arabic fricative)

j̲ pronounced like the English *z*; the same as the consonant represented by *z* in Anglicized 'gha*z*i' (Persian-Arabic fricative)

d̲ retroflex like *ḍ*, but distinguished from the latter by flapping the tongue for slight, transient contact with the hard palate (unaspirated)

d̲h̲ retroflex like *ḍh*, but distinguished from the latter by flapping the tongue for slight, transient contact with the hard palate (aspirated)

f pronounced like the English *f*; distinguished from *ph* (Persian-Arabic fricative)

For the few words transliterated from Tamil and Kannada, see the explanation of symbols in Ramanujan 1973.

GLOSSARY

ādi : 'first, primary, foremost, original; the beginning' (Sanskrit, Hindi, Punjabi). Used in *ādi sant* to mean a saintly man who is chronologically or qualitatively the foremost among such men. Used in the title *Ādi Granth* (see below). Also used in *ādivāsī*, which means 'first inhabitant' (Sanskrit, Hindi), and denotes the aborigine peoples of India.

Ādi Granth : 'the first or foremost book' (Punjabi); the scripture of Sikhism, as composed and canonized by the fifth Guru, Arjan, in 1604. Its normative manuscript form survives in the *Kartarpur Pothi* (see entry). Also see entries on *Dasam Granth* and *Guru Granth Sāhib*.

Advaita Vedānta : 'non-dualist culmination of the Veda' (Sanskrit); classical school of Hindu-Indian philosophy, which flourished under the influence of Shankarācharya (eighth century); also known as Uttar Mīmāṃsā. It opposes *dvaita* (dualism) and *viśiṣṭadvaita* (qualified non- dualism). See Hiriyanna 1985.

āgamin : see *karma* below.

Akāl Purakh : An epithet for God or godhead in Sikh theology (Punjabi); derived from Sanskrit 'akāla' (deathless, timeless) and 'puruṣa' (primordial being, undifferentiated godhead, male life-principle). See Mann 2001; Pashaura Singh 2000.

ākār : 'shape, outward or physical form' (Sanskrit, Hindi, Punjabi); an object may be *sākār*, 'with shape, formed' or *nirākār*, 'without shape or form'; *nirañkār* is a variant of *nirākār*. Some varieties of nirguṇa *mat* claim that God is *nirañkār*, formless, rather than completely without qualities; the Nirankaris (believers in a 'formless' ultimate reality), for example, constitute a separate community under the umbrella of 'Sikhism'.

akshar : 'indestructible'; a letter of the alphabet, or the unit of sound it represents (Sanskrit, Hindi). In the Kabir tradition, as in some older Indian systems of thought, the fifty-two *akshars* of the Nagari alphabet are part of a 'secret code', and therefore have esoteric or mystical meanings. For a Kabir experiment with a 'mystical acrostic' in the *Ādi Granth*, see Dass 1991.

Allāh : The proper 'name' of God in the Qur'ān and in Islam (Arabic). The canon also lists 99 other epithets for God; those used here include 'Khudā', 'Karīm', 'Rahīm' and 'Kabīr' itself.

añga : 'limb, well-defined part of a body or structure' (Sanskrit). Middle-period Indian texts, especially those of composite authorship or form, are often divided into thematic or other *añgas*; Rajjabadas' *Sarbañgī* (1620) places poems by 137 authors in 144 thematic *añgas*.

añjan : literally, 'lampblack', used as a cosmetic pigment to line the eyelids (similar to modern eyeliner); figuratively, 'stain, soil, taint, flaw, blackening, tarnish' (Sanskrit, Hindi). Its opposite is *nirañjan*, stain-less, flawless, pure, untarnished. The Niranjani Panth's basic theological position is that only nirguṇa or attributeless God is *nirañjan*; everything else is part of the created universe, and hence is *añjan*, stained, flawed or contaminated.

antahkaraṇa : 'inner agent of action' (Sanskrit); within an individual, the complex that consists of the capacities of sensory perception (*indriyas*), the capacities of motor action (*karmendriyas*) and the 'mind' (*manas* or *man*). The *antahkaraṇa* does not include the *ātmā* (true self).

anuśaya : : a 'residue' that an action and its consequences leave on its agent (Sanskrit). See *karma*.

aril : also *arilla*; a metrical form with sixteen *mātrās* or morae per verse (Hindi).

āsan : 'sitting posture, position; seat, throne'; term for 'posture' in *haṭha*-yoga (Sanskrit, Hindi).

ashrāf : plural of *sharīf*, 'good man, gentleman, one born into a family of rank and status' (Arabic); *ashrāf* denotes members of the upper classes, the political, economic and social elite.

āshrama : also *aśrama* (Sanskrit); here, 'stage of life'. In classical India, *varṇāśrama* dharma enjoined *dvija* Hindus (brahmins, kshatriyas, vaishyas) to live by the codes of the caste-system, and to follow the codes appropriate for specific 'stages' in life. This system of beliefs divided the normal life-cycle into four clear *āśramas* or stages, namely, *brahmachārya* (student and apprentice; childhood and youth), *grihastha* (householder; early adulthood and middle age), *vānaprastha* (retirement 'in the forest'; late middle age), and *saṃnyāsa* (final renunciation; old age). Such a normative scheme sought to create an ideal moral and ethical balance in the human order, paying equal attention to the needs of individual, family and society.

ashṭapadī : also *aṣṭapadī* (Sanskrit); describes 'a poem containing eight verses'. Here 'Sapling and Seed' is an *ashṭapadī* ramainī, a ramainī with eight verses. A *baḏī ashṭapadī ramainī* is a 'large' or extended poem in the same form; see 'Moth' which has two opening verses (first stanza in English), followed by eight main verses (four stanzas in English). See *ramainī*.

asura : category of beings in Paurāṇic mythology who are 'enemies of the gods', and display great cruelty and violence. In his Buddha avatar, Vishṇu destroys *asuras* who terrorize the earth.

atishūdra : 'very lowly' (Sanskrit). In the caste-system, the class of 'untouchables'. See *varṇa* below.

ātmā : also *ātman* (Sanskrit); literally, 'self'. In Hinduism, an individual's 'true self', which corresponds to, but is very different from, the 'soul' in Christianity. In most branches of Hindu philosophy and theology, in each cycle of creation, the material-physical universe (*prakṛti*) is created out of a primordial substance (*puruṣa*) which is identical with godhead or God; living things come to life in the universe because they contain 'fragments' of *puruṣa*; every human being contains an *ātmā* that is identical in substance (but not in form) to *puruṣa*, which serves as the 'principle of life' within him or her. (The *Bhagavad-gītā*, a key text for bhakti, uses the term *ātmā* only once; for the rest, it refers to the 'self' only deictically, or indexically as the *dehin*, 'the one who is embodied'. See *karma* and *mukti* below.

Avadhi a language used in the region of Avadh, north of Banaras in eastern-central north India. It has served as the speech-variety of that region for at least 600 years; it became a literary medium by the fifteenth century, and developed a significant literature in the next 200 years. It is now classified as a major language or sub-language within 'Hindi', which is a constellation of seventeen such 'regional dialects'. The Avadhi in the early Kabir texts is 'Old Avadhi', earlier than that in the poetry of Tulsidas (sixteenth century). See Chaturvedi 1954, Allchin 1966, Vaudeville 1974 and Lutgendorf 1994.

avadhūt a *saṃnyāsī*, one who has renounced 'life in the world'; a member of a distinct order of sādhus, such as the Nath Panth; someone who practises Tantra and yoga. A fairly high proportion of the Kabir poems in the eastern and western manuscript-lines address their imagined interlocuters as *avadhūt* or *avadhū*.

avatar a 'descent or descended form', an incarnation of a god. Among the major Hindu deities, Vishṇu 'descends' to the human world in a variety of human, semi-human and non-human incarnations. He has twenty-four past and future avatars in human history, ten of which are regarded as the principal ones. See note on the poem 'The Ten Avatars'.

baḏī ashṭapadī see entry on *ashṭapadī*.

bait verse; poem; couplet (Arabic). A genre of verse with compositions in Persian found in the *sarbañgī*-style anthologies of the Dadu Dayal Panth in Rajasthan.

Bali in Paurāṇic mythology, another name of a demonic king, Daitya, son of Virochana; Vishṇu incarnated Himself on earth as Vāmana (the Dwarf avatar) to destroy him.

bāṇī	:	derivative, in Hindi and Pujabi, of Sanskrit *vāṇī* (see the entry below).
bārahapadī	:	describes a poem 'containing twelve verses' (Hindi). See *ashṭapadī* and *ramainī*.
bastā	:	bag, packet (Hindi). A term sometimes used in archives for a packet of unbound manuscripts.
bhagat	:	Punjabi variation on *bhakta* (see below).
Bhagavad-gītā	:	embedded in the *Mahābhārata*, it has been a constant reference for bhakti poets. It provides an influential formulation of three 'equivalent' yogas, each leading to God and mukti: *karma-yoga*, *jñāna-yoga* and *bhakti-yoga* (the disciplines of action, knowledge and devotion, respectively; see the entries on these terms). For the Kabir poets, the perspective of the *Gītā* is important because they are often divided between *jñāna*-yoga and *bhakti*-yoga, with the former predominating in the Niranjani and Kabir Panthi traditions, and the latter in certain parts of the Dadu Panthi and *Ādi Granth* traditions. Also see *ātmā* and *yoga*.
bhajan	:	'act of service (to God); worship; song of praise' (Sanskrit, Hindi). In everyday practice, a *bhajan* is usually sung in a congregational setting, with a small group of instrumental musicians accompanying a lead singer; the congregation joins in as a 'chorus' for the refrain.
bhakta	:	male 'devotee' (Sanskrit, Hindi); someone who has made an unqualified commitment to the worship and service of a particular god, and who then devotes himself 'totally' to the spiritual life. A female devotee is called a *bhaktin*. See entry on *bhakti*.
bhakti	:	'loving devotion' to a god or some other appropriate object of worship (Sanskrit, Hindi). As a religious practice, bhakti arose as a 'critical reaction' to classical Hinduism (which focused on temples, priests, rituals, pilgrimages, donations to institutions, hierarchical social divisions and rigid, discriminatory codes of conduct). Bhakti started in the southernmost regions of the peninsula before the eighth century, and

gradually spread northwards and eastwards, until it had reached most parts of the subcontinent by the fourteenth century. As a productive literary movement, bhakti drew to a close by the eighteenth century, as European powers consolidated their colonization of India; but as a 'religious institution' it remains alive today, having permeated every aspect of Hinduism in daily life. The practice, discourse and theory of bhakti are internally multifarious: major divergences appear between saguṇa and nirguṇa theologies; among the bhaktas of Shiva, Vishṇu and the Devi (the Goddess); between 'sober' and 'intoxicated' styles of devotion; among formations defined by criteria such as male and female, upper-caste and low-caste, *dvija*-caste and untouchable, and wealth and poverty; and socially between conservative and progressive communities. On this broad spectrum of possibilities, the Ḳabir poets mostly adopt positions of radical theological, philosophical, social and political reform across religious and other lines. See entry on *Bhagavad-gītā*. See Ramanujan 1973 and 1981; Dharwadker 1999.

bhakti-yoga : the 'discipline of devotion' (Sanskrit); in the *Bhagavad-gītā* Krishna states that unqualified devotion to Him results in mukti. Bhakti poets pursue this ideal very frequently; the Kabir poets uphold it even as they pursue a parallel 'path to salvation' through *jñāna*-yoga, the 'discipline of knowledge'. See entry on *Bhagavad-gītā*.

bhāshā : 'language' (Sanskrit, Hindi); distinguished from *bolī*, 'speech-variety' (Hindi). Indian scholars classify a verbal medium as a *bhāshā* only when, in addition to its oral dimension, it possesses a script and a tradition of writing and literary production; without the written tradition, the medium remains merely a *bolī*. A *bhāshā* has one or more written standards, and may have many *bolī*s (speech-varieties) associated with it. Hindi scholars also distinguish between a *bhāshā* and an *upa-*

bhāshā, the latter a 'sub-language' or 'supra-language' that has a written standard of its own, but may not be as widespread, comprehensive or dominant as the *bhāshā* that subsumes it; if a *bhāshā* includes several *upa-bhāshās*, it may choose the written standard of one of the sub-languages to serve as the norm for the whole cluster of mediums. This perspective is especially useful in understanding the complex structure of 'Hindi' and its seventeen principal sub-languages and speech-varieties. See *Hindi* below.

Bhavānī : name for Shiva's consort, also known in her other aspects as Parvati and Shakti.

Bhojpuri : speech-variety used in the Bhojpur region, east of Banaras; although it has been in use for oral communication for several hundred years, it has not yet emerged as a significant literary language (and hence remains a *bolī*). Bhojpuri vocabulary and locutions appear in many Kabir poems, especially in the eastern tradition. See *bhāshā* and *Hindi*.

Bījak : the principal text of the 'eastern tradition' in the Kabir corpus. The *Bījak* has been produced and is maintained in several versions by different branches of the Kabir Panth; see the Introduction for details.

bolī : 'speech-variety' (Hindi). See discussion under *bhāshā* above.

Braj Bhāshā : the speech-variety and literary language of the Braj region, around Mathura. It entered the sphere of writing early in the last millennium; developed a major literature between the sixteenth and nineteenth centuries; and remained the dominant standard in the 'Hindi' world until the mid-nineteenth century. The syntax of Braj provided a basic 'indigenous frame' upon which both 'Hindi' and 'Urdu' emerged as 'mixed' mediums of communication in the presence of Persian and Arabic between the twelfth and eighteenth centuries. Braj words, expressions and grammatical forms appear quite frequently in the Kabir corpus.

Brahmā : saguṇa god; with Vishṇu and Shiva, He is part of the classical Hindu 'trinity'. The 'giver of the Vedas' to the human race, He is linked with 'creation'; His consort is Saraswati, goddess of knowledge.

Brahman : in the Upanishads, Brahman is undifferentiated godhead, absolute reality; this concept sought to replace the older, Ṛg-vedic concept of *Puruṣa* (see entry).

brahmin : caste-group of priests in Hindu society; placed highest in ritual rank among castes.

Buddha : Gautama, the Buddha who historically founded Buddhism; in the classical period, he was also absorbed into Hindu mythology, where he appears as one of Vishṇu's ten main avatars.

chakra : 'circle, wheel' (Sanskrit, Hindi); used as a technical term in *yoga* (see entry).

charitra : often translated as 'character'; but also represents 'conduct, behaviour; nature, temperament; life-story, biography' (Sanskrit, Hindi).

chaupada : a poem consisting of 'four verses' (Sanskrit, Hindi, Punjabi). One of the categories used to order poems in the *Ādi Granth*.

chaupāī : a widely-used verse-form in pre-modern Hindi, composed of 'four feet', each with sixteen *mātrās* or morae. The final verse of a *ramainī* is in this form (see entry). Rarely used on its own by the Kabir poets; but aphorism 33 is a *chaupāī* in the original.

chhanta : a poetic genre in the *Ādi Granth* (Punjabi); not used by the Kabir poets. See Mann 2001.

cowrie : Anglicization of Hindi *kauḏī*; hard, durable mollusk shell, often glossy and colourful, used as money in the Indian Ocean and South Pacific economies for much of the past millennium.

crore : Anglicized form of Hindi *karoḏ*; cardinal number, equals ten million or 100 *lakh* (see entry).

Dadu Dayal Panth : one of the principal religious communities associated with the production, preservation and circulation of the Kabir text; founded in the sixteenth century, and based mainly in Rajasthan. See Introduction for details.

dargāh : mausoleum of a sufi *pīr* or master (Persian); also called a *rozā*. Often a destination for pilgrims, especially those attending annual festivals commemorating the buried master.

Dasam Granth : 'tenth book' (Punjabi); title given to the collection of poetic texts, his own and others', compiled by Guru Gobind Singh, the tenth Sikh Guru, which he added to the *Ādi Granth* by about 1692. See entries on *Ādi Granth* and *Guru Granth Sāhib*.

Dasharath : in the *Rāmāyaṇa*, ruler of Kosala and father of Rāma, the epic's hero. See *Rāma*.

dashāvatār : 'the ten avatars' (Sanskrit, Hindi). Name of artistic form that celebrates Vishṇu's ten main avatars in various expressive mediums. See note on the poem 'The Ten Avatars'.

Devakī : see entry on *Krishṇa*.

dhyān : 'concentration' (Sanskrit, Hindi); the activity of disciplining the mind to concentrate on a specific object of contemplation, excluding all other possible objects of consciousness. The concept of *dhyān* migrated from India to China, where it was translated as *chan*; and from there to Japan, where it was translated as *zen*. The Kabir poets inherit *dhyān* from classical and Nath yoga as well as Tantra.

dīkshā : 'the act of teaching a mantra' (Hindi); more generally, religious instruction to an initiate. A *dīkshā*-guru is a spiritual master who transmits (often esoteric or secret) knowledge of texts and practices to a (worthy) student. In middle-period north India, teachers who became *dīkshā*-gurus were legitimized by an intricate network of institutions, most of them controlled by upper-caste communities; these institutions also determined who could 'enroll' as a student or novitiate. The Kabir poets devote much poetic energy to attacking and dismantling this exclusionary system of transmission and legitimation.

Dīvān : chief administrator of a kingdom; prime minister to the ruler (Persian).

dvaita : 'dualism' (Sanskrit). A philosophical position that argues for the ontological difference between Creator and Creation, God and Self, cause and effect, etc. See *Advaita Vedānta* above. See Hiriyanna 1985 for details.

dvija : 'twice born' (Sanskrit). Categorization of castes whose members go through a 'second birth' when they participate in rituals designed to confirm their caste status. Only brahmins, kshatriyas and vaishyas are 'born twice'. *Dvija* status insurmountably separates the three upper caste-groups from the shūdras, as also from the untouchables. See entry on *āshrama*.

fakir : in modern English usage, 'Muslim religious mendicant', or 'Hindu ascetic or religious mendicant, especially one who performs feats of magic or endurance'; the word, derived from Arabic, is used in Hindi and Urdu to mean 'beggar; Muslim or Hindu mendicant'.

fana' : 'destruction, dissolution' (Arabic); in sufi theology, *fana'* designates the dissolution of difference between God and individual human soul, or object of worship and worshipper.

Farsi : used in this book interchangeably with 'Persian'; refers both to the literary language and its script (a modified form of the Arabic script, with distinctive codes and writing styles).

gaddī : 'seat, cushion' (Hindi, Punjabi); ceremonial and ritual centre of a religious organization.

Ganesha : Ganeśa in Sanskrit; elephant-headed son of Shiva and Parvati, saguṇa god of memory, writing, accounting and auspicious beginnings, who also helps humans overcome obstacles.

Ganga : the principal river of north India; it rises in the Himalayas, flows in a south-easterly direction across the north-central plain, and empties into the Bay of Bengal. In Hindu theology and mythology, the most sacred of rivers on earth.

gāyatrī : the most famous mantra in the *Ṛg-veda*; recited at initiation ceremony for *dvija*-caste members.

Goindval Pothis : notebooks compiled by the third Sikh Guru, Amardas, and his companions between 1570 and 1572. Originally a set of four, only two *pothīs* have survived into the twenty-first century. They record texts of poems probably first collected by Guru Nanak, the founder of Sikhism, and augmented and arranged later by Guru Amardas. They provided a paradigm for content, editing and organization that the fifth Guru, Arjan, adapted for the much larger *Ādi Granth* some three decades later. See Mann 1996 and 2001 for details.

Gokul : a village near Vrindavan (in the proximity of Mathura), where Nanda and Yashodā lived, and where they raised Balarāma and Krishṇa (Vishṇu's avatar). See entry on *Krishṇa*.

gopī : 'cowgirl' (Braj Bhāshā, Hindi); in Vaishṇava mythology and literature, term for the women in the Vrindavan region associated with the erotic god *Krishṇa* (see entry).

Govind : an epithet of Vishṇu in his avatar as Krishṇa in the Vrindavan region, highlighting his erotic and playful aspects as a 'cowboy' who seduces all the 'cowgirls' around him.

granth : 'book, collection of texts, sacred or valorized text' (Sanskrit, Hindi, Punjabi).

Granthāvalī : title used in the Dadu Panthi and other Rajasthani manuscript traditions for a large and highly valued anthology of Kabir texts. In 1961 Parasanath Tivari adopted this traditional title for his modern scholarly edition, *Kabīr Granthāvalī*.

guṇa : 'strand; quality, attribute, distinguishing feature; nature' (Sanskrit, Hindi). Since an early stage in their history, Indian religion and philosophy have distinguished between objects that have determinate attributes or qualities, and therefore are saguṇa, 'with attributes, qualified'; and objects that do not, and hence are nirguṇa, 'without attributes or qualities'. Thus, even God and godhead may be either saguṇa or nirguṇa. Most schools of thought agree that *prakṛti*, 'that which has been created', or the entire order of physical-material Creation, consists of objects that are saguṇa. According to the *Bhagavad-gītā* and other texts, everything in the sphere of *prakṛti* is made up of three 'great qualities': *tamas*, 'darkness and inertia'; *rajas*, 'energy and momentum'; and *sattva*, 'truth and light'. The 'nature' of an object is thus determined by the great quality that predominates in its constitution. For the Kabir poets, these ideas are vital: godhead is nirguṇa; all of Creation is Māyā, and everything saguṇa is part of that 'universal illusion'; Māyā controls physical-material existence with her 'noose' woven out of the three 'strands' of *tamas*, *rajas*, and *sattva*; and, in the final analysis, mukti can be attained only by renouncing everything saguṇa. See Hiriyanna 1985.

Gurmukhi : 'that which has issued from the mouth of the Guru' (Punjabi); name of the script created and refined by the early Sikh Gurus, mainly for the task of establishing the Sikh scripture. Used widely since the seventeenth century to write the Punjabi language.

guru : 'heavy, large, great, dear, powerful, worthy of being worshipped; father, elder, teacher, master' (Sanskrit, Hindi, Punjabi). The most common term for a spiritual master or teacher. (See entries on *dīkshā* and *shikshā* also.) In the Kabir canon, God is also a guru; He is the *Satguru*, the 'True Master', the Guru of all gurus. In Indian traditions generally, the primary relationship in education and spiritual discipline is between guru and *shishya* (student, pupil, disciple). In Punjabi, the word for *shishya* is *sikh*; the very term for a Sikh (and hence for the religion itself, Sikhism) indicates that the faith is defined by its process of transmission, which occurs through the paradigm of the guru-*shishya* relationship (guru-*sikh* in Punjabi). The old Indian guru-*shishya* institution parallels the later sufi institution of *pīr-o-murīd* (master-and-disciple). For the Kabir poets, all human gurus and *pīrs*, and hence all guru-*shishya* and *pīr-o-murīd* relationships in the human world, are false. This position creates much internal and external tension in their poetry, but they stand by it in order to stave off the hypocrisy and fraud they find in faiths centred around human gurus and *pīrs*. The Sikh Gurus resolve such tensions pragmatically at different historical moments, until Guru Gobind Singh closes the line of human gurus and declares the augmented *Ādi Granth* to be the *Guru Granth Sāhib*, the book that is the authoritative 'living guru' into perpetuity.

Guru Granth Sāhib : the title of the final, canonical version of the *Ādi Granth*, assigned to it by Guru Gobind Singh shortly before his death in 1708; this version of the scripture functions as the authoritative living 'master' of the faith and its human community. See *guru* above.

hajj : Arabic term for the annual pilgrimage to Mecca during the holy month of Ramadān, enjoined upon all Muslims as a primary objective of their religious lives.

haṃsa : 'goose or swan'; Upanishadic term for 'true self' or *ātmā* (Sanskrit). See notes on the poems 'Fable', 'Swan' and 'Parting'. Also see entries on *ātmā* and *prāṇa*.

Hari : an ancient name of Vishṇu in His universal aspect; Shiva's complementary name is Hara.

Hindi : usually classified as a 'language', but more appropriately conceived of as a 'hyper-language' that was constructed retroactively in the late nineteenth and early twentieth centuries at the complex ideological juncture of linguistics, politics, ethnicity, religion and culture. Indian scholars now label Hindi a *bhāshā* (full-fledged 'language') with five *upa-bhāshās* (sub-languages or supra-languages), each of which contains two or more major *bolīs* (speech-varieties; see the entry on *bhāshā* above), for a total of seventeen regionally-distributed dialects:

LANGUAGE	SUB-LANGUAGE	SPEECH-VARIETIES
Hindī	I. Western Hindī	1. Khaḏī Bolī (Kauravī)
		2. Braj Bhāshā
		3. Hariyāṇī
		4. Bundelī
		5. Kannaujī
	II. Eastern Hindī	6. Avadhī
		7. Baghelī
		8. Chhattisagaḏhī
	III. Rajasthānī	9. Mārawāḏī
		10. Jaipurī
		11. Mewātī
		12. Mālawī
	IV. Pahāḏī	13. Western Pahāḏī
		14. Mid-region Pahāḏī (Kamāyunī-Gaḏhavālī)
	V. Bihārī	15. Bhojpurī
		16. Magahī
		17. Maithilī

(This table is based on Nagendra and Gupta 1973.) Of the *bolīs*, Khaḏī Bolī, Braj Bhāshā, Avadhī, Mārawāḏī and Maithilī developed written standards and major or significant literary cultures before the middle of the past millennium. During the middle period, what is now identified as Khaḏī Bolī, together with Braj, provided much of the linguistic basis for the formation of what was long (and confusingly) known as 'Hinduī' or 'Hindavī', and for what emerged after the eighteenth century as 'Urdū', 'Hindustānī' and 'Hindī'. Historically, Hindi stands on a linguistic continuum with Urdu and Punjabi, even though the three languages use three different script-systems (Nagari, Farsi, Gurmukhi). The varieties of Hindi used in the Kabir texts (Avadhī, Bhojpurī, Braj, Rajasthānī, Khaḏī Bolī) appear in some of their oldest recorded historical forms. See the entries on individual speech-varieties and sub-languages; also see *bhāshā* above.

Hiraṇyakashipu : son of Kashyapa and Aditi, and father of the famous bhakta Prahlāda; Vishṇu descended to earth in the avatar of Narasiṃha (the man-lion), and burst out of a stone pillar to take the evil Hiraṇyakashipu by surprise and destroy him. See note on 'The Ten Avatars'.

Ik Oṃkār : 'the One and Only articulation of the sacred syllable OṂ'; epithet for nirguṇa God, godhead or ultimate reality in Sikhism (Punjabi).

Indra : the chief god of the Vedic pantheon; corresponds roughly to Zeus in the Greek pantheon.

Iñgalā : see entry on *nāḍī*.

jañgama : 'that which (or he who) is in perpetual motion'; term in Kannada for a Vīrashaiva practitioner. See Ramanujan 1973.

jap : usually a silent, repetitive recitation of a god's name. See entry on *nām*.

jāti : primary Sanskrit and Indian-language term for 'caste'; etymologically, 'genealogy; class or group to which membership is conferred by birth'. See entry on *varṇa*.

jīvan-mukta : 'one who has attained liberation from karma and rebirth while still alive' (Sanskrit).

jīvātmā : complex of 'living creature' and the particular 'Self' to which it is attached (Sanskrit).

jñāna-yoga : 'discipline of knowledge' (Sanskrit); one of the three main 'paths' to God and mukti advocated in the *Bhagavad-gītā* (see entry). Also see *yoga*.

jugi : Bengali word for 'yogi'; used as the name for a specific caste in the Bengal countryside.

julāhā : 'weaver' (Persian); used mostly for Muslim weavers. See Introduction for discussion.

Ka'aba : derived from the Arabic *ka'b*, 'cube'. The name of the cube-shaped shrine in Mecca, at the holiest site of Islam. Muslim pilgrims undertake the hajj to worship at the Ka'aba; when Muslims pray five times a day in any part of the world, they must face in the direction in which the Ka'aba lies from wherever they are.

Kabir Panth : multifaceted religious organization and community founded on the 'legacy' of the historical Kabir; based in the eastern parts of north-central India, the Panth has several branches, institutional centres and theological and textual traditions. See the Introduction.

Kaithi : a form of the *Nagari* script (see entry); it contains fewer symbols in the alphabet, and is written more rapidly, without a line drawn over the top of the letters; employed widely in the middle period for administrative and commercial records. A few Kabir manuscripts are recorded in this script (rather than in Nagari or Farsi).

Kaligrahi : see entry on *Kalki*.

Kalki : the avatar that Vishṇu will take when he descends at the end of the (present) Kali Age, in order to rid the earth of its evil (represented by a cruel and terrifying future tyrant, Kaligrahi).

Kamāl : the name of Kabir's son, as reported by several texts that entered circulation after the poet's death. In one set of accounts, Kamāl rejected his father's impractical spirituality and became a successful merchant or trader; in another, Kamāl became a spiritual figure himself, and achieved some renown in eastern India.

Kamalā : one of the names of Vishṇu's consort, Lakshmi, goddess of wealth and prosperity; Kamalā corresponds to Vishṇu's benevolent aspect as Keshav.

Kaṃsa : see entry on *Krishṇa*.

kārakhānā : 'workshop' (Urdu, Hindi); used in the modern period also for 'factory'.

Karīm : an epithet of Allāh listed in the Qur'ān.

karma : 'action, deed' (Sanskrit). The word basically denotes an individual act; but it also invokes a large theory of action that first appeared in outline in the Upanishads and acquired its most elaborate philosophical form in the classical period. According to this theory, every deed has consequences; for its agent, the 'fruit' of an action (*karmaphala*) may be either good or bad, and morally it may result in either 'merit' (*puṇya*) or 'demerit' (*pāpa*). Once performed, neither a deed nor its consequences can be erased; and its consequences have further inescapable consequences. Within the law of karma, the only way to 'undo' an action and its multiple proximate and remote effects would be to perform another action which is exactly contrary, in itself and in its consequences, to the first action; but that would only multiply the number of actions and effects in play. According to the Advaita Vedānta analysis of karma, every action produces a 'residue' (*anushaya*) in the agent, which is either 'meritorious' (*dharma*) or 'unmeritorious' (*adharma*); and which is accompanied by 'dispositional tendencies' (*saṃskāras*). The principal difficulty with karma is that these *saṃskāras* are 'stored' in the agent until they 'mature' or come to 'fruition'—at some unpredictable time in the future, which includes time beyond the agent's present lifetime. The residual *anushayas* of an action are of three kinds: (*a*) *prārabdha*, stored residues from one or more past lives, the *saṃskāras* of which were determined at the time of this birth to be fructified in this lifetime; (*b*) *sañchita*, also residues from previous lives, but the *saṃskāras* of which are determined at birth to remain dormant during this lifetime; and (*c*) *āgamin* or *krīyamāṇa*, residues of actions from this lifetime, the *saṃskāras* of which will mature and fructify in some future lifetime. At maturation in this lifetime, the *anushayas* and accompanying *saṃskāras* from past actions combine to produce a *bhoga* or 'experience of pleasure or pain' that is the 'experiential component' of the 'fruit of action'; and to produce the *kāma* or 'desire' that propels the agent into further (reactive) action. What creates the bondage of karma over many lifetimes is that the *anushayas* and their accompanying *saṃskāras* are stored in the 'indestructible' part of the agent (in the *chitta* or consciousness that is attached to his *ātmā*), and once they come into existence (as soon as an action is performed) they cannot be erased. In bhakti, God intervenes to 'free' the bhakta from the insurmountable 'bonds' of karma that he has accumulated over numerous lifetimes. See the Introduction; also Potter 1980.

karma-yoga : 'discipline of action' (Sanskrit); one of the three 'paths' to God and mukti recommended in the *Bhagavad-gītā* (see entry).

Kartarpur Pothi : manuscript of the *Ādi Granth*, as compiled by the fifth Sikh Guru, Arjan, in 1604; preserved in the Punjab in the form of a large bound notebook. It serves as the copy-text for a large portion of the canonical *Granth*. See Mann 2001 for details.

Kashyapa : (*a*) Name of Vishṇu's tortoise avatar, in which He destroyed Shaṅkhāsura in the ocean and retrieved the stolen Vedas. (*b*) Name of a powerful ancient *rishi* ('seer', visionary sage) who, with his various wives, fathered numerous *suras* ('good beings'), *asuras* ('demons'), humans, animals and other types of creatures; with his wife Aditi, he fathered the demonic Hiraṇyakashipu, whom Vishṇu destroyed by descending in His Narasiṃha (man-lion) avatar. See the entries on *Shaṅkhāsura* and *Hiraṇyakashipu*.

kavitta : a genre of text represented in the Dadu Panthi *sarbaṅgī* anthologies (see below).

Keshav : name for Vishṇu in his avatar as the erotic god Krishṇa (see below).

Khaḍī Bolī : also called Kauravī; speech-variety of the region around Delhi, in use since early in the past millennium.

Between the twelfth and eighteenth centuries, early forms of Kha<u>d</u>ī Bolī were loosely labelled as Hinduī or Hindavī; they provided much of the linguistic basis for the formation of what subsequently became 'Hindī', 'Urdū' and 'Hindustānī'. Modern Kha<u>d</u>ī Bolī (the medium of the nineteenth and twentieth centuries) now serves as the 'standard' for 'Hindī', both in its spoken and written forms. The literary culture of Kha<u>d</u>ī Bolī in its earliest form begins in the thirteenth century. See the entry on *Hindi*.

Khudā : epithet for Allāh in the Qur'ān (Aarabic); used widely in the Indian languages.

Krishṇa : Kṛṣṇa in Sanskrit. Avatar of Vishṇu; eighth among the ten main incarnations. According to the elaborate mythology surrounding him, Krishṇa was born to Vāsudev and Devakī in the Yādav clan of the Braj region. Devakī's brother, Kaṃsa, was then king of Mathura; he was a wicked ruler, and when he heard a prophecy that Devakī's child would kill him, he tried to murder all her children. But Vāsudev and Devakī arranged to send Krishṇa and his brother Balarāma across the River Jamuna to a village called Gokul (in the Vrindavan region), where they were raised by the cowherd Nanda and his wife Yashodā. In his infancy in that household, Krishṇa revealed his divine nature as a mischievous child-god; later, in his youth and early adulthood, he became a cowherd or 'cowboy', and turned into an erotic god. His flute-playing drew all the *gopī*s ('cowgirls', the daughters, sisters and wives of the cowherds) to the forest, where they danced ecstatically with him; though he had 16,000 lovers, Rādhā remained his favourite. Subsequently, Krishṇa and Balarāma returned to Mathura and killed Kaṃsa; still later, Krishṇa led the Yādavs to Dwaraka (Kathiawar), where he ruled the clan for many decades. As a warrior-god in his mature years, he sided with the Pāṇḍavas against their cousins, the Kauravas, in the epic conflict of the *Mahābhārata*.

krīyamāṇa	:	see entry on *karma*.
korī	:	'weaver' (Sanskrit, Hindi); common term for Hindu weaver. See *julāhā*.
kosha	:	'envelope' (Sanskrit). See entry on *sharīra*.
kshatriya	:	the warrior caste-group, second in rank to the brahmins (Sanskrit). See *varṇa*.
lakh	:	Anglicization of Hindi *lākh*; cardinal number, equals 1,00,000. See entry on *crore*.
Mādhav	:	name of Vishṇu in His 'sweet' or enchanting aspect as an erotic god.
mādhurya	:	'sweetness' (Sanskrit, Hindi); used often to describe melodiousness and mellifluousness.
man	:	Hindi variation on Sanskrit *manas*, 'mind' or, more precisely, 'heart-mind'.
mandala	:	'circle' (Sanskrit, Hindi, Marathi); used in Tantra and yoga to represent processes or phenomena pictorially or conceptually; also used metaphorically to describe an association, group or meeting, such as a 'circle of friends'.
mantra	:	a verbal formula, used in Vedic ritual; also a formula with transformative powers, used outside ritual to exercise control over an object or an environment.
mat	:	'opinion, view, position' (Sanskrit, Hindi); corresponds closely to Latin *doxa*, 'opinion'.
maṭh	:	an institutional residence for sādhus and *saṃnyāsīs*; an ashram for a religious group.
Matsya	:	Vishnu's Fish avatar. See *Shaṅkhāsura* below.
Māyā	:	'illusion' (Sanskrit); generally, a representation of the world around us as 'unreal', and as consisting of illusory appearances. See Introduction; also see note to the poem 'Māyā'.
maulavī	:	a teacher of Arabic and Farsi; a scholar of Muslim *sharia*, law (Arabic, Persian).
Mecca	:	the holiest city of Islam; birthplace of the Prophet Muhammad; destination of the *hajj*.

Meru : short name for Mount Sumeru (Sanskrit). According to Paurāṇic mythology, Mount Sumeru is a golden mountain located in one of the nine regions of Jambudvīpa (which is one of the seven 'great islands' or continents on earth). It defines the *axis mundi* or axis of the world, and stands at the centre of the universe; it spans the height and depth of the universe, rising up to the heavens and going down to the bottom of the nether regions. All the gods have their celestial abodes on or near it, and their devotees dwell there after death, while waiting to be reborn on earth. The Himalayas form the foothills of Meru, and Bhāratavarsha ('India') stretches to its south, occupying the next region of Jambudvīpa. (The Hindu temple is modelled on Meru, with its steep *shikhar* or crown representing the majestic mountain.)

mlechchha : 'foreigner, outsider' (Sanskrit); xenophobic orthodox Hindu label for people of a foreign race or religion.

mokśa : Sanskrit term for the Self's liberation from karma and rebirth; origin of the term *mukti*.

mukti : in Hindi and other languages, 'liberation or final release' of the *ātmā* from the bondage of karma and *saṃsār*; derived from Sanskrit *mokśa*. See entries on *ātmā*, *karma* and *saṃsār*.

mullāh : 'master' (Persian, Turkish, Urdu; derived from Arabic); title for a Muslim religious teacher or leader belonging to a Sunni order.

nāḍī : in yogic physiology, a cord-like 'channel' for the body's 'vital airs' (Sanskrit, Hindi, Marathi). The 'body' here consists of a *sthūla sharīra* (gross body) and a *sūkshma sharīra* (subtle body); see entry on *sharīra*. Numerous *nāḍīs* traverse the *sharīra*; for yogic bodily and spiritual discipline, the three most important of these are the Iñgalā (also called the Iḍā), the Piñgalā and the Sushumnā, which are channels in the 'subtle body'. In relation to the 'gross body', the Sushumnā rises straight from the anus region to the top of the head; the Iñgalā (based on the left of the Sushumnā) and the Piñgalā (based on the right), curve sinusoidally and symmetrically across the central *nāḍī*, intersecting with each other five times (at points corresponding to the genitals, navel, heart, throat and forehead). The Iñgalā and Piñgalā convey breath through the subtle body; physical discipline (*haṭha*-yoga) and *prāṇāyāma* (breath-control) enable the yogi to channel his breath alternately through these two 'tubes', which induces an 'alchemical transformation' of his entire 'body'; after this transformation, the yogi can 'awaken his *kuṇḍalinī*' and cause it to ascend the Sushumnā, up to the *sahasrāra-chakra* just above the top of his head, which results in the blissful state of 'union' with godhead, or mukti. See entry on *sahasrāra*.

Nagari : short for 'Devanagari', a script developed to write Sanskrit; also used for Hindi and Marathi.

nām : 'name' (Sanskrit, Hindi); *nām-sumiran* is the ritualized activity of repeating God's name, usually in silence, as an aid to concentration and worship. See *jap*.

Nanak Panth : 'Nanak's path, way' (Punjabi, Hindi); original name, still in use, for the community of Guru Nanak's followers, now the Sikh community.

Nanda : see entry on *Krishṇa*.

Nārad : a sage or seer of the ancient period, whose absolute, unwavering devotion to God made him a model of bhakti during the middle period.

Narasiṃha : Vishṇu's avatar as a 'man-lion', half human and half animal. See *dashāvatār* above.

Nath Panth : a 'path' or order of sādhus, founded by Gorakhnath and his guru, Matsyendranath (probably twelfth century); its members are known equally commonly as *siddhas*, yogis and *avadhūts*, and thus are perceived as inheritors of much older *siddha*, yogic and Tantric traditions, as also more specifically of Sahajiya (or Tantric) Buddhism, Vaishṇava Sahajiya Tantra, Shaiva-Shakta Tantra, Gauḍiya (or Bengali) Vaishṇavism, and sufism. See Nagendra and Gupta 1973; Salomon 1995. Also see the Introduction.

Nath yoga : a 'vernacular' version of classical yoga. While classical yoga is expounded in Sanskrit (from Patanjali to Vāchaspati Mishra), Nath yoga is elaborated in a medium at the intersection of Apabhramsha and Hindavī or Hinduī (one of the oldest forms of Khaḏī Bolī). Nath yoga retains the entire metaphysics and theology of classical *rāja*-yoga, but builds on a variant conception of the 'body' as *kāyā*, with new emphasis within the system of *haṭha*-yoga (bodily discipline of 'strength'). See Nagendra and Gupta 1973; Varenne 1976; Salomon 1995.

nawab : Anglicized form of Arabic *nawwāb*; a royal administrator, appointed to govern a particular region or province on behalf of a Muslim ruler.

nirañjan : 'without blackening', stain-less, flawless, untarnished (Sanskrit, Hindi). Some Kabir texts characterize nirguṇa godhead as *nirañjan*, the opposite of *añjan* (see entry).

nirañkār : 'formless' (Hindi). See entry on *ākār*.

Niranjani Sampradaya : a religious community based in Rajasthan, probably founded in the fifteenth century; closely connected to the Dadu Dayal Panth. See Introduction.

nirguṇa : 'without qualities or attributes; unqualified' (Sanskrit, Hindi). In the Kabir canon, used to describe God (nirguṇa Rāma) or godhead (Brahman). See entry on *guṇa*.

nirvana : 'snuffing out' (Sanskrit; *nibbāna* in Pali). The moment at which a Buddhist 'extinguishes' the 'self' altogether; the culmination of all spiritual effort in Buddhism. The Kabir poets adopt the term on a few occasions, even though it differs starkly from the nirguṇa concept of mukti.

OṂ : sacred 'compound syllable' (*aum*), regarded by Hindus, Sikhs and others as the purest, most primordial and most important sound in the universe, identical with 'ultimate reality' itself. Sikh tradition represents nirguṇa godhead as *Ik Oṃkār* (see above).

pada : 'verse, poem, song' (Sanskrit, Hindi). The term may be used to designate either a single verse or an entire poem; it may also be used as a mass-noun to designate 'verse'. As a poem, a pada may be in any metre or form; in the Kabir canon, especially in the Rajasthani tradition, 'pada' designates one of the three principal poetic forms, the other two being the sākhī and the ramainī. Although the Kabir padas vary in structure and metre, the basic pattern has two parts: an opening verse that serves as a refrain, with a short first 'line' (using only one foot of the verse-form, instead of two); and a main body composed of multiple verses in a specific metrical form. The Kabir padas often use one metre for the refrain and another for the main verses; sometimes they also use two or more different metres in the main body of the poem. Commonly used metres include the *dohā* (four feet, with a 13–11–13–11 distribution of *mātrā*s or morae); the *chaupāī* (four feet, with sixteen *mātrā*s each); and the *sār* (with a 16–12–16–12 distribution of *mātrā*s). The *Ādi Granth* uses the term 'shabad' (a Punjabi derivative of the Sanskrit *śabda*, meaning 'sound, word, speech, discourse') in relation to the Kabir poems much as the Rajasthani manuscripts use 'pada'; the *Bījak* uses the Hindi term 'shabda' (borrowed without change from Sanskrit) for the same purpose. 'Pada' is a term from prosody and aesthetics; 'shabad' and 'shabda', which have an import comparable to that of the Greek word *logos*, are more theologically freighted terms.

pañchavāṇī : 'the discourse of five (saints)' (Hindi); genre of anthology which brings together the works of five major authors canonized by the Dadu Panth. Contrasted with *sarbaṅgī*.

paṇḍā : a brahmin priest who officiates at a temple, pilgrim-station or holy cremation site (Hindi).

paṇḍit : a brahmin scholar trained in the *shāstras* (Hindu codebooks and disciplinary texts); a man of high learning (Sanskrit).

panth : 'path, way' (Sanskrit, Hindi, Punjabi); common term for a 'sect', a religious community or organization, or even an independent faith. See *Kabir Panth* and *Nanak Panth*.

pāpa : 'demerit' (Sanskrit); a measure of the 'wrongness' of an action in relation to *dharma*, moral law. See entry on *karma*.

paraṃparā : 'tradition' (Sanskrit). See Introduction for discussion.

Parashurāma : a human avatar of Vishṇu; see entry on *dashāvatār.*

Paurāṇic : adjective; 'belonging to, derived from or related to the Purāṇas' (Sanskrit, Hindi).

Piṅgalā : a major *nāḍī* in yogic physiology; see the entry on that term.

pīr : 'master' (Persian); sufi term for spiritual mentor or teacher; contrasted with *murīd*, disciple, student. Persian and sufi *pīr-o-murīd* (master-and-pupil) parallels the older Sanskrit guru-*shishya*; see the entry on *guru*.

prāṇa : 'breath; life; sign of life; principle of life' (Sanskrit); in the Upanishads, *prāṇa* is *ātmā* or *haṃsa*, the 'true self' within. See entry on *ātmā*.

prārabdha : a technical term in the analysis of *karma* (see entry).

pratibhā : 'lustre, brilliance; intellect; intelligence, understanding; great intellectual power' (Sanskrit).

Punjabi : the language of the people of Punjab, a region now divided between western India and eastern Pakistan. Punjabi emerged as a speech-variety of the region between Delhi and Lahore in the opening centuries of the past millennium; modern Punjabi stands on a continuum with modern Hindi, Urdu and Farsi, among other languages used in the northern portion of the subcontinent. The history of the language and its literature is closely connected to the history of the Sikhs in the Punjab. See entry on *Gurmukhi*.

puṇya	:	'merit' (Sanskrit); a measure of the 'rightness' of an action in relation to *dharma*, moral law. See entry on *karma*.
Purāṇa	:	'old or ancient text' (Sanskrit). A category of texts, mostly composed in encyclopaedic forms during the first millennium A.D. or within a few centuries afterwards; Purāṇas are devoted primarily to theology and mythology, but many of them also bring together narrative and poetry, as well as history, social theory, politics, ethics, aesthetics and other such subjects. The Purāṇas contain much of the discourse that defines the theory and practice of 'classical Hinduism'; they also provide many of the stories, fables, concepts and structures that animate bhakti literature in later centuries.
qāzī	:	a Muslim judge who applies *sharia* (law); a scholar of that law (Arabic).
Qur'ān	:	the holy book or scripture of Islam. For the Kabir poets, also simply the *Kateb* or 'Book'.
Rādhā	:	see entry on *Krishṇa*.
Radhasoami Satsang	:	a new nirguna 'sect', founded in the nineteenth century. See Introduction.
rāga	:	'colour; musical mode' (Sanskrit *rāgah*). A tonal structure, with a framework of progressions and melodic and rhythmic patterns, upon which a performer improvises variations in order to articulate the mood and meaning of a particular theme. In the case of a vocal rendition, the theme is provided and the mood (*rasa*) indicated by a lyric that is 'religious' in nature. A rāga (classified as a 'male' structure) is associated with one or more rāginīs (classified as 'female' structures), which elaborate subsidiary tonal, melodic and other alternatives to the primary framework. Rāgas themselves are grouped into 'families', with each family grounded quite systematically in a master-structure called a *mela* or *thāṭa*, each of which constitutes a basic combination

of tones and semitones. In the seventeenth century, the 'Hindustānī' classical system of music, which evolved its present form in the middle period (roughly, 1200 to 1750) in north India, could be described using twelve *thāṭas*; the 'Karnatak' or Carnatic classical system, which evolved contemporaneously in south India, had a theoretical basis in thirty-six *melas* (these classifications and their theoretical bases have changed in the modern period). In principle, each *thāṭa* or *mela* can generate a family of twenty to thirty rāgas and rāginīs. The musical structures of the Kabir texts and the *Ādi Granth* evolved *before* theorists of the middle period systematized *melas* and rāgas; the two canons are therefore premier sites of innovation in the multidimensional aesthetics of language, music, mood and communication. The approximately 3,000 poems in the *Ādi Granth* (in its final form as the *Guru Granth Sāhib*) are set to thirty-one rāgas and rāginīs; the Kabir canon uses a comparable range of musical structures in its totality. The thirty-nine padas translated from the Punjabi and Rajasthani traditions in this book belong to ten rāgas and rāginīs: Āsā or Āsāvarī, Basanta, Basanta Hiṇḍolā, Bhairava, Bihāga, Gauḏī, Prabhātī, Rāmakalī, Soraṭhī and Sūhī. The variants of some of the translated padas are set differently, and thus bring other rāgas and rāginīs also into play: Bilāvala; Gauḏī Chetī, Jañgalī Gauḏī and Mālī Gauḏī; Bibhāsa Prabhātī; and Sārañga. In the final analysis, the 'meaning' of a Kabir poem that is set to music in the original cannot be understood without reference to this intricate musical system, which deeply 'colours' its text.

Raghu : see the entry on *Rāma*.

rāginī : see the entry on *rāga*.

Rahīm : an epithet of Allāh in the Qur'ān.

rajas : quality of 'energy and force or momentum' (Sanskrit); see *guṇa*.

Rajasthani : an ensemble of speech-varieties and literary standards that have evolved steadily over the past millennium, and that, in tandem, constitute the large western branch or sub-language of 'Hindi'. Historically, the principal dialects of Rajasthani are: Mārawāḏī (western Rajasthani); Jaipurī (eastern Rajasthani); Mewātī (northern Rajasthani); and Mālawī (southern Rajasthani). Distinctive speech-varieties within this classification, associated with specific places in Rajasthan, include Ajmerī, Bikānerī, and Jodhpurī. Much of Rajasthan is semi-arid; its climate has provided exceptionally salubrious conditions for the survival of manuscripts in India, making the region home to a large proportion of middle-period archives. Many of the earliest surviving works in the history of 'Hindi' literature, including Chandabardai's *Prithvīrāj-rāso* and the 'folk ballad' *Dholā-Māru rā dūhā* (both twelfth century), are composed in old forms of Rajasthani. The Rajasthani tradition has played a shaping role in the formation of the Kabir canon, even though the poet presumably belonged to the Banaras-Magahar region.

Rāma : (*a*) Name of the seventh of Vishṇu's ten main avatars; Rāma in this saguṇa form is the epic hero of the *Rāmāyaṇa*. He was a prince in the clan of Raghu; his father, Dasharath, was the ruler of the republic of Kosala. When Rāma was ready to succeed his father to the throne, a palace-intrigue deprived him of his kingship; he went into a long exile in the southern forests with his wife, Sītā, and his younger brother, Lakshmaṇa. During their sojourn, Sītā was abducted by a demon-king, Rāvaṇa, and imprisoned in his island-kingdom; Rāma and Lakshmaṇa, using the help of an army of monkeys, invaded the island, defeated Rāvaṇa and his brothers, and rescued Sītā. Although the Kabir poets reject this mythology, they nevertheless allude to this story and its elements several times. (*b*) Most often in the Kabir texts, 'Rāma' is an invocation of 'Nirguṇa Rāma', the poets' paradoxical term for godhead or ultimate reality without attributes. See the Introduction for details.

Ramadān : the ninth month of the Muslim calendar, during which the faithful fast daily from sunrise to sunset as an act of spiritual discipline (Arabic).

Ramananda Sampradaya : a 'sect' or religious order founded by Rāmānanda (fourteenth century), an influential brahmin philosopher and renowned 'activist'; its texts and practices define a socially and theologically conservative Vaishṇava conception of bhakti.

ramainī : one of the three principal poetic forms of the Kabir canon, found primarily in the *Bījak* and to a lesser extent in the Rajasthani collections; absent from the northern texts. A ramainī contains two 'parts': the main body of the poem, which is composed with multiple verses in the *dohā* form (a couplet-like rhymed verse with four feet, the first and third of which contain thirteen *mātrā*s or morae each, and the second and fourth of which contain eleven *mātrā*s each); and the concluding verse, which is in the *chaupāī* form (a quatrain-like rhymed verse with four feet of sixteen *mātrā*s each). A ramainī is designed esoterically to induce a state of 'bliss' in the listener or reader. See Sharma 1969.

Rāmāyaṇa : ancient Indian epic, which tells the life-story of Rāma, an avatar of Vishṇu. See *Rāma*.

re<u>kh</u>tā : (*a*) A verse or poem, often a 'couplet', composed with different parts of the poem (particular 'feet' or 'lines') in different languages; Persian and Hindavī were often the languages of choice in such an exercise. (*b*) A verse or poem composed throughout in a less-structured 'mixture' of Persian and Hindavī, a 'mongrel medium'. (*c*) The 'mixed' speech-variety that evolved in Delhi and other regions of north India, in which Persian and Arabic words were superposed on a largely Hindavī or Braj syntax to create what later came to be called 'Hindustānī' in its spoken form, and 'Urdū' and 'Hindī' in their early modern written forms. See Faruqi 2001 and Pollock 2003.

Rukmiṇī : Krishṇa's first wife. See *Krishna* above.

rūp : 'form, outward shape, appearance' (Sanskrit, Hindi); see entry on *ākār* above.

sādhu : a Hindu ascetic, a holy man who has 'renounced' life in the everyday human world.

sādhukkaḏī : the jargon of sādhus (Hindi); synonym of *sant bhāshā* (see entry).

saguṇa : 'with qualities, attributes; qualified' (Sanskrit, Hindi); see *guṇa*.

sahaj : 'easy, spontaneous, natural, accessible, casual, simple' (Sanskrit, Hindi, Punjabi, Marathi). For the Kabir poets, the *sahaj sthiti* is the 'simple state' in which an individual merges with his *ātmā*, which is identical with nirguṇa godhead or ultimate reality. See Introduction for details.

sahasrāra : the *chakra* or circle 'with a thousand petals' (Sanskrit). In classical yoga, conceptualized as an inverted thousand-petalled lotus, located just outside the *sthūla sharīra* or gross body (the physical, flesh-and-blood body), above the head, but still inside the *sūkshma sharīra* or subtle body. The yogi's goal is to raise his *kuṇḍalinī* to the *sahasrāra*, where it achieves 'liberation' or 'release', leading to a final state of 'bliss' (which corresponds to the *ātmā*'s *mukti*, 'union' with ultimate reality). See the entries on *nāḍī*, *sharīra* and *yoga*.

sākhī : with the pada and the ramainī, one of the three principal poetic forms in the Kabir tradition. It is usually composed as a *dohā*, a rhymed verse-form with four feet, with a 13–11–13–11 distribution of *mātrā*s or morae. The second and fourth feet have end-rhymes, so the effect is often similar to that of a 'heroic couplet' in English. A sākhī is conceived of as a poem of 'witness' or 'testimony', and offers spiritual and practical wisdom in the shape of a witty, satirical or proverb-like aphorism.

samādhī : 'to put together, join, unify; to be fixed in one location' (Sanskrit, Hindi). To achieve union with God, godhead or nirguṇa reality; to enter into the final 'bliss' in yoga; to attain *mukti* in a final trance. Also, a monument built to mark the place where a bhakta 'enters *samādhī*.'

saṃnyāsī : one who has renounced the everyday human world; a 'world-renouncer' (Sanskrit).

saṃpradāya : an organized community, usually of the followers of a shared faith; a religious order, a 'sect' (Sanskrit, Hindi).

saṃsār : 'confluence; karmic cycle of life, death and rebirth; the everyday human world in its totality; full round of daily existence' (Sanskrit, Hindi). See *karma*.

sañchita : see entry on *karma*.

sant : a true or good man; a pious or holy man; a gentle, morally upright person (Hindi). Used as a term to distinguish the followers of nirguṇa *mat* from other types of bhaktas.

sant bhāshā : 'the language of the *sants*' (Hindi); term for jargon used by north Indian nirguṇa authors in the middle period. Synonymous with *sādhukkaḏī* (above); also see Introduction.

sarbañgī : 'that which has all the parts together' (Hindi); from Sanskrit *sarvāñgī*. Genre of anthology in Dadu Panthi tradition that collects texts by different authors in different forms on a broad range of themes. See discussion in Introduction; contrasted to *pañchavāṇī* (see entry).

Satguru : 'the True Master' (Sanskrit, Hindi, Punjabi). One of the epithets of nirguṇa God or godhead in the Kabir texts; also used widely in other nirguṇa traditions, including Sikhism. No human being can be the *Satguru*. The conceptualization of God as the True Guru obviates the necessity of a human guru, or of institutional intercession between worshipper and deity. It places bhakti, devotion, on an axis defined by a direct connection between bhakta and God, a line of 'total freedom' from interference by others; it also prepares the way for the 'interiorization' of both nirguṇa reality and mukti within the devotee's 'self'.

sattva : the great quality of 'light and truth' (Sanskrit). See *guṇa*.

saulabhya : 'ease of access' (Sanskrit); bhakti term for God's accessibility to His devotees.

shabad : Punjabi variation on Sanskrit *śabda* or Hindi *shabda* (see entry).

shabda : Sanskrit form of the word, which means 'sound, word, speech'; this spelling is retained in the *Bījak* tradition to designate the genre of the short (to medium-length) lyrical poem which, in the Rajasthani tradition, is called the *pada* (see entry).

shah : 'master, lord' (Persian); an honorific title, given to or taken by a ruler, usually a regional ruler within a larger imperial order. Also a title higher than *sheikh* (see below) given to a sufi master in India, in recognition of extraordinary influence.

Shaiva : a worshipper of Shiva; term used to describe communities and practices associated with Shiva. Shaiva devotees are also often called Shāktas, especially in eastern India.

shākhā : 'branch' of a tree (Sanskrit, Hindi); figuratively, a branch of an organization or structure.

shalok : also *salok*; Punjabi variations on Sanskrit *śloka* (see entry).

Shankara : (*a*) One of Shiva's names, used frequently by his worshippers to invoke his more benevolent aspect. (*b*) Name of famous eighth-century philosopher of the Advaita Vedānta or Uttar Mīmāṃsā school.

Shaṅkhāsura : an *asura* or *rākshasa* (demonic creature) who stole the text of the Vedas from Brahmā (the god of the Vedas) and hid it in the ocean; Vishṇu descended to earth in the form of a fish (the Matsya avatar) to destroy Shaṅkhāsura and restore the Vedas.

sharīra : 'body' (Sanskrit, Hindi). In classical yoga, the human body is conceptualized as consisting of an 'outer' *sthūla sharīra* (gross body), the body of flesh, blood and bone; and an 'inner' *sūkshma sharīra* (subtle body), made up of a series of imperceptible *kosha*s or envelopes, each of which is wrapped around a particular component of the individual's 'self' (the *buddhī*, the *chitta*, the *ātmā*, etc.), one inside the other in succession (like a set of Chinese boxes). Yogic bodily and spiritual discipline is designed to use this structure of the 'body' to attain the *mukti* of the *ātmā* from *karma* and rebirth. See entries on *ātmā*, *karma* and *yoga*.

sheikh : alternative transliteration, *shekh* (Arabic). An honorific title with a complex and varied history of usage in the Muslim world. In middle-period India, a title given to and used by sufi masters; and also by members of the 'upper classes' in the subcontinent's indigenous population that converted to Islam.

Shesha : name of a mythical serpent who supports the earth on his hood.

shikshā : 'instruction, education' (Sanskrit, Hindi). In middle-period north Indian social and religious life, only male children from the *dvija* castes could be educated by a legitimate *shikshā*-guru, whose legitimacy as a teacher was determined by norms and institutions controlled by the upper caste-groups. See entry on *dīkshā* for the corresponding system of controls in the domain of religious instruction and legitimation.

Shiva : With Vishṇu, one of the two 'great gods' of Hinduism; with Brahmā and Vishṇu, one of the Hindu 'trinity'. Shiva is the master-yogi, the prototype of the 'wandering ascetic'; he is also the 'outlaw' god of Shāktism, the ultimate Tantric. His consort is Parvati, with whom he has a son, the elephant-headed Ganesha; Parvati is also Shakti.

shloka : *śloka* in Sanskrit; a verse in *anuṣṭubh* metre, with four feet containing eight syllables each.

shūdra : caste-group of 'servants', placed below the three *dvija* caste-groups. See *varṇa.*

silsilāh : 'chain; continuous line, sequence' (Arabic). Sufi institution of passing down spiritual practice and legitimacy from master to pupil, from one generation to the next; to be legitimate, a sufi must demonstrably be a 'link' in a continuous 'chain' of precursors.

Sirjanhār : Hindi derivative of Sanskrit *sṛjanahāra*, 'creator, compiler, constructor'; epithet for God in his aspect as the Creator of the universe.

Sītā : wife of Rāma, the hero of the *Rāmāyaṇa*; see *Rāma.*

smṛti : 'that which is remembered; memory' (Sanskrit). The category of discourse in ancient India that contains what has been composed by human authors, but nevertheless deserves the status of 'canon'. The two major epics, the *Rāmāyaṇa* and the *Mahābhārata*, for example, are *smṛti* literature (though the *Bhagavad-gītā*, which is part of the latter epic, is sometimes called 'the fifth Veda', and hence accorded the status of *śruti*). See entry on *śruti.*

śruti : 'that which is heard' (Sanskrit); major category of discourse that defines what constitutes the 'law' or 'canon' given by the gods to humans; the Vedic corpus is *śruti*. See *smṛti.*

sthūla : 'gross' (Sanskrit); used to describe the structure of the 'body' in yoga and other systems of thought. See entry on *sharīra.*

sūkshma : 'subtle' (Sanskrit); used to describe the structure of the 'body' in yoga and other systems of thought. See *sharīra.*

Sushumnā : one of the major *nāḍī*s in yogic physiology; see the entry on *nāḍī.*

tamas : the quality of darkness and inertia; see *guṇa.*

Turk : the term that north Indians used most often between the thirteenth and nineteenth centuries to designate Muslims, especially those of Central and West Asian origin or descent. This usage in Hindi parallels that of 'Turk' and 'Moor' in early modern English.

tyāg : 'renunciation' (Sanskrit, Hindi). Voluntary relinquishment of something desirable; more broadly, relinquishment of life in the everyday human world, in the quest for *mukti*.

ulaṭabāṃsī : 'upside-down speech or discourse' (Hindi). A genre of poetry, primarily in the nirguṇa tradition of the middle period in north India, shaped by the topos that 'the world at present is upside down'. See note on 'The Way' above; also see 'Rāma's Essence' and 'Creation'.

Upanishad : a large, varied and complex class of texts, composed and canonized between the Vedic period and the classical period of Indian history, that provides the early basis of much of Hindu philosophical, religious and mystical thought. The number of important Upanishads is variously placed at eighteen, fifty-two and 108. See Olivelle 1996.

upāsak : a worshipper, devotee, or follower (Hindi). Used instead of 'bhakta' for a nirguṇa devotee.

upāsanā : worship, devotion (Hindi). Used for nirguṇa devotion, to distinguish it from saguṇi bhakti.

Urdu : The language that emerged slowly but steadily in north India after about 1100 out of a mixture of Farsi and various north Indian languages and speech-varieties, and acquired its early modern spoken and written forms in the eighteenth century. It stands on a linguistic, social, historical and cultural continuum with what we now call 'Hindi', but the two languages use two different scripts (mostly Farsi for Urdu and Nagari for Hindi since the late nineteenth century). Especially see Faruqi 2001 and Pollock 2003. Also see entry on *rekhtā*.

Uttar Mīmāṃsā : In the history of Indian philosophy (*darshan*), the name for the school better known as *Advaita Vedānta* (see entry).

vachana : 'speech, utterance' (*vacana* in Sanskrit); in Vīrashaiva literature in Kannada, a genre of poetic utterances recorded in 'prose', attributed to its major 'saints'. See Ramanujan 1973.

Vaikuṇṭha : the celestial 'abode of Vishṇu', hence *swarga* or 'heaven' (Sanskrit).

Vaishṇava : a worshipper or follower of Vishṇu.

vaishya : the caste-group of traders, merchants and common folk; see *varṇa*.

Vāmana : the 'Dwarf' avatar of Vishṇu. See entry on *dashāvatār*.

vāṇī : 'speech, utterance,' discourse (Sanskrit); its derivative in Hindi and Punjabi is often *bāṇī*. In the Sikh tradition, the Gurus distinguish between *pakkī bāṇī*, solid, fixed or permanent, and therefore indispensable, discourse; and *kachchī bāṇī*, weak, shaky and dispensable discourse. Only *pakkī bāṇī* can be admitted to the textual canon of Sikhism.

vāra : a genre of composition in the *Ādi Granth*. See Mann 2001.

Varāha : the 'Boar' avatar of Vishṇu. See *dashāvatār*.

varṇa : 'colour, class, group' (Sanskrit). The *Ṛg-veda* and other canonical texts in Hinduism offer a primary division of society into four (or five) main *varṇas*, groups of classes; these define the principal caste-groups labelled as brahmin, kshatriya, vaishya, shūdra (and *atishūdra*).

varṇāśrama : a Sanskrit term that combines *varṇa* and *āshrama* (see both entries).

Vāsudev : see entry on *Krishṇa*.

Veda : 'knowledge' (Sanskrit); an extensive body of texts composed and compiled starting around 1000 B.C., which became the founding 'scripture' of Hinduism. It includes four *saṃhitas* or collections of hymns—the *Ṛg-veda*, the *Sāma-veda*, the *Atharva-veda*, and the *Yajur-veda*—that form the liturgical core of a significant part of Hindu religious practice. It also includes texts in the genres, such as the Brāhmaṇas and Upanishads, that provide the discursive basis for much of subsequent Hindu philosophy, theology, morality and ethics, and social and political theory. The Vedic canon, 'given by the gods', lays down the 'law' in most spheres of Hindu life, though the later *shāstras* and *sūtras*, *itihāsas* and *purāṇas*, *kāvyas* and *kathās* provide many of the practical guidelines. 'Veda' therefore consistently signifies authority, and serves as the source for the legitimation of authority.

vichār : 'thought, thinking' (the Sanskrit verbal root denotes 'roaming' quite haphazardly); in bhakti literature, sometimes designates 'meditation'.

Vīrashaiva : a 'school' of Shaiva practice, specific to the Kannada-speaking region in south-central India, whose members launched a major movement of social and religious reform around the twelfth century. See Ramanujan 1973.

Vishṇu : with Shiva, one of the two principal anthropomorphic gods in Hinduism; with Shiva and Brahmā, one of the gods in the Hindu 'trinity', in which His function is 'preservation' (as distinguished from Brahmā's 'creation' and Shiva's 'destruction'). Each of the gods in the trinity has multiple 'aspects'; both Shiva and Vishṇu also have multiple names; but unlike the others, Vishṇu alone 'descends' to earth in various avatars (incarnations) at particular times. Vishṇu has a total of twenty-four avatars, of which ten are 'primary'. Four of these are human incarnations in the past; two of them are particularly famous in Hindu mythology and literature: Rāma, prince of the clan of Raghu in the kingdom of Kosala, hero of the epic *Rāmāyaṇa*; and Krishṇa, a cowherd in Vrindavan, near Mathura, child-god and adult erotic god, later transformed into the warrior-god of the epic *Mahābhārata* and the ruler of the western city of Dwaraka. Vaishṇavism, which claims Vishṇu as the supreme God, demographically defines the majority of Hindus; it portrays Vishṇu as a benevolent preserver of order, whose consort, Lakshmi, is the goddess of wealth and prosperity. Its core also constitutes the most 'conservative' sector of Hinduism.

viśiṣṭadvaita : 'qualified non-dualism' (Sanskrit); a school of Vedānta philosophy associated with the philosopher Ramanauja, who produced a variation on Shankarācharya's Advaita Vedānta, 'unqualified non-dualism'. See Mohanty 1995.

viveka : discrimination; capacity to distinguish between good and bad, to weigh choices (Sanskrit).

yajña : Vedic sacrificial ritual, which is central to the practice of the 'religion' of the Veda (Sanskrit).

yantra : 'instrument' (Sanskrit); technically, a device used in a particular spiritual exercise or practice, designed to aid the attainment of a specific goal.

yoga : act of 'yoking together'; discipline (Sanskrit). In its general sense, any ancient Indian spiritual discipline and practice, such as the various yogas mentioned in the *Bhagavad-gītā* (see above). More specifically, a system of spiritual discipline and practice based on a distinctive and comprehensive philosophy and theology, initially formulated by the middle of the epic period, and subsequently systematized in the classical period as one of the six principal *darshans* or Indian philosophical systems. Classical yoga is divisible into numerous branches or varieties, with *rāja*-yoga serving as the dominant or comprehensive 'master-system' and *haṭha*-yoga ('discipline of strength'), among others, serving as a popular subsidiary practice. Early in the middle period, the

Nath Panth became an influential institution of yogic theory and practice, providing the immediate reference-point for most of the speculation and discourse in the subcontinent's new 'vernacular' languages that alluded to yoga after about 1200. *Nath yoga* exercised a pervasive influence on nirguṇi as well as saguṇi bhakti until the eighteenth century (see the entry above).

yogi : a practitioner of one or more types of yoga; a member of an order committed to a particular 'school' of yoga; in general, a holy man who practises a rigorous spiritual discipline.

BIBLIOGRAPHY

Ahmad, Aijaz. 1992. *In Theory: Classes, Nations, Literatures*. London: Verso.

Alam, Ishrat. 1997. 'A Dutch Memoir of 1603 on Indian Textiles'. In Habib 1997. Pp. 294–97.

Alam, Muzaffar, and Sanjay Subrahmanyam, ed. 1998. Rpt. 2000. *The Mughal State 1526–1750*. New Delhi: Oxford University Press.

Ali, M. Athar. 1997. 'The Perception of India in Akbar and Abū'l Fazl'. In Habib 1997. Pp. 215–24.

Allchin, F. R., trans. 1966. *Tulsī Dās. The Petition to Rām: Hindi Devotional Hymns of the 17th Century*. London: George Allen and Unwin.

Auden, W. H. 1991. *Collected Poems*. Ed. by Edward Mendelson. New York: Vintage, Random House.

Azad, Muhammad Husain. [1880, 1883] 2001. *Āb-e hayāt: Shaping the Canon of Urdu Poetry*. Ed. and trans. by Frances Pritchett, with Shamsur Rahman Faruqi. New Delhi: Oxford University Press.

Bahura, Gopal Narayan, ed. 1984. *Pada sūradāsajī kā. The Padas of Surdas*. With an essay by Ken Bryant. City Palace, Jaipur: Maharaja Sawai Man Singh II Museum.

Barthwal, P[itambar]. D[utta]. [1930] 1978. *Traditions of Indian Mysticism Based upon Nirguna School of Hindi Poetry*. New Delhi: Heritage.

———, ed. [1942] 3rd ed. 1960. *Gorakh-bāṇī*. Prayag [Allahabad]: Hindi Sahitya-sammelan.

Bassnett, Susan, and Harish Trivedi, eds. 1999. *Post-colonial Translation: Theory and Practice*. London: Routledge.

Bayly, Susan. 1999. *Caste, Society and Politics in India from the Eighteenth Century to the Modern Age*. Vol. 4, pt. 3 of *The New Cambridge History of India*, ed. by Gordon Johnson. Cambridge: Cambridge University Press.

Behl, Aditya, and Simon Weightman, trans. 2000. *Manjhan. Madhumālatī: An Indian Sufi Romance*. Oxford: University of Oxford Press.

Bhajan-saṃgraha. [1981] 1994. Gorakhpur: Gita Press.

Bharadwaj, Surinder Mohan. 1973. *Hindu Places of Pilgrimage in India: A Study in Cultural Geography*. Berkeley: University of California Press.

Bharucha, Rustom. [1998] 2001. *In the Name of the Secular: Contemporary Cultural Activism in India*. New Delhi: Oxford University Press.

Bose, N. K. [1949] 1975. *The Structure of Hindu Society*. Trans. by Andre Beteille. New Delhi: Sangam Books, Orient Longman.

Bryant, Kenneth E. 1978. *Poems to the Child-God*. Berkeley: University of California Press.

———. 1984. 'The Manuscript Tradition of the *Sursagar*: The Fatehpur Manuscript'. In Bahura 1984. Pp. vii–xx.

Callewaert, Winand M. 1978. *The Sarvāngī of the Dādūpanthī Rajab*. Leuven, Belgium: Department Orientalistiek, Katholieke Universiteit Leuven.

———. 1996. *Śrī Guru Granth Sāhib: With Complete Index*. 2 vols. Delhi: Motilal Banarsidass.

———, with Swapna Sharma and Dieter Taillieu. 2000. *The Millennium Kabīr Vāṇī: A Collection of* Pad-*s*. New Delhi: Manohar.

Chattopadhyaya, Brajadulal. 1994. Rpt. 1999. *The Making of Early Medieval India*. New Delhi: Oxford University Press.

Chaturvedi, Parashuram. [1950] 2nd ed. 1964. *Uttarī bhārat kī sant-paraṃparā*. Allahabad: Bharati Bhandar, Leader Press.

———. 1954. *Kabīr-sāhitya kī parakh*. Prayag [Allahabad]: Bharati Bhandar, Leader Press.

———, ed. 1966. *Dādūdayāl: granthāvalī*. Varanasi: Nagari Pracharini Sabha.

Chitre, Dilip, trans. 1991. *Says Tuka: Selected Poetry of Tukaram*. New Delhi: Penguin.

Currie, P. M. [1989] 1992. *The Shrine and Cult of Mu'īn al-dīn Chistī of Ajmer*. Delhi: Oxford University Press.

Curtius, Ernst Robert. [1953] Bollingen paperback ed. 1973. *European Literature and the Latin Middle Ages*. Trans. by Willard R. Trask. Princeton: Princeton University Press. [Original German ed. 1948.]

Dalmia, Vasudha. 1996. 'Introduction'. In Vaudeville 1996. Pp. 1–14.

Damrosch, David, gen. ed. 1999. *The Longman Anthology of British Literature*. Vol. 2. New York: Longman.

Dasgupta, S. N. [1927] 1959. Rpt. 1971. *Hindu Mysticism*. New York: Frederick Ungar.

Dass, Nirmal, trans. 1991. *Songs of Kabir from the Adi Granth*. Albany: State University of New York Press.

Davis, Richard H. 1995. 'Introduction: A Brief History of Religions in India'. In Lopez 1995. Pp. 3–52.

Dharwadker, Vinay. 1995a. 'Kabir'. In Lopez 1995. Pp. 77–91.

———. 1995b. 'Poems of Tukaram'. In Lopez 1995. Pp. 92–103.

———. 1999a. 'A. K. Ramanujan's Theory and Practice of Translation'. In Bassnett and Trivedi 1999. Pp. 114–40.

———, gen. ed. 1999b. *The Collected Essays of A. K. Ramanujan*. New Delhi: Oxford University Press.

Dimock, Edward C., Jr., and Denise Levertov, trans. 1967. *In Praise of Krishna: Songs from the Bengali*. New York: Anchor, Doubleday.

Dvivedi, Hazariprasad. [1941] 1955. *Kabīr: kabīrake vyaktitva, sāhitya aur dārshanik vichāroṃkī ālochanā*. 5th rev. ed. Bombay: Hindi-Granth-Ratnakar. [1990 ed. 8th reprint. New Delhi: Rajkamal Prakashan.]

———. [1952] 6th ed. 1990, third rpt. 1999. *Hindī sāhitya: udbhav aur vikās*. New Delhi: Rajkamal Prakashan.

———. [1959] 1997 ed. *Hindī sāhitya kī bhūmikā*. New Delhi: Rajkamal Prakashan.

Dwyer, William J. 1981. *Bhakti in Kabīr*. Patna: Associated Book Agency.

Eaton, Richard M. [1993] new ed. 1994, 1997; 2nd impression 2000. *The Rise of Islam and the Bengal Frontier, 1204–1760*. New Delhi: Oxford University Press.

Eck, Diana. 1982. 'Kashi: City of All India'. In Madan 1992. Pp. 138–55.

———. 1985. *Darśan: Seeing the Divine Image in India*. 2nd rev. and enlarged ed. Chambersburg, Pennsylvania: Anima.

Embree, Ainslie T., ed. 1971. *Alberuni's India*. Trans. by Edward C. Sachau. Abridged ed. New York: W. W. Norton.

Faruqi, Shamsur Rahman. 2001. *Early Urdu Literary Culture and History*. New Delhi: Oxford University Press.

Feuerstein, Georg, trans. [1979]. American ed.1989. *The Yoga-Sūtra of Patañjali: A New Translation and Commentary*. 2nd ed. Rochester, Vermont: Inner Traditions International.

Flood, Gavin. 1996. *An Introduction to Hinduism*. Cambridge: Cambridge University Press.

Freitag, Sandra B., ed. [1989] 1992. *Culture and Power in Banaras: Community, Performance, and Environment, 1800–1980*. Berkeley: University of California Press.

Gandharva, Kumar. 1985. *The Genius of Kumar Gandharva*. 2 cassettes. CBS Gramophone Records and Tapes (India).

Gangasharan Shastri, ed. 1989. *Bījak ṭīkā manoramā*. Varanasi: Kabir Vani Prakashan Kendra.

Ghose, Sisirkumar. 1995. 'Religious Experience: The Experience of Mysticism'. *The New Encyclopaedia Britannica*. 15th ed. Vol. 26. Pp. 582–90.

Gold, Ann Grodzins. [1988] 1990. *Fruitful Journeys: The Ways of Rajasthani Pilgrims*. Berkeley: University of California Press.

Grewal, J. S. 1997. 'The Sikh Movement During the Reign of Akbar'. In Habib 1997. Pp. 243–55.

Gupta, Mataprasad, ed. 1969. *Kabīr-granthāvalī*. Allahabad: Lokabharati Prakashan.

Habib, Irfan, ed. 1992. *Medieval India 1: Researches in the History of India*

1200–1750. Centre of Advanced Study in History, Aligarh Muslim University. Delhi: Oxford University Press.

———, ed. 1997. Rpt. 2000. *Akbar and His India*. New Delhi: Oxford University Press.

Hawley, John Stratton. 1984. *Sūr Dās: Poet, Singer, Saint*.

———. 1995. 'The *Nirguṇ/Saguṇ* Distinction in Early Manuscript Anthologies of Hindu Devotion'. In Lorenzen 1995a. pp. 160–80.

———, and Mark Juergensmeyer, trans. 1988. *Songs of the Saints of India*. New York: Oxford University Press.

Henry, Edward O. 1995. 'The Vitality of the *Nirguṇ* Bhajan: Sampling the Contemporary Tradition'. In Lorenzen 1995a. Pp. 231–50.

Hess, Linda, and Shukdev Singh, trans. 1983. *The Bījak of Kabir*. San Francisco: North Point Press.

Hiriyanna, M. [1949] 1985. *Essentials of Indian Philosophy*. London: George Allen and Unwin.

Husain, Iqbal. 1992. 'Hindu Shrines and Practices as Described by a Central Asian Traveller in the First Half of the 17th Century'. In Habib 1992. Pp. 141–53.

Jafri, Ali Sardar. [1965] New ed. 1998; 2nd rpt. 2001. *Kabīr bāṇī*. New Delhi: Rajkamal Paperbacks.

Jairazbhoy, Nazir A. 1995. 'South Asian Arts: Music'. *The New Encyclopaedia Britannica*. 15th ed. Vol. 27. Pp. 652–60.

Juergensmeyer, Mark. 1988. 'The Logic of Religious Violence'. In Madan 1992. Pp. 382–93.

———. 1995. 'The Social Significance of Radhasoami'. In Lorenzen 1995a. Pp. 67–93.

Kabīr vāṇī. 1995. Haridwar: Randhir Prakashan.

Keay, F. E. 1931. *Kabir and His Followers*. Calcutta: Association Press and Oxford University Press.

Kermode, Frank. [1975] rev. ed. 1983. *The Classic: Literary Images of Permanence and Change*. Cambridge, Massachusetts: Harvard University Press.

Khan, M. A. Saleem. 1997. *Early Muslim Perception of India and Hinduism*. New Delhi: South Asian Publishers.

King, Christopher R. 1989. 'Forging a New Linguistic Identity: The Hindi Movement in Banaras, 1868–1914'. In Freitag 1992. Pp. 179–202.

———. [1994] 1999. *One Language, Two Scripts: The Hindi Movement in Nineteenth Century North India*. New Delhi: Oxford University Press.

Klostermaier, Klaus K. 1994. *A Survey of Hinduism*. 2nd ed. Albany: State University of New York Press.

Krishan, Yuvraj. 1997. *The Doctrine of Karma: Its Origin and Development in Brahmanical, Buddhist and Jaina Traditions*. Delhi: Motilal Banarasidass.

Kumar, Nita. 1989. 'Work and Leisure in the Formation of Identity: Muslim Weavers in a Hindu City'. In Freitag 1992. Pp. 147–70.

———. 1992. *Friends, Brothers, and Informants: Fieldwork Memoirs of Banaras*. Berkeley: University of California Press.

Lapidus, Ira M. 1988. Rpt. 1995. *A History of Islamic Societies*. Cambridge: Cambridge University Press.

Lopez, Donald S., Jr., ed. 1995. *Religions of India in Practice*. Introduction by Richard H. Davis. Princeton: Princeton University Press.

Lorenzen, David N. 1991. *Kabir Legends and Ananta-das's* Kabir Parachai. Albany: State University of New York Press.

———, ed. 1995a. *Bhakti Religion in North India: Community Identity and Political Action*. Albany: State University of New York Press.

———. 1995b. 'Introduction: The Historical Vicissitudes of Bhakti Religion'. In Lorenzen 1995a. Pp. 1–32.

———. 1995c. 'The Lives of *Nirguṇī* Saints'. In Lorenzen 1995a. Pp. 181–211.

———. 1996. *Praises to a Formless God: Nirguṇī Texts from North India*. Albany: State University of New York Press.

Lutgendorf, Philip. 1992. 'Rām's Story in Shiva's City: Public Arenas and Private Patronage'. In Freitag 1992. Pp. 34–61.

———. 1994. *The Life of a Text: Tulsīdās'* Rāmcharitmānas *in Performance*. Berkeley: University of California Press.

———. 1995. 'Interpreting Rāmrāj: Reflections on the *Rāmāyaṇa*, Bhakti, and Hindu Nationalism'. In Lorenzen 1995a. Pp. 253–87.

Madan, T. N. 1988. 'Secularism in Its Place'. In Madan 1992. Pp. 394–409.

———, ed. [1991] 1992. *Religion in India*. 2nd and enlarged ed. New Delhi: Oxford University Press.

Makaryk, Irena R., gen ed. 1993. *Encyclopedia of Contemporary Literary Theory: Approaches, Scholars, Terms*. Toronto: University of Toronto Press.

Mann, Gurinder Singh. 1996. *The Goindval Pothis: The Earliest Extant Source of the Sikh Canon*. Cambridge, Massachusetts: Department of Sanskrit and Indian Studies, Harvard University.

———. 2001. *The Making of Sikh Scripture*. Oxford: Oxford University Press.

Mathur, K. S. 1964. 'Hindu Values of Life: Karma and Dharma'. In Madan 1992. Pp. 63–77.

McLeod, W. H., ed. and trans. [1984] 1990. *Textual Sources for the Study of Sikhism*. Chicago: University of Chicago Press.

______. 1999; 3rd impression 2000. *Sikhs and Sikhism*. New Delhi: Oxford University Press. [Omnibus edition of four books published earlier by Oxford University Press: *Guru Ṅanak and the Sikh Religion* (1968); *The Evolution of the Sikh Community* (1976); *Early Sikh Tradition* (1980); and *Who Is a Sikh?* (1989).]

Miller, Barbara Stoler, trans. 1998. *Yoga, Discipline and Freedom: The Yoga Sutra Attributed to Patanjali*. New York: Bantam Books.

Mishra, Sharad Kumar. 1985. *Sant dādūdayāl aur madhyakālīn bhaktikāvya*. New Delhi: Pramod Prakashan.

Mohanty, J.N. 1995. 'Indian Philosophy'. *The New Encyclopaedia Britannica*. 15th ed. vol. 21. Pp. 191–212.

Monegal, Emir Rodriguez, and Alastair Reed, eds. 1981. *Borges: A Reader. A Selection from the Writings of Jorge Luis Borges*. New York: E. P. Dutton.

Nabokov, Vladimir. 1955. 'Problems of Translation: *Onegin* in English'. In Schulte and Biguenet 1992. Pp. 127–43.

Nagendra, ed., and Suresh Chandra Gupta, co-ed. 1973. *Hindī sāhitya kā itihās*. Delhi: National Publishing House.

Oberoi, Harjot. 1994. *The Construction of Religious Boundaries: Culture, Identity, and Diversity in the Sikh Tradition*. Chicago: University of Chicago Press.

O'Flaherty, Wendy Doniger, ed. 1980. *Karma and Rebirth in Classical Indian Traditions*. Berkeley: University of California Press.

______, ed. and trans. [1988] 1990. *Textual Sources for the Study of Hinduism*. Chicago: University of Chicago Press.

Olivelle, Patrick, trans. 1996. *Upaniṣads*. Oxford: Oxford University Press.

Pandey, Shyam Manohar. 1989. *Hindī aur fārasī sūfī kāvya: maulānā dāūd, hāfiz, nizāmī tathā jāyasī saṃbandhī kuchh adhyayan*. Allahabad: Sahitya Bhavan.

______, and Norman Zide. 1966. 'Sūrdās and His Krishna-*bhakti*'. In Singer 1966. Pp. 173–99.

Pollock, Sheldon. 1998. 'India in the Vernacular Millennium: Literary Culture and Polity, 1000–1500'. *Daedalus*, vol. 127, no. 3 (Summer): 41–74. Special issue on Early Modernities.

______, ed. 2003. *Literary Cultures in History: Reconstructions from South Asia*. Berkeley: University of California Press.

Potter, Karl H. 1980. 'The Karma Theory and Its Interpretation in Some Indian Philosophical Systems'. In O'Flaherty 1980. Pp. 241–61.

Rahman, Fazlur. 1979. 'The Qur'an'. In Madan 1992. Pp. 26–37.

Ramanujan, A. K. 1973. *Speaking of Śiva*. Harmondsworth: Penguin.

______, trans. 1981. *Hymns for the Drowning: Poems for Viṣṇu by Nammāḻvār*. Princeton: Princeton University Press.

———, trans. 1985. *Poems of Love and War: From the Eight Anthologies and the Ten Long Poems of Classical Tamil*. New York: Columbia University Press.

Reichenbach, Bruce R.1990. *The Law of Karma: A Philosophical Study*. Honolulu: University of Hawaii Press.

Rippin, Andrew, and Jan Knappert, ed. and trans. [1986] 1990. *Textual Sources for the Study of Islam*. Chicago: University of Chicago Press.

Salomon, Carol, 1995. 'Bāul Songs'. In Lopez 1995. Pp. 187–208.

Sen, Kshitimohan. 1961. Rpt. 1987. *Hinduism*. London: Penguin.

Schelling, Andrew, trans. [1993] 1998. *For Love of the Dark One: Songs of Mirabai*. Rev. ed. Prescott, Arizona: Hohm Press.

Schimmel, Annemarie. [1990] 1992. *Islam: An Introduction*. Albany, New York: State University of New York Press.

Schulte, Rainer, and John Biguenet, eds. 1992. *Theories of Translation: An Anthology of Essays from Dryden to Derrida*. Chicago: University of Chicago Press.

Sekhon, Sant Singh, and Kartar Singh Duggal. 1992. *A History of Punjabi Literature*. New Delhi: Sahitya Akademi.

Shapiro, Michael C. 1995. 'The Theology of the Locative Case in Sacred Sikh Scripture (Gurabani)'. In Lorenzen 1995a. Pp. 145–59.

Sharma, Ramvilas. 1996. Rpt. 1998. *Bhāratīya sāhitya kī bhūmikā*. New Delhi: Rajkamal Prakashan.

Sharma, Sarnamasingh. 1969. *Kabīr: vyaktitva, krititva evaṃ siddhānta*. Gulabapura, Rajasthan: Bharatiya Shodha-samsthan.

Shastri, Gangasharan. *See* Gangasharan Shastri.

Shukla, Dinesh Chandra. 1992. *Rājasthān ke pramukh sant evaṃ loka devatā*. Jodhpur: Rajasthani Sahitya Samsthan.

Shyamsundardas, ed. [1930] 7th ed. 1959. *Kabīr granthāvalī*. Varanasi: Nagari Pracharini Sabha.

Siddiqui, Iqtidar Husain. 1992. 'Social Mobility in the Delhi Sultanate'. In Habib 1992. Pp. 22–48.

Singer, Milton, ed. 1966. *Krishna: Myths, Rites, and Attitudes*. Honolulu: East-West Center Press.

Singh, Ajaib, ed. and trans. [1982]; 2nd printing with index 1984. *The Ocean of Love: The* Anurāg Sāgar *of Kabir*. Sanbornton, New Hampshire: Sant Bani Ashram.

Singh, Jayadev, and Vasudev Singh, ed. 1981. *Kabīr vañmaya*. Vol. 2: *Shabad: bhāvārthabodhinī vyākhyā sahit*. Varanasi: Vishvavidyalaya Prakashan.

Singh, Kedarnath. 1995. *Uttar kabīr aur anya kavitāeṃ*. New Delhi: Rajkamal Prakashan.

Singh, Namvar. [1952] 1971. *Hindī ke vikās meṃ apabhraṃsh kā yoga*. 5th rev. ed. Allahabad: Lokabharati Prakashan.

Singh, Pashaura. 2000. *The Guru Granth Sahib: Canon, Meaning and Authority*. New Delhi: Oxford University Press.

Singh, Pushpapal. 1962. *Kabīr granthāvalī saṭīk*. Introduction by Govind Trigunayat. Delhi: Ashok Prakashan.

Singh, Shukdev, ed. 1972. *Kabīr-bījak*. Allahabad: Nilabh Prakashan.

———, and S. Atibal. 1981. *Kabīr ke smaraṇatīrtha*. Varanasi: Kabiravani Prakashan Kendra, Kabir Chaura.

Singh, Trilochan, Bhai Jodh Singh, Kapur Singh, Bawa Harkishen Singh, and Khushwant Singh, trans. 1973. *Selections from the Sacred Writings of the Sikhs*. Rev. by George S. Fraser. Introduction by S. Radhakrishnan. Foreword by Arnold Toynbee. New York: Samuel Weiser.

Singhal, Dharmapal, ed. 1990. *Sant shrī rajjab dvārā saṃkalit sarbaṅgī, gun gañjanāmā sahit*. Jalandhar, Punjab: Dipak Publishers.

Spear, Percival. 1965. Rpt. with revisions 1979. *A History of India*. Vol. 2. Harmondsworth: Penguin.

Stein, Burton. [1998] 2001. *A History of India*. New Delhi: Oxford University Press.

Subrahmanyam, Sanjay.1998. 'Hearing Voices: Vignettes of Early Modernity in South Asia, 1400–1750'. *Daedalus*, vol. 127, no. 3 (Summer): 75–104. Special issue on Early Modernities.

Tagore, Rabindranath, trans. [1915] 1995. *Songs of Kabir*. York Beach, Maine: Samuel Weiser.

Thapar, Romila. 1966. *A History of India*. Vol. 1. Harmondsworth: Penguin.

Tharu, Susie, and K. Lalita, eds. 1991. *Women Writing in India: 600 B.C. to the Present*. Vol. 1: *600 B.C. to the Early 20th Century*. New York: The Feminist Press at the City University of New York.

Thukral, Uma. 1995. 'The Avatar Doctrine in the Kabīr Panth'. In Lorenzen 1995a. Pp. 221–30.

Tivari, Parasanath, ed. 1961. *Kabīr-granthāvalī*. Prayag [Allahabad]: Hindi Parishad, Prayag Vishvavidyalaya.

Tulpule, Shankar Gopal. 1984. *Mysticism in Medieval India*. Wiesbaden: Otto Harrassowitz.

Upadhyaya, Ayodhyasingh, 'Hariaudh', ed. [1946] 12th ed.1964. *Kabīr vachanāvalī*. Kashi [Varanasi]: Nagari Pracharini Sabha.

Varenne, Jean. [1973] 1976. *Yoga and the Hindu Tradition*. trans. by Derek Cottman. Chicago: University of Chicago Press.

Vaudeville, Charlotte. 1974. *Kabīr*. Vol. 1. Oxford: Clarendon Press.

_______. 1993. *A Weaver Named Kabir: Selected Verses, with a Detailed Biographical and Historical Introduction*. Delhi: Oxford University Press.

_______. *Myths, Saints and Legends in Medieval India*. Ed. by Vasudha Dalmia. Delhi: Oxford University Press.

Waines, David. [1995] 1996. *An Introduction to Islam*. Cambridge: Cambridge University Press.

Wescott, G. H. [1907]1961 microfilm-xerox rpt. by University Microfilms, Ann Arbor, Michigan. *Kabir and the Kabir Panth*. Cawnpore [Kanpur]: Christ Church Mission Press.

Wink, Andre. [1990] 1999. *Al-Hind: The Making of the Indo-Islamic World*. Vol. 1: *Early Medieval India and the Expansion of Islam 7th-11th Centuries*. New Delhi: Oxford University Press.

Yeats, W. B. 1916. 'The Wild Swans at Coole'. In Damrosch 1999. P. 2310.

Zaehner, R. C. [1966] 1973. *The Bhagavad-Gītā: With a Commentary Based on the Original Sources*. London: Oxford University Press.

Zaidi, Ali Jawad. 1993. *A History of Urdu Literature*. New Delhi: Sahitya Akademi.

Zelliott, Eleanor, and Maxine Bertsen, eds. 1988. *The Experience of Hinduism: Essays on Religion in Maharashtra*. Albany: State University of New York Press.

Read more in Puffin

Puffin Handbooks: Looking Good

Dr Rekha Sheth

Packed with clear information for curious minds, *The Puffin Handbooks* are small enough for quick reading, but big enough to provide the answers to all your questions. Find out more about a subject that you are interested in, or discover a whole new area from an expert in these lucid, fact-filled, illustrated books.

Looking good in your teens is something that doesn't only happen in fairytales ...

We all want to look good. But with teenage hormones, pollution, and exam stress, often this seems a goal virtually impossible to achieve. Yet all it requires to have a glowing complexion and gleaming hair is some simple steps. This book explains the theory behind why your body reacts in certain ways, and tells you what you can do about it. Renowned dermatologist Dr Rekha Sheth's no-nonsense, practical advice, interspersed with amusing anecdotes from her casebook, make this handbook both useful and reassuring.

READ MORE IN PUFFIN

Puffin Handbooks: Careers
Usha Albuquerque

Packed with clear information for curious minds, *The Puffin Handbooks* are small enough for quick reading, but big enough to provide the answers to all your questions. Find out more about a subject that you are interested in, or discover a whole new area from an expert in these lucid, fact-filled, illustrated books.

It is never too early to start planning for the rest of your life ...

We all have dreams about what we would like to do with our lives. But often we do not know how to translate these into concrete career possibilities. In this book, career management specialist Usha Albuquerque uses tests and questionnaires to show you how the person you are and things you love can all be brought to bear on this important decision. She illustrates how you need to start thinking about this early, identify your likes and dislikes, and set yourself realistic short-term and long-term goals which will enable you to fulfil your dreams. The book also includes diverse career profiles to bring you in touch with the reality of working.